Terminological Ontologies

SEMANTIC WEB AND BEYOND
Computing for Human Experience

Series Editors:

Ramesh Jain
University of California, Irvine
http://ngs.ics.uci.edu/

Amit Sheth
Wright State University
http://knoesis.wright.edu/amit/

As computing becomes ubiquitous and pervasive, computing is increasingly becoming an extension of human, modifying or enhancing human experience. Today's car reacts to human perception of danger with a series of computers participating in how to handle the vehicle for human command and environmental conditions. Proliferating sensors help with observations, decision making as well as sensory modifications. The emergent semantic web will lead to machine understanding of data and help exploit heterogeneous, multi-source digital media. Emerging applications in situation monitoring and entertainment applications are resulting in development of experiential environments.

SEMANTIC WEB AND BEYOND
Computing for Human Experience
addresses the following goals:

➢ brings together forward looking research and technology that will shape our world more intimately than ever before as computing becomes an extension of human experience;
➢ covers all aspects of computing that is very closely tied to human perception, understanding and experience;
➢ brings together computing that deal with semantics, perception and experience;
➢ serves as the platform for exchange of both practical technologies and far reaching research.

Additional information about this series can be obtained from
http://www.springer.com/series/7056

Javier Lacasta • Javier Nogueras-Iso
Francisco Javier Zarazaga-Soria

Terminological Ontologies

Design, Management and Practical Applications

 Springer

Javier Lacasta
University of Zaragoza
Maria de Luna 1
50018 Zaragoza
Spain
jlacasta@unizar.es

Javier Nogueras-Iso
University of Zaragoza
Maria de Luna 1
50018 Zaragoza
Spain
jnog@unizar.es

Francisco Javier Zarazaga-Soria
University of Zaragoza
Maria de Luna 1
50018 Zaragoza
Spain
javy@unizar.es

ISSN 1559-7474
ISBN 978-1-4614-2644-8   ISBN 978-1-4419-6981-1 (eBook)
DOI 10.1007/978-1-4419-6981-1
Springer New York Dordrecht Heidelberg London

Springer is part of Springer Science+Business Media (www.springer.com)

To María del Carmen, Aurelio and Elena.
To Ascensión, Fermín and María Jesús.
To Esther, Victor and Silvia.
41.6839, -0.8892 —— 41.6677, -0.8788

Preface

Information infrastructures are integrated solutions based on the fusion of information and communication technologies. An information infrastructure is defined as an advanced, seamless web of public and private communications networks, interactive services, interoperable hardware and software, computers, databases, and consumer electronics to make available vast amounts of information. The term started to be commonly used after the launching of the US plan for National Information Infrastructures [195]. Since then, the term has been widely used to describe national and global communication networks like the Internet and more specialized solutions for communications within specific business sectors. For example, following the US path, the European Union published some years later its own plan for the creation of European information infrastructures [46].

Information retrieval is a basic functionality in any information infrastructure. Information retrieval deals with the representation, storage, organization, and access to information items [13]. It consists in determining which documents of a collection are relevant to the user information request. The primary goal of an information retrieval system is to retrieve all the documents that are relevant to the user information need while retrieving as few non-relevant documents as possible. To do so, it has to be able to extract syntactic and semantic information from the documents, and use this information to rank the documents according to the degree of match with respect to the user information need. However, the interpretation of the user need is not an easy task. It is limited by the expressivity of the user query language and by the inherent ambiguity and terminological dispersion of the written text.

An information infrastructure requires an efficient and effective information retrieval system to provide the users with access to the items stored in the infrastructure. It does not really matter how much information about a subject an infrastructure contains; if it is not possible to find it, it is useless. Therefore, it is important to distinguish between an information retrieval and a data retrieval process. While data retrieval systems are focused on determining which records stored in a catalog system contain the words specified in the user query, information retrieval ones are more concerned with obtaining information about a subject or topic than retrieving the data which satisfies exactly a given query. Data retrieval techniques are applicable to systems with well structured data where returning a single erroneous item means a total failure. However, in systems working with natural language text, which is not always well structured and could be semantically ambiguous, information retrieval systems could be a better option if some inaccuracies and small errors are acceptable.

An information infrastructure is composed of several services and components that have to interact to provide the desired functionality. If each component uses a different set of interfaces and formats, the interoperability between them becomes a difficult task. The use of standards is of great help to solve syntactic interoperability problems establishing a common way to access to information (they provide a common syntax). However, syntactic interoperability is not enough for information retrieval. Natural language terms used in classification, indexing and querying contain semantic relations between them (e.g., synonymy, polysemy, homonymy, meronymy, hyponymy, lexical variants, or misspellings) may make difficult the creation of effective search services.

In order to increase semantic interoperability in search systems, libraries, museums, and archives have traditionally used controlled vocabularies (list of terms about a certain subject) to describe resources, reducing in that way the possible terms used in classification and search to the selected ones. Their use increases the homogeneity in the descriptions, simplifies the query process and improves the results. Controlled vocabularies are used in classification steps to describe (and index) the resources. In the search components, they provide the user with the appropriate terminology for constructing queries. And in information browsing, they are used to provide a browsing structure through the resources based on the selected vocabulary. The selection of an appropriate vocabulary represents nevertheless an important challenge [74], it has to be adapted to the collection requirements avoiding terms irrelevant for the desired context.

Having in mind the increase of terminological precision, the use of simple controlled vocabularies has been progressively displaced by the use of more sophisticated knowledge models. This tendency has been greatly increased in the last years with the impact of Internet and the Semantic Web. The knowledge models stored in paper (taxonomies, thesauri) by libraries and other institutions have been computerized and transformed into more formal ontology models to provide a higher level of semantics. The term ontology is used in information systems and in knowledge representation systems to denote a knowledge model, which represents a particular domain of interest. A body of formally represented knowledge is based on a conceptualization: the objects, concepts, and other entities that are assumed to exist in some area of interest and the relationships that hold among them. And an ontology provides "an explicit formal specification of a shared conceptualization" [69]. Some ontology types are classification schemes that organize materials at a general level (such as books on a shelf), subject headings that provide more detailed access, authority files that control variant versions of key information (such as geographic names and personal names), or semantic networks and formal ontologies that provide a complete set of formally defined relations. Depending on the formalism level, Sowa [178] distinguishes two main classes of ontologies: terminological (also called lexical) and axiomatized (also called formal). Terminological ontologies are not fully specified by axioms and definitions and the relations are limited to subtype/supertype or part/whole relations. On the other hand, axiomatized ontology concepts and relations have associated axioms and definitions that are stated in logic or in some computer-oriented language that can be automatically translated to logic.

Nowadays, ontologies play an important role in the information retrieval context. Usually, the retrieval of resources through an information retrieval system implies successive iterations of resource discovery, followed by resource evaluation, and a final stage of access (direct as a data set, or indirect via a data access service) and exploitation of the resource. In all these stages, different ontology models can help to improve the produced results.

As concerns **resource discovery**, some of the most remarkable problems that affect the interoperability and cooperation of discovery systems are metadata schema heterogeneity and content heterogeneity [156].

In order to facilitate discovery and access, the content of a collection is summarized into small descriptions, usually called metadata (data about the data), which can be either introduced manually or automatically generated (index terms automatically extracted from a collection of documents). Most Digital libraries define their structured metadata in accordance to recognized standards such as MARC21 [149] or the Dublin Core Metadata Element Set [85] (proposed by the Dublin Core Metadata Initiative[1]) but other models can be used. This heterogeneity makes difficult the integration of collections using different metadata models. In this context, given that a metadata schema is a model that contains a set of concepts with properties and relations to other concepts, their structure can be modeled as a formal ontology, where metadata records are instances of this ontology [17]. This kind of formal ontologies may be used to profile the metadata needs of a specific resource and its relationships with metadata of other related resources, or to provide interoperability across metadata schemas.

On the other hand, metadata try to describe in an accurate way information resources to enhance information retrieval, but this improvement depends greatly on the quality of metadata content. Even in the same collection, the content of each metadata can be quite heterogeneous. Here, terminological ontologies facilitate classification of resources and information retrieval. One way to enforce the quality is the use of selected terminology for some metadata fields in the form of lexical ontologies. These ontologies are used to describe contents but also allow computer systems to reason about them. This role of terminological ontologies is even more significant in the case of developing multilingual systems because they can provide the translations of the terms used for classification to all the required languages.

Regarding **resource evaluation**, an information retrieval system and must provide enough means to visualize the data appropriately. In this scenario, one could consider multilinguality and other specific issues related with the type of data stored.

In the case of viewing metadata in a specific language required by the user, one may face the problem of having to translate it. Once again, formal ontologies and

---

[1] http://www.dublincore.org

terminological ontologies may facilitate the work in two important aspects. Firstly, a formal ontology may provide the labels, in the appropriate language, for the elements of the metadata schema. Secondly, terminological ontologies may be used in the task of automatic translation of metadata to increase accuracy of translations.

Depending on the processed data, other issues where the use of ontologies helps may raise. For example, in a map repository, developers must consider the internationalization of legends and the display of internationalized attribute information.

Finally, the **resource access** step may benefit as well from the use of ontologies to facilitate data sharing and system development. Once again, formal ontologies help to define the meaning of features or a resource and they can provide a "common basis" for semantic mapping, e.g. to find similarity between two features that represent the same object but that have been defined using different language representations.

From the different types of ontologies, terminological ones are the most commonly used in every aspect of an information retrieval process. Their uses range from classification to query construction and results visualization. However, if all these different models are created, used and managed independently, the complexity of the system increases in a great deal. This book focuses on providing a coherent framework for the integration of terminological ontologies in an information retrieval system, with the objective of facilitating its creation, management, and use for the different components requiring it. The integration problems that have been faced can be divided into three main general categories: representation, acquisition and access:

- Related to the **representation** problem, it is common to find that each organization has created a new ontology using an ad-hoc representation format, which is only useful in its specific context. This has led to a big heterogeneity of representation models that increases the difficulty and the cost of integrating the models into a homogeneous system. In this context, a single and homogeneous representation mechanism for terminological models is vital to provide uniform ontology models to the components that require them. An additional problem is the need to provide a single and homogeneous access to different data collections classified with different terminological ontologies. For example, when integrating data from different countries classified according to different terminological models in different languages. To provide a homogeneous access to the resources, the used ontologies have to be related to be able to identify equivalences and obtain complete results. The process of matching ontologies (called ontology alignment) is difficult and costly but other collections using the same terminological models can reuse it. Therefore, in a similar way as it is required a representation format for individual terminological models, it is required another one for storing the mappings between them.
- Regarding the ontology **acquisition** problem, the needed ontologies have to be obtained or created, and adapted to integrate them in the required systems. However, this is not an easy task. On the one hand, the heterogeneity in the creation of terminological models limits their reusability in contexts different from the original ones. Therefore, even if a suitable terminology is found, it has to be

transformed to facilitate its integration with the rest used in the system. This requirement involves additional integration issues due to the need of a different transformation process for each required ontology. On the other hand, the creation of a new one from scratch is very costly in time and resources. In this context, to reduce the development effort, it is useful to reuse sections of other ontology models that contain suitable terminology. An additional issue that has been taken into account is the overlapping of the acquired models. Here, the common elements of different models have to be properly managed to avoid classification problems.

- Finally, with respect to the **access** problem, the applicability of these models in a wide range of application domains has led to the creation of a great variety of terminological ontologies with very different levels of specificity, language coverage (i.e., from monolingual list of terms to multilingual thesauri covering dozens of languages), formalization (i.e., from simple glossaries to well-structured thesauri), or size (e.g., AGROVOC thesaurus [126] contains more than 16,000 concepts). Additionally, it is important to note that they are distributed to the public through ad-hoc services created for each institution providing them. This ad-hoc distribution is not appropriate in an information infrastructure where it is required to provide the ontologies to all components in a simple and common way. In this context, it is needed a coordinated view of the ontologies that can only be obtained through a homogeneous management and access not dependent of the original providers.

In order to solve these specific problems, this book describes a homogeneous solution for each of these discovery scenarios. These solutions are interrelated in such a way that they can be combined to facilitate all the steps required to integrate a new terminological ontology into an information retrieval system.

1. In order to deal with the representation issues, the existent representation formats for terminological models have been analyzed. From them, the most appropriate has been selected, extending it to cover those information requirements that were not fulfilled in the original format model. A similar work has been done with respect to the representation of mappings between different terminological models. In this case, given that no suitable format exists, a new one based on textual recommendations indicated in the terminological ontology standards has been designed.

2. With respect to the acquisition issue, each problem described has required a different approach as part of a global transformation process. First, a general transformation process is proposed to harmonize the way a terminological ontology is converted to the selected representation format. The format allows defining the structure of the source and destination models and simplifies the definition of relations between them. The proposed architectural pattern helps to reuse the common elements of the different transformations. Secondly, to simplify the construction of a new ontology, a process that uses a set of ontologies as base and combines them into a new model is described. To focus the result into the desired domain, the process limits the content of the new ontology pruning the

non-relevant concepts. Finally, with the objective to increase the formalization of the models when required, a process that helps in the identification of the existent *is-a* relationships has been developed.

3. In the ontology management context, it has been identified the need for an efficient and common ontology management service to filter and select the most appropriate ontology for each specific context. However, before the creation of these services, the design of a common repository is proposed to store all the required terminological ontologies. On top of this repository, the design of an efficient editor and other GUI widgets is proposed to facilitate the annotation and the update of terminological ontologies. Additionally, a centralized ontology service, called Web Ontology Service (WOS), which enables uniform management of terminological ontologies (including discovery services) has been developed to provide access to terminological ontologies via Web services. To provide a full integration with the rest of components of a typical information retrieval system, it follows and extends standard interfaces used by the Semantic Web community.

This book consists of seven chapters describing in detail the integration problems and the proposed solutions. The content of these chapters is organized as follows:

- Chapter 1 reviews the types of ontologies and the techniques used for establishing alignments between them. The concepts, ideas and techniques described are used along the entire book.
- Chapter 2 focuses on the problems of representation of terminological ontologies. It starts analyzing the problematic of representation of simple models, and then follows with the issues related to representing the relationships between overlapping models.
- Chapter 3 analyzes the issues related to the creation of terminological ontologies using data from different sources such as data corpora, dictionaries, schemata and other knowledge models.
- Chapter 4 describes the issues related to the lack of formalism in terminological models and how to increase it in order to provide additional semantic functionality.
- Chapter 5 analyzes the way to provide access to terminological models. It describes the structure of a terminological ontology repository, a tool for managing and editing the ontologies, and a web service for providing access to them.
- Chapter 6 describes how the components proposed in chapter 5 can be integrated into an information retrieval system. As a result of this integration we present: tools for creating metadata facilitating the management of terminological models for classification; search clients able to use the stored ontologies to improve the search results; and browsing systems providing access to the resources on the basis of the structure of a terminological ontology.
- Chapter 7 contains some concluding remarks and an outlook of future areas of work.

Zaragoza,   *Javier Lacasta*
April 2010   *Javier Nogueras-Iso*
                                                                                   F. Javier Zarazaga-Soria

Acknowledgements

There are many people to whom we are grateful for their support during the evolution of this book.

First of all, we would like to thank to the members and friends of the Advanced Information Systems Laboratory (IAAA) of the University of Zaragoza, making a especial mention to Pedro R. Muro-Medrano, Rubén Béjar, and F. Javier Lopez-Pellicer by their comments and suggestions that have been so valuable for improving this book. We also have to include other members and ex-members from the staff of IAAA and GeoSpatiumLab S.L. that have provided us with the required technical support and advice, specially to Juanjo, Jesús, Mariano, Rodolfo, Covadonga, Christian, Aneta, and Miguel Ángel. Besides, we cannot forget the support of our colleagues at the Computer Science and Systems Engineering Department, specially Jose Ángel Bañares, Joaquín Ezpeleta and Pedro Álvarez.

Finally, we are absolutely grateful to our families and friends for all their patience, support and love. Much time have been stolen from our personal lives for the creation of this text. Undoubtedly, without their generous understanding this work would never have come into existence.

Contents

Chapter 1
Ontology basic concepts

1.1 Introduction

According to Gruber [69], an ontology is an explicit specification of a conceptualization. A conceptualization is an abstract, simplified view of the world that we wish to represent for some purpose. A body of formally represented knowledge is based on a conceptualization: the objects, concepts, and other entities that are presumed to exist in some area of interest and the relationships that hold between them. Every knowledge base, knowledge-based system, or knowledge-level agent is committed to some conceptualization, explicitly or implicitly.

Following a more technical perspective, Sowa [178] defines an ontology as a specification of the kinds of entities that exist or may exist in some domain or subject area. Formally, an ontology is specified by a collection of names for concept and relation types organized in a partial ordering by the *type/subtype* relation. In a similar way, Guarino [71] defines an ontology as an engineering artifact, constituted by a specific vocabulary used to describe a certain reality, plus a set of explicit assumptions regarding the intended meaning of the vocabulary words. This set of assumptions has usually the form of a first-order logical theory where vocabulary words appear as unary or binary predicate names, respectively called concepts and relations. In the simplest case, an ontology describes a hierarchy of concepts related by subsumption relationships; in more sophisticated models, suitable axioms are added in order to express other relationships between concepts and to constrain their intended interpretation.

This chapter analyzes the different ontology types, and the processes to establish relations between them with the objective of selecting those that are more suitable for the information retrieval context. A study of families and types of ontology models is shown to compare them and detect the common characteristics and the differences. This analysis has the objective of providing the context in which the terminological ontologies are placed and showing how each of model is related to the rest. Additionally, an analysis of the available mapping technology used to relate

J. Lacasta et al., *Terminological Ontologies: Design, Management and Practical Applications*, Semantic Web and Beyond 9, DOI 10.1007/978-1-4419-6981-1_1,
© Springer Science+Business Media, LLC 2010

ontologies is performed, focusing on those most useful for terminological ontologies and in the types of relations that may be established between the models.

1.2 Ontology families

Ontologies are usually classified according to the amount and type of structure of their conceptualization. Following this criteria, Sowa [178] distinguishes two main families: terminological (also called lexical) and axiomatized (also called formal).

Terminological/Lexical ontology: An ontology whose concepts and relations are not fully specified by axioms and definitions that determine the necessary and sufficient conditions of their use. The concepts may be partially specified by relations such as *subtype/supertype* or *part/whole*, which determine the relative positions of the concepts with respect to one another, but do not completely define them.

Axiomatized/Formal ontology: A terminological ontology whose concepts and relations have associated axioms and definitions that are stated in logic or in some computer-oriented language that can be automatically translated to logic. There is no restriction on the complexity of the logic that may be used to state the axioms and definitions.

Sowa [178] states that a terminological ontology may be expressed in logic, but the logic required is usually simpler, less expressive, and more easily computable than full first-order predicate calculus. The distinction between terminological and axiomatized ontologies is one of degree rather than kind. They are models of different complexity in the same category. Axiomatized ontologies tend to be smaller than terminological ones, but their axioms and definitions can support more complex inferences and computations.

van Heijst et al. [199] propose another classification that divides ontologies into terminological, information and knowledge modeling. According to this classification, terminological ontologies specify the terms that are used to represent knowledge in the domain of discourse; information ontologies do the same with the record structure of databases (e.g., database schemata); and knowledge modeling ontologies are used to specify conceptualizations of the knowledge. Matching this classification with the one proposed by Sowa [178], terminological ontology definitions would be equivalent, knowledge modeling ontologies would fit into the axiomatized class, and information ontologies would lie somewhat in the middle of the two since they have many of the features of the formal ones but they lack some key elements such as clearly defined *is-a* relationships.

The treatment provided to the *is-a* relationship can be considered as the crucial point that separates terminological from axiomatic ontologies. Not everybody considers terminological models as ontologies, due to the lack of a formal explicit *is-a* hierarchy. The name Knowledge Organization Systems (KOS) is then used to refer to all the different models used to organize knowledge, reserving the name of ontology to axiomatized ontologies. As it is described by Hodge [77], the term "Knowledge Organization Systems (KOS)" intends to encompass all those types of schemas for organizing information and promoting knowledge management. A KOS serves as a bridge between the user information need and the material in the collection. Knowledge organization systems include: classification schemes that organize materials at a general level such as books on a shelf; subject headings that provide more detailed access; and authority files that control variant versions of key information such as geographic names and personal names.

In addition to the classifications based on the structure, ontologies can also be classified according to the subject of the conceptualization, i.e. their content. Guarino [71] describes the following classes:

Top-level ontologies: They describe very general concepts which are independent of a particular problem or domain (e.g., space, time, matter, object, event and action). Therefore, it seems reasonable, at least in theory, to have unified top-level ontologies for large communities of users.

Domain and Task ontologies: These ontologies describe, respectively, the vocabulary (conceptualizations) related to a generic domain (like medicine, or automobiles) or a generic task or activity (like diagnosing or selling), by specializing the terms introduced in the top-level ontology.

Application ontologies: These ontologies contain all the definitions that are needed to model the knowledge required for a particular application. They describe concepts depending on a particular domain and/or task. Therefore, they are often specializations of ontologies of these classes. These concepts often correspond to roles played by domain entities while performing a certain activity.

The classification of Mizoguchi et al. [145] is quite similar to the one proposed by Guarino [71] but dividing the ontologies into general/common ontologies (top-level), domain ontologies and task ontologies. Another content-based classification is also proposed by van Heijst et al. [199], which includes application ontologies, domain ontologies, generic ontologies (top-level) and representation ontologies. Representation ontologies describe the conceptualizations about knowledge representation formalisms [37], which are intended to be neutral with respect to world entities [72]. That is to say, they provide a representational framework without making claims about the world. Representation ontologies provide the primitives to formally represent and share the rest of the ontologies (top, domain, task and application).

1.3 Ontology classification

The main difference between ontology models is their capacity to express semantics. Focusing on the terminological vs. axiomatized ontology classification, terminological models do not have enough expressivity to represent the relationship complexity required by many applications, but they are much easier to create and integrate than formal ones. In this context, the selection of a terminological or a formal model depends exclusively on the required functionality. For example, to provide a list of possible values in a search service, the use of an ontology with hundreds of values and relations is not adequate. Here, a very limited terminological model adjusted to the collection content is much better. However, to model the information structure of a system where reasoning is needed, a formal model is required.

Lassila and MacGuinness [123] propose a classification of ontologies types according to the degree of formalism and semantics provided in their specification (figure 1.1). They range from simple lists, passing by subject sets, to complex reasoning models. Following this classification, terminological ontologies correspond with the models on the left part of figure 1.1, and axiomatic ones with the models on the right.

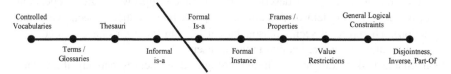

Fig. 1.1: Categorization of ontologies extracted from Lassila and MacGuinness [123]

A complementary classification is described by Sigel [175] as shown in figure 1.2. This model focuses on explaining the different types of ontologies from the semantic interoperability point of view and focusing on the ability to express hierarchical relations. The categories range from taxonomies, which are able to express few semantics (subclassification relationship) and only provide syntactic interoperability, to logical theory models, which thanks to their strong semantics provide the most complete form of semantic interoperability. In this categorization, terminological models are those that provide syntactic and structural interoperability, and the axiomatic ones those that provide semantic interoperability.

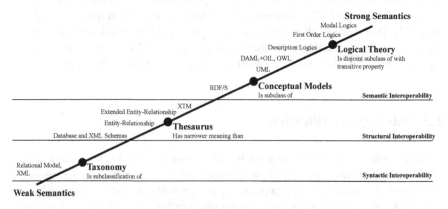

Fig. 1.2: Categorization of ontologies extracted from Sigel [175]

The evolution from one model to another one can be done by adding semantics. For example, moving from taxonomies to thesauri involves the addition of the syndetic structure (connecting elements) which comprises the system of *see* and *see also* cross references to other indexing terms. And moving from thesauri to topic maps adds a greater number of typed semantic relations, internal attributes, typed links to external information resources, and sophisticated searching and displaying capabilities.

The most common types of ontologies are described next following the categorization by Lassila and MacGuinness [123] in figure 1.1. Additionally, some models that do not completely fit in any of its divisions are included within the most similar category or in a new one (if they are too different).

1.3.1 Controlled vocabularies

The simplest type of knowledge structure is the controlled vocabulary. It can be defined as a finite list of terms about a certain subject. Controlled vocabularies can be seen as lists of items published by a certain body that provide them with an unambiguous interpretation in the form of pairs Term-Identifier. A simple example of controlled vocabulary is the list of themes in a library where a unique code associated to each theme is used to classify the books.

More sophisticated controlled vocabularies are authority files (also called authority records). They are lists of terms used to control variant names for an entity or the domain values for a particular field. Authority files contain information to identify common type instances (e.g., geographic entities or administration departments), and they provide a normative preferred name for resource classification and indexing. Their main function is to provide enough identifying information so that humans can identify the entity and associate it to a unique identifier and a preferred name. Standards such as ISAAR (CPF) [79] and MARC 21 Format for Authority Data [148] define their structure and properties. Authority files do not include a deep organization or complex structure, no hierarchical relations are used and the syndetic structure is quite poor (i.e., there are not *see* and *see also* references to other indexing items). Examples of Authority Files are the Library of Congress Name Authority File[1] and the Virtual International Authority File[2]. Figure 1.3 shows an entry of the Library of Congress Name Authority File. In the table, *LC Control Number* field contains the unique identifier, *Heading* has the authorized label of the entry, *Used For* identifies the unauthorized forms of headings and other variants not chosen as an authorized form, and *Found In* has the source of the authorized label.

---

[1] http://authorities.loc.gov/

[2] http://orlabs.oclc.org/viaf/

LC Control Number	n 86807672
Heading	Senate Democratic Caucus (Calif.)
Used For	California. Legislature. Senate. Democratic Caucus
Found In	nuc86-13536: Patino, L. The key that locks the records ...[MI] 1973 (hdg. on PSt rept.: California. Legislature. Senate. Democratic Caucus; usage: Senate Democratic Caucus)

Fig. 1.3: Entry of the Library of Congress Name Authority File

1.3.2 Glossaries

A glossary is a list of terms that usually contains definitions and cross-reference entries. The terms are defined within a specific environment and rarely include variant meanings. The definitions are directed to humans and therefore specified as natural language statements. Two examples are the terms of environment from the USA Environmental Protection Agency[3] and the UK National Statistics Geography glossary[4].

A dictionary can be considered as an enrichment of a glossary. Similarly to glossaries, dictionaries are alphabetical lists of words in a specific language with their definitions but including synonyms, spelling and morphological variants, multiple meanings across disciplines, etymologies, pronunciations, and other information. A terminology is a kind of domain specific dictionary including phrases instead of single words. Additionally, when the dictionary terms include translations in another language, they are known as lexicons. An example of dictionary is provided by the *Real Academia de la lengua*[5] (Royal Academy of Language) that contains the definitions of the words used in Spanish language. The Cambridge Dictionary[6] does the same for the English language but additionally it provides translations to other languages. Therefore, it can also be considered as a lexicon. Figure 1.4 shows an element of this dictionary, showing the properties that it provides.

1.3.3 Subject headings and taxonomies

Two types of models providing more semantics than a glossary and less than a thesaurus (subsection 1.3.4) are subject headings and taxonomies. These models are more complex than glossaries because of their hierarchical structure. They cannot be considered as thesauri because they lack their explicit definition of relationship types.

---

[3] http://www.epa.gov/OCEPAterms/

[4] http://www.statistics.gov.uk/geography/glossary/default.asp

[5] http://buscon.rae.es/draeI/

[6] http://dictionary.cambridge.org/

geography Show phonetics
noun [U]
1 the study of the systems and processes involved in the world's weather, mountains, seas,
lakes, etc. and of the ways in which countries and people organize life within an area
See also physical geography.

2 the geography of *somewhere* the way all the parts of an area are arranged within it:
We learnt about the geography of Australia.
It's impossible to work out the geography of this hospital.

geographer Show phonetics
noun [C]
a person who studies geography

geographical Show phonetics
adjective (MAINLY US geographic)
a geographical region

geographically Show phonetics
adverb

(from Cambridge Advanced Learner's Dictionary)

Fig. 1.4: Definition of geography according to Cambridge dictionary

A subject heading is a uniform group of words used to describe the subject of library materials. It provides a set of controlled terms to represent the subjects of items in a collection. They have a very limited hierarchical structure and their terms can be coordinated to provide more specific concepts. Examples include the Medical Subject Headings[7] and the Library of Congress Subject Headings[8]. Figure 1.5 shows a subset of the Medical Subject Headings showing the structure and the description of one of its terms. As main elements, it provides *Unique ID* field as identifier, *MeSH Heading* as preferred label and two *Entry Terms* as alternatives. The other elements described provide additional information about the term such as *Annotation*, *Scope Note* and *History Note*, or for management, such as *Date of Entry*.

Subject categories are quite similar but their main objective is to group concepts as clusters of preferred and non-preferred terms that share a single characteristic. Each subject category may have a number of characteristics, but only one is selected to collect and arrange the terms into a hierarchical order and create sub-categories. Subject categories are often used to group thesaurus terms in broad topic sets that lie outside the hierarchical scheme of the thesaurus. The AGRIS (international bibliographic information system for the agricultural sciences and technology) subject category[9] provided by FAO (Food and Agriculture Organization of the United Nations) is an example of this model.

A taxonomy (also called classification or categorization scheme) is a controlled vocabulary designed for classifying or categorizing resources. It provides aggregation of concepts using a (poly-)hierarchical broader concept based structure. Exam-

---

[7] http://www.nlm.nih.gov/mesh/

[8] http://www.loc.gov/aba/cataloging/subject/

[9] http://www.fao.org/scripts/agris/c-categ.htm

ples of classification schemes include the Library of Congress Classification[10], the Dewey Decimal Classification[11], or the Universal Decimal Classification[12].

1. ⊞ Anatomy [A]
2. ⊟ Organisms [B]
    o Animals [B01] +
    o Algae [B02] +
    o Bacteria [B03] +
    o Viruses [B04] +
    o Fungi [B05] +
    o Plants [B06] +
    o Archaea [B07] +
    o Mesomycetozoea [B08] +
3. ⊞ Diseases [C]

(a) Subset of the hierarchy

MeSH Heading	Animals
Tree Number	B01
Annotation	NIM as check tag; Manual 18.7+ ...
Scope Note	Unicellular or multicellular ...
Entry Term	Animal
Entry Term	Animalia
History Note	2004 (1974); was check tag only ...
Date of Entry	19750725
Unique ID	D000818

(b) *Animal* term

Fig. 1.5: *Animal* term in the Medical Subject Headings

A folksonomy is a social variant of a taxonomy. It is a classification scheme created by normal users instead of being created by experts in the area. They have become popular since the massive use of social web applications such as social bookmarking or photograph annotation. A well-developed folksonomy is ideally accessible as a shared vocabulary that is both originated by, and familiar to, its primary users. However, as they are created by many different non-technical users, they usually lack consistency and reliability in structure and content.

Another taxonomy related model is a gazetteer. A gazetteer can be viewed and modeled as a specialized kind of glossary, but nowadays they are modeled as taxonomies, thesauri or even more formal models. A classical basic gazetteer is a list of place names published as books or as indexes. In addition to a description, each element contains a feature type (e.g., city, road and mountain) and the coordinates for locating the place on the earths surface (if it is geo-spatially referenced). An example is the U.S. Code of Geographic Names[13].

1.3.4 Thesauri

A thesaurus is a set of terms describing the vocabulary of a controlled indexing language, formally organized so that the a priori relationships between concepts (e.g.,

---

[10] http://www.loc.gov/catdir/cpso/lcco/

[11] http://www.oclc.org/dewey/

[12] http://www.udcc.org/about.htm

[13] http://geonames.usgs.gov/

synonymous terms, broader terms, or narrower terms) are made explicit [9, 81, 92]. The vocabulary is arranged in a known order and structured so that the different relationships among terms are displayed clearly and identified by standardized relationship indicators that should be employed reciprocally.

According to Foskett [57], the main purposes of a thesaurus are to provide a standard vocabulary for indexing, to assist users with locating terms for proper query formulations, and to provide classified hierarchies that allow the broadening and narrowing of the current query request according to the user needs. The thesaurus structure was first defined to be used in the classification of resources (books, documents) to organize them thematically. Nowadays, their digital versions are used in data repositories (e.g., data libraries, management systems, geospatial catalogs) for classification and search purposes.

Thesauri have properties also present in some of the previous models, such as definitions or synonyms, but they add an explicit definition of concept relationships that can be interpreted unambiguously by agents. Different national and international standards have been developed to harmonize their structure. They can be divided into standards for the development of monolingual thesauri such as Z39-19 [9], BS-5723 [26] and ISO-2788 [81], and those having into account multilingual needs such as BS-6723 [25] and ISO-2788[81].

Relationships commonly expressed in a thesaurus include hierarchy represented using the notation BT (broader term) and NT (narrower term); equivalence described as SYN (synonym), and association or relatedness with RT (associative or related term). The root of the broader term hierarchy is described through the TT (top term) relationship. Additional properties such as SN (scope note) are usually included to identify the scope of use of each term. Thesaurus standards define three specializations of the broader-narrower relationship: the generic relationships, the instance relationships and the whole-part relationships.

Generic relationship (NTG/BTG): It identifies the link between a class and its members or species. This type of relationship is often identified with the *is-a* relation (e.g., Fruits NTG Citrus).

Instance relationship (NTI/BTI): It describes the link between a general category of things or events, expressed by a common noun, and an individual instance of that category, often a proper name. In more formal models these relations are managed as class instances and not as concept relationships (e.g., Mountains Regions NTI Alps).

Whole-Part relationship (NTP/BTP): It covers situations in which the meaning of one concept is inherently included in another one, regardless of context, so that the terms can be organized into logical hierarchies, with the whole treated as a broader term (e.g., Canada NTP Ontario).

Traditionally, the model to represent thesauri has been term-based (see figure 1.6a). Following this model, the term (lexical label) is the core of the structure and it is used as identifier. All the relations are between terms, not only including the BT/NT, RT and TT relations but also the synonymy between labels. Synonymy is managed with the USE/UF (used for) relationship that allows identifying which of

the synonyms is the preferred one. Multilingualism is managed as translations of
the terms and included as additional properties. Therefore, there is a main language
used as core of the structure and translations of those terms to other languages.

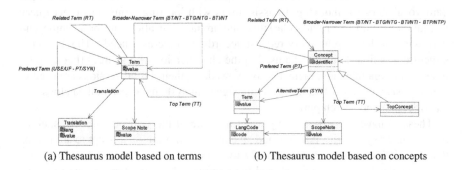

(a) Thesaurus model based on terms   (b) Thesaurus model based on concepts

Fig. 1.6: Alternative thesaurus models

Nowadays, in the information science community, the used thesaurus model
is concept-based (see figure 1.6b). In this model, the core element is the concept, which has a unique identifier used to distinguish each one from the rest. The
BT/NT, RT and TT relations are relations between concepts. USE/UF relationship
is replaced for the PT/SYN (preferred/synonym) relationship between concepts and
terms containing the labels of the concept. Multilingual features are easily managed
since all language dependent labels are managed uniformly. Two terms in different languages are associated to the same concept as *preferred/alternative* labels but
each one containing a language code to indicate the language they are written. The
same happens with other optional properties that are language dependent such as
the *scope note* indicating the use of the concept and the *definition* of the concepts.

Some examples of thesauri used along this book are the following:

GEneral Multilingual Environmental Thesaurus[14](GEMET):   It has been created
  by the European Environment Agency (EEA) and the European Topic Centre on
  Catalogue of Data Sources to the European Environment Information and Obser-
  vation Network for the classification of the developed environmental resources.
  It is available in 23 different languages (two of them different English dialects)
  and contains around 6500 concepts and 200000 descriptors.

AGROVOC thesaurus[15]:   It is provided by the Food and Agriculture Organization
  of the United Nations (FAO) for the classification of geographic information resources (with special focus on agriculture resources) [126]. It is available in 19
  languages (being 4 more under construction) and contains around 28000 concepts and 600000 elements between properties and relationships.

---

[14] http://www.eionet.europa.eu/gemet

[15] http://www.fao.org/aims/ag_intro.htm

European Vocabulary[16](EUROVOC):   It is a multilingual thesaurus created by European Communities covering the fields in which the European Communities are active. For example, it provides a means of indexing the documents in the documentation systems of the European institutions and of their users. It is published in 23 languages containing around 6600 different concepts and 100000 descriptors.

UNESCO thesaurus[17]:   It is a general-purpose thesaurus created by the United Nations Educational, Scientific and Cultural Organization (UNESCO) for its use in the indexing and retrieval of information in the UNESCO Integrated Documentation Network [194]. Published in English, Spanish and French contains around 4400 concepts.

geography
Concept definition:
The study of the natural features of the earth's surface, comprising topography, climate, soil, vegetation, etc. and man's response to them. (Source: CED)

broader terms	عربي:	الجغرافيا
science	Български:	География
narrower terms	Čeština:	geografie
biogeography	Dansk:	geografi
cartography	Deutsch:	Geographie
economic geography	Ελληνικά:	γεωγραφία
geodesy	English (US):	geography
geomorphology	Español:	geografía
hydrography	Eesti keel:	geograafia, maateadus
orography	Euskara:	geografia
physical geography	Suomi:	maantiede
political geography	Français:	géographie
	Magyar:	földrajz
	Italiano:	geografia
Scope note:	Nederlands:	geografie
scope note is not available	Norsk:	geografi
	Polski:	geografia
Themes:	Português:	geografia
geography	Русский:	геграфия
research	Slovenčina:	geografia
	Slovenščina:	geografija
Groups:	Svenska:	geografi
RESEARCH, SCIENCES		

Fig. 1.7: The geography concept in the GEMET thesaurus

Figure 1.7 shows the content of the *geography* concept in the GEMET thesaurus (the concept identifier of is not shown in the figure but it is required to identify and locate the concept). Some of the relations described previously are shown: the left part of the figure displays the *broader* and *narrower* relations; the right area contains the *preferred labels* for the available languages; and on the top there is a *definition*. Besides, GEMET includes themes and groups similar to the subject categories described in section 1.3.3 to group thesaurus terms in broad topic sets that lie outside the hierarchical scheme of the thesaurus.

In addition to the use of subject categories in thesauri such as GEMET, it is also common to structure thesauri information according to facets integrated in the thesaurus hierarchy. In this context, facet refers to a set of fundamental categories

---

[16] http://europa.eu/eurovoc/

[17] http://www.ulcc.ac.uk/unesco/

and their combination according to (synthesis) rules. This definition comes from Ranganathan [168], who uses it to denote aspects or viewpoints in library classification systems. Usually, one problem with classification systems is that items can be classified differently based on different purposes. Ranganathans idea was that class hierarchies can be built and combined for different purposes. For example, a piano is a musical instrument in an abstract typology of instruments but a piece of furniture for the purpose of interior design.

1.3.5 Semantic Networks

A semantic network can be seen as a generalization of a thesaurus where the relationship structure between concepts and terms is not hierarchical but a net of relationships. The relationships generally go beyond the standard BT, NT, RT and usually include specific *whole-part*, *cause-effect*, or *parent-child* relationships. An example is WordNet[18], a lexical database of English created by the Princeton University [52]. WordNet is a large English lexical database that groups nouns, verbs, adjectives and adverbs into sets of cognitive synonyms (synsets), each expressing a distinct concept. Those synsets are interlinked by means of conceptual-semantic and lexical relations.

WordNet is structured in a hierarchy of synsets, defining a synset as a set of strict synonyms representing one underlying lexicalized concept, and providing semantic relations (synonymy, hypernymy, hyponymy, meronymy, holonymy ...) among these synsets. Evolving from WordNet, EuroWordNet [203] was developed as its multilingual version consisting of a set of cross-related WordNets in several languages (French, German, Spanish, Dutch, Italian, Czech, Estonian and English). It includes the semantic relations between words of each provided European language and the relations among each word and the equivalents in the other languages. Although WordNet and EuroWordNet hypernymy/hyponymy relationships could be mapped to an *is-a* (in the sense described in section 1.3.6 most of the times), they are not used homogeneously, involving a fairly loose semantic association. An example in the medical field is the semantic network of UMLS (Unified Medical Language System) [132].

A specific type of semantic network is a topic map. It is a representation of knowledge with an emphasis on the find-ability of information. A topic map defines a multidimensional topic space in which the locations are topics, and the kinds of relationships define the path from one topic to another [86]. It can be seen as an aggregated semantic network that group similar items into topics, associations, and scopes. The term "topic" refers to the object or node in the topic map that represents the subject being referred to. Each topic can be assigned to a type of resource to classify it and to an explicit name to refer to it. ISO-13250 standard [86] defines a topic map with the characteristic of being able to assign multiple base names to a

---

[18] http://wordnet.princeton.edu/

single topic, and to provide variants of each base name for use in specific processing contexts. In the standard, variants were limited to *display name* (used for presentation) and *sort name* (using for alphabetic sorting). There is a one-to-one relationship between topics and subjects, with every topic representing a single subject and every subject being represented by just one topic.

```
<topic id="entry.60.10.34.01">
    <instanceOf>
        <topicRef xlink:href="#commodity"/>
    </instanceOf>
    <subjectIdentity>
        <subjectIndicatorRef xlink:href="urn:x-unspsc:60.10.34.01"/>
    </subjectIdentity>
    <baseName>
        <baseNameString>Geography charts or posters</baseNameString>
    </baseName>
</topic>
<association>
    <instanceOf>
        <topicRef xlink:href="#assoc-class-commodity"/>
    </instanceOf>
    <member>
        <roleSpec>
            <topicRef xlink:href="#class"/>
        </roleSpec>
        <topicRef xlink:href="#entry.60.10.34.00"/>
    </member>
    <member>
        <roleSpec>
            <topicRef xlink:href="#commodity"/>
        </roleSpec>
        <topicRef xlink:href="#entry.60.10.34.01"/>
    </member>
</association>
```

Fig. 1.8: XTM *Geography charts or posters* node of UNSPSC topic map

A topic may be linked to one or more information resources called occurrences that are relevant to the topic. Such occurrences are generally external to the topic map document and they are referenced using URIs or a similar mechanism. Occurrences may be of different types; such distinctions are supported in the standard by the *occurrence role*, and identified by an *occurrence role type*. To be able to describe relationships between topics, the topic map standard provides a construct called *topic association* where the associations between topics are described and grouped by their type. Each topic that participates in an association plays a role in that association called the *association role*. A topic map example is the UNSPSC Topic Map[19] that documents the entire Universal Standard Products and Services Classification (UNSPSC). UNSPSC is a schema that classifies and identifies commodities. It is used in sell side and buy side catalogs and as a standardized account code in analyzing expenditure (Spend Analysis). Figure 1.8 shows the content of *Geography charts or posters* node of UNSPSC in XTM format [163]; property *id* in

---

[19] http://www.techquila.com/tmsamples/xtm/unspsc/unspsc_11.zip

topic tag contains the identifier of the topic; *instanceOf* shows the topic type; *base-Name* has the topic label; and *subjectIdentity* references to the subject that is reified by the topic. *Association* shows the structure of a relation of a topic with another one, with *instanceOf* containing the type of relation, *member* specifying each topic that is part of the relation and *roleSpec* containing the role that each topic plays in the relation.

In the same way as thesauri provide additional built-in relationships and properties with respect to taxonomies, topic maps extend thesauri adding a more flexible model with an open vocabulary. For topic maps, the representation of simple ontology models can be done by establishing the structure of the required classification using topic map roles [59].

1.3.6 Is-a Hierarchies and Formal Instances

Formal hierarchies include strict *is-a* subclass relationships. According to Brachman [24], *is-a* hierarchies can be divided into two major subtypes: one relating two generic nodes (classes) where usually the associated node is less general; and the other relating a generic node with an individual being described by the general description (instantiation). From the categories of each subtype described by Brachman [24], *superset/subset* and *generalization/specialization* for relations between generic nodes, and *set membership* between a generic and a individual node are the most commonly used. *Instance-of* nomenclature is commonly used for generic to individual relationships leaving *is-a* for generic to generic relationships. From now on, this is the way the nomenclature *is-a* and *instance-of* are going to be used.

An *is-a* relationship is transitive in the way indicated in equation 1.1 where *ISA(x,y)* stands for *x "is-a" y*. *Subset* relationship adds the additional requirements shown in equation 1.2 where *SUBSET(x,y)* means *x "is-a-subset-of" y* and *MEMBER(z,x)* (defined in equation 1.4) means that z is member (instance) of the collection (class) x (e.g., *SUBSET(Citrus, Fruits)*. On the other hand, *specialization* relationship is a relation between predicates that affects two arbitrary predicates (P_1 and P_2 in equation 1.3) where *SPECIALIZATION* (P_1,P_2) stands for P_1 *"is-a-specialization-of" P_2* (e.g., *SPECIALIZATION (creation date, date)*. Thesaurus NTG relationship is similar to *is-a* relationship, but mostly defined with the *subset* meaning.

$$ISA(x,y) \wedge ISA(y,z) \rightarrow ISA(x,z) \tag{1.1}$$

$$SUBSET(x,y) \rightarrow \forall z(MEMBER(z,x) \rightarrow MEMBER(z,y)) \tag{1.2}$$

$$SPECIALIZATION(P_1,P_2) \rightarrow \forall x(P_1(x) \rightarrow P_2(x)) \tag{1.3}$$

$$MEMBER(x,y) \rightarrow x \in y \tag{1.4}$$

Richer models include *instance-of* relationships, i.e., formal membership (instances) associated to the model entities. Equation 1.4 shows the membership relationship explained before (e.g., *MEMBER(Alps, Mountains Regions)*). Membership is a transitive relation with respect to the *is-a* relationships (equation 1.5).

$$\text{MEMBER}(x, y) \wedge \text{ISA}(y, z) \rightarrow \text{MEMBER}(x, z) \tag{1.5}$$

This property is intensely used in information discovery for expanding query and indexing terms. It is difficult to find an equivalence of *Membership* in simpler ontology models; the most similar is the NTI relationship but with the lack of explicit transitivity. Equation 1.6 cannot be automatically deduced (it has to be specifically stated).

$$\text{NTI}(x, y) \wedge \text{NTG}(y, x) \rightarrow \text{NTI}(x, z) \tag{1.6}$$

There is a great difference between *is-a* used as a formal relationship and previously described similar relationships, such as the NT used by thesauri. Each *is-a* subtype provides a strong semantics and it is used coherently and homogeneously in the models (e.g., *subset* is not merged with *instance-of*). However, for thesaurus construction, NT is the relationship used by default, merging the different semantics of NTG, NTI and NTP under the same relation name.

1.3.7 Frame based ontologies

A *frame* is a named data structure which is used to represent a concept in a domain. According to Schaerf [172], a *frame* usually represents a concept (or a class) and it is defined by an identifier, and a number of data elements called *slots*, each one corresponding to an attribute that the members of the class can have. The values of the attributes are either elements of a concrete domain (e.g., integers, strings) or identifiers of other frames. Frame based ontologies include classes and property information that is specified at a general class level and inherited by subclasses and instances. For example, if a class *travel* has as properties *origin* and *destination*, a specific travel instance may have *origin:Zaragoza* and *destination:London*. Any subclass in the *is-a* hierarchy of travel, such as for example *low cost travel*, has all *travel* properties and relations, and it can add additional specific ones. This structure of organizing knowledge is similar to the classic software object oriented modeling techniques.

Frame models usually include other elements of knowledge representation such as *facets*. A facet is used here to represent information about a *slot* containing a series of descriptive properties informing about the corresponding attribute and constraining the possible values. They are used to specify default values, value restrictions and attached procedures for computing values when needed or for propagating side effects when the slot is filled. The most commonly used constraints types are: *Cardinality, Minimum-Cardinality, Maximum-Cardinality, and Value-Type*. An example of *Value-Type* facet can be the restriction to a specific range of numbers to the value associated to a relation called *price*. The meaning of facet in this context must not be confused with the sense of facet used in section 1.3.4 for thesauri.

```
<rdf:RDF xmlns:rdf="http://www.w3.org/1999/02/22-rdf-syntax-ns#"
         xmlns:owl="http://www.w3.org/2002/07/owl#"
         xmlns:rdfs="http://www.w3.org/2000/01/rdf-schema#">
    <owl:Class rdf:ID="City"/>
    <owl:Class rdf:ID="Travel">
        <rdfs:subClassOf>
            <owl:Restriction>
                <owl:onProperty>
                    <owl:ObjectProperty rdf:ID="Origin"/>
                </owl:onProperty>
                <owl:cardinality rdf:datatype=
                    "http://www.w3.org/2001/XMLSchema#int">1
                </owl:cardinality>
            </owl:Restriction>
        </rdfs:subClassOf>
        <rdfs:subClassOf rdf:resource=
            "http://www.w3.org/2002/07/owl#Thing"/>
    </owl:Class>
    <owl:ObjectProperty rdf:about="#Origin">
        <rdfs:range rdf:resource="#City"/>
        <rdfs:domain rdf:resource="#Travel"/>
    </owl:ObjectProperty>
    <owl:DatatypeProperty rdf:ID="Name">
        <rdfs:range rdf:resource="http://www.w3.org/2001/XMLSchema#string"/>
        <rdfs:domain rdf:resource="#City"/>
    </owl:DatatypeProperty>
</rdf:RDF>
```

Fig. 1.9: Example of OWL-Lite ontology

An example of frame based ontologies is the one proposed by Chaudhri et al. [29], which provides a uniform model based on a common conceptualization of classes, individuals, slots, facets and inheritance to share knowledge. Protégé [158] and Ontolingua Server [50] are examples of two ontology construction tools that support the construction of frame based ontologies (between other models). In this context, but related with software engineering, UML language provides all the needed elements ('is-a' hierarchy, classes, property definitions, cardinality specification and value restrictions) to construct frame based models but with representation capabilities more reduced than the provided with some complex frame based models.

In the Semantic Web context, the Web Ontology Language (OWL) [16] has become the "de facto" standard to represent formal ontologies. It has a subset called OWL-Lite that supports the set of characteristics required to create frame based ontologies. OWL is constructed on top of RDF-Schema, and therefore it shares many RDF-Schema properties. It can be said, that RDF-Schema provides the basic structure to construct basic frame based ontologies, and OWL-Lite enriches it by allowing adding *facets* to the model. Figure 1.9 shows a very simple example of a frame based ontology in OWL-Lite format. In the example the classes *city* and *travel* are defined; the property *name* is added to the *city* class but limiting their values to strings. It adds the relation *origin* between a *travel* and a *city*, but adding a constraint to indicate that it must be unique (*owl:cardinality*).

1.3.8 General Constraints and Disjointness

Frame based ontologies are limited in their capability to express complex constraints between elements, not being able to support some requirements of the information systems. For example, the value of one property may be based on the value of two other properties; or it may be needed to express disjointness between classes, stating explicitly that an instance of a class A cannot be an instance of a different class B.

```
<rdf:RDF xmlns:rdf="http://www.w3.org/1999/02/22-rdf-syntax-ns#"
         xmlns:owl="http://www.w3.org/2002/07/owl#"
         xmlns:rdfs="http://www.w3.org/2000/01/rdf-schema#">
    <owl:Class rdf:about="#MusicDrama">
        <owl:equivalentClass>
            <owl:Class>
                <owl:unionOf rdf:parseType="Collection">
                    <owl:Class rdf:about="#Opera"/>
                    <owl:Class rdf:about="#Musical"/>
                </owl:unionOf>
            </owl:Class>
        </owl:equivalentClass>
    </owl:Class>
    <owl:Class rdf:about="#Opera">
        <rdfs:subClassOf rdf:resource="#MusicDrama"/>
    </owl:Class>
    <owl:Class rdf:about="#Musical">
        <rdfs:subClassOf rdf:resource="#MusicDrama"/>
        <owl:disjointWith rdf:resource="#Opera"/>
    </owl:Class>
</rdf:RDF>
```

Fig. 1.10: Example of OWL extracted from Bechhofer et al. [16]

The ontologies on top of the formal ontology classification are able to express this additional complexity with arbitrary logical statements using first order logic constraints between terms, but at the cost of an increased complexity that make them to lack computational completeness (all conclusions are guaranteed to be computable) and decidability (all computations will finish in finite time). For example, a class can be treated simultaneously as a collection of individuals and as an individual in its own right, but no reasoner can automatically make use of it. Figure 1.10 shows an ontology containing the *union of* and *disjointness* properties typical of these ontologies.

These ontologies can be represented using different family of languages focused on expressing first order predicates, each one with their limitations in the statements able to define or use. A first family is the one based on frames such as the described by Minsky [143], Fikes and Kehler [54], that are used in knowledge tools such as Protégé [158] and Ontolingua Server [50], CycLp [128] or the Frame Logic lan-

guage used by OntoEdit[20] [183]. Another family is based on Description Logics
such as Classic [20], KIF [61], its successor CL [89] and Ontolingua language [70]
(also based on KIF). OWL [16] has also an explicit logical basis for the language
based on description logics, but the limitations of the RDF-Schema based representations make difficult the expression of some types of predicates (see Horrocks
and Patel-Schneider [78]). The last family contains general-purpose declarative languages such as CLIPS [62] o JESS [58].

1.4 Alignment of ontologies and ontology mappings

Nowadays, in the information retrieval context, there is a great need to provide single homogeneous access to different data collections independently of the type. The
diversity of the used knowledge models hinders in great extent the possibilities of
integration. Data collections created by different organizations usually use different ontologies (or different versions of the same ontology) to classify and index the
resources. Along the years, each organization with the need to describe a collection has created specific "ad hoc" ontologies for the required purpose. Additionally,
the different requirements of data collection, which can range from legacy systems
to new electronic data catalogues, have made that the used ontologies vary in the
degree of formalism.

The definition of equivalence relations between the ontologies used in data collections is a solution usually adopted to provide a unified view. In the information
retrieval field, there are four main types of ontology harmonization processes with
a high level of interrelation needs:

- Integration: It focuses on reusing one or more ontologies to create a new ontology. The source ontologies are related without losing their independence. It is
  usually used to increase the domain of the resulting model.
- Merging: It is the combination of two or more ontologies into a new unified
  one that replaces the originals. Individual elements of the original ontologies are
  present in the new one, but they cannot be traced back to their source.
- Transformation: It changes the semantics of an ontology to make it suitable for
  other purposes. It is needed to model the changes from the original to the transformed ontology. Versioning of ontologies can be viewed as a kind of transformation where the final objective is to obtain an improved model.
- Translation: It refers to changing the representation format of an ontology. There
  is the need to interrelate the equivalent concepts of the each representation model
  to be able to perform the translation.

The existent ontology models of any area of knowledge are not completely independent; they usually have fragments also contained in other ones. For example, focusing on the thesauri models, the classification needs in numerous areas of

---

[20] http://www.ontoknowledge.org/tools/ontoedit.shtml

knowledge have promoted the creation and diffusion of well-established electronic thesauri that partially overlap in their content (with others of the same area). However, the structure provided in each ontology model for the overlapping areas is usually different. For instance, both GEMET and UNESCO thesauri (see section 1.3.4) contain equivalent terminology about the natural environment (among other subjects). However, in GEMET this terminology is concentrated in a branch, and in UNESCO it is distributed throughout the thesaurus.

Some initiatives have tried to harmonize the existent models creating general ontologies that can be used in multiple situations. Some examples are: CYC [127], a universal schema of roughly 10^5 general concepts spanning human reality (it has an open version called OpenCYC[21]); the Descriptive Ontology for Linguistic and Cognitive Engineering (DOLCE) [134], that aims at capturing the ontological categories underlying natural language and human commonsense; WordNet [52], a lexical database designed as a semantic network based on psycholinguistic principles; or the Suggested Upper Merged Ontology (SUMO) [150], developed for research and applications in search, linguistics and reasoning. However, these projects are far from creating a single shared ontology. As Lesk [129] states, while a single ontology would be advantageous, it is unlikely that such a system will ever be developed. Culture constrains the knowledge classification scheme, so that, what is meaningful to one culture is not necessarily meaningful to another one. This is not only true with different cultures but also in the same area of knowledge, by the difficulty of obtaining the agreement of different groups about a unified classification scheme.

An additional problem is the semantic heterogeneity of natural languages. In natural languages, many concepts can be characterized in different ways imposing each one a slightly different view of the world. This ambiguity is expressed through semantic relations between the language terms. From the different relations in natural languages, the following ones are the most frequent:

Synonymy: A relationship between two terms that have the same meaning. Two exact synonyms are equivalent and can be used indistinctly; however, it is very common to have partial synonyms that share the meaning only in some contexts.

Polysemy: It is the capacity of a term to have multiple meanings (related in some way).

Homonymy: The relation between two words that are spelled and/or pronounced the same way but differ in meaning. The difference with respect to polysemy is that while homonymy is a relation between two different words, polysemy represents the multiple meanings of a single word.

Meronymy / Holonymy: Meronymy denotes the relation in which a term is a constituent part of, or a member of other one. Its opposite is holonymy.

Hyponymy / Hypernymy: Hyponymy is the semantic relation in which one word meaning is included within other one. Its opposite is hypernymy.

Gender equivalence: Languages such as Spanish and English have terms that change completely depending on the gender (e.g., cow, bull). In some contexts

---

[21] http://www.opencyc.org/

they can be considered equivalent for search purposes. Therefore, the equivalence
between them has to be stated.

Translations: Terms from different languages can also be equivalents in the way
   described by synonymy (having exactly the same meaning). However, is much
   more habitual to have terms in different languages that only partially overlap in
   meaning, making difficult the definition of equivalence relations.

Most ontology models are able to represent subsets of these relations. Synonymy
and translations are managed through the use of alternative labels (gender equivalence can be represented in a similar way); polysemy and homonymy is reduced
by adding definitions, examples and scope notes; and meronymy and hyponymy is
represented using subset and specialization relations. However, the models generated are not complete; they only include the information required for the purpose
for which they were created. Therefore, queries to systems combining data classified according to different ontologies may perform poorly independently of which
ontology has been used in the query construction (many of the records may contain
terms different from the ones used in the query).

The identification of these relationships (e.g., equivalence or subsumption) between entities of different ontology models allow reducing the semantic heterogeneity problem and provide a unified view. As remarked by Koch et al. [112],
the identification of relations is a complex process that depends on imprecise objec-
tives such as the desired browsing structure, display needs, depth, use of non-topical
classes, and the trade-off between consistency, accuracy and usability. The process
of finding these relationships is known as ontology alignment or ontology matching,
and the representation of these alignments into a format that can be understood for a
computer system to perform a specific task is called ontology mapping. Doerr [43]
defines a matching as "the process of identifying terms, concepts and hierarchical
relationships that are approximately equivalents".

An alignment between two ontologies means to find for each entity (concept,
relation or instance) in the first ontology, a corresponding entity with the same
intended meaning in the second one. Alignment is not only restricted to identity
functions, other possible alignment relations such as subsumption and instantiation
can also be used. Ehrig [45], (chap. 2) defines an ontology alignment as a partial
function according to equation 1.7, where E is the set of all entities, O the set of
possible ontologies, and R the set of possible alignment relations. Given two ontologies $o_1, o_2 \in O$, an entity $e \subset o_1$ is aligned with an entity $f \subset o_2$ according to an
alignment relation $r \in R$ if $align_{o_1,o_2}(e,r) = f$.

$$align = E \times O \times O \rightharpoonup E \times R \qquad (1.7)$$

From the computer science perspective, an alignment is a set of correspondences
$\langle e, f, r, l \rangle$ with e and f being the two aligned entities, r representing the relation
holding between them, and l expressing the level of confidence if it is needed. The
directionality of the alignments depends on the alignment relation. For symmetric
relations, the alignment is bidirectional; in any other case, to provide an alignment

in the opposite direction an inverse alignment relation have to be identified, or two different unidirectional alignments have to be provided (one for each direction).

Ontology alignment is used in any mediation process where it is needed to obtain inter-operation between ontology models for any specific task (e.g., query rewriting or instance transformation).

Related to ontology integration, alignment is used to detect overlapping between the integrated ontologies. Fernández-Breis and Martínez-Béjar [53] describe a framework for the integration of ontologies supplied by a predetermined set of expert users. Every user could benefit from what other users had already contributed to create his integration-derived ontology. Calvanese et al. [28] present another framework for ontology integration, where a global ontology is used to provide a unified view for querying local ontologies. It addresses the problem of specifying the mapping between the global and the local ontologies.

In a merging scenario, alignment between the source ontologies is used to identify their equivalences and perform the merging. McGuinness et al. [136] show an ontology editing, merging, and diagnostic environment called Chimaera. Kotis and Vouros [113] describe the HCONE approach on ontology merging. It is based on capturing the intended informal interpretations of concepts by mapping them to WordNet senses using lexical semantic indexing, and exploiting the formal semantics of concepts by means of description logics reasoning services.

When the objective is to perform a model transformation, the alignment is needed to model the changes from the original to the transformed ontology. Klein and Fensel [111] discuss the problem of ontology versioning comparing it with database schema and program library versioning; they propose building blocks for the most important aspects of a versioning mechanism. Tennis [185] focuses on versioning representation and suggests extensions to SKOS Core [94, 139] to make explicit differences between versions.

Finally, for translation processes, alignment is needed not for the ontology itself but for the meta-models of the source and destination format, that is, to relate each element of the source and destination format models. van Assem et al. [198] describe a method for converting existing thesauri and related resources (terminological ontologies) from their native format to RDF(S) and OWL. van Assem et al. [197] advance in the same line, improving the process to provide transformation to SKOS.

With the objective to perform in a better way some of these interrelation tasks, along the years different approaches for identifying the similarities and equivalences between different vocabulary concepts have been developed. Euzenat and Shvaiko [48], Kalfoglou and Schorlemmer [104], and Rahm and Bernstein [166] remark the following ones as the most relevant:

Techniques based on the analysis of entity names: They match names (classes, attributes ...) and name descriptions of ontology entities. These *terminological* techniques work directly with strings and some matching algorithms use them to analyze textual element descriptions in natural language to find equivalences. They analyze entities (or instances) in isolation, ignoring their relations with other entities (*element level* techniques) and use only the existent data without using additional elements (*syntactic* techniques). They can be divided into *string-based*, and *linguistic* or *language-based* techniques. *String-based* techniques consider terms as sequences of characters and suppose that the more similar the strings, the more likely they denote the same concepts. Cohen et al. [32] and Noy and Musen [159] describe techniques such as string normalization (case, accent, separator removal), equality, edit distance, token and path comparison. *Linguistic* or *language-based* techniques interpret terms as linguistic objects and exploit morphological properties of the entity names to perform linguistic normalization and compare them. Some examples are lemmatization, term extraction and stop-words removal [47, 53].

Techniques based on the analysis of the entities structure: They analyze the structure between the entities (*structure level* techniques). Additionally, since these techniques do not use external elements to work, they are also *syntactic* techniques. They can be subdivided into *internal* and *relational* techniques. *Internal* techniques are based on the use of constraints in the structure of the entities (e.g., types, names or multiplicity of attributes) to find equivalences [166, 33]. *Relational* techniques use the relations between the entities of each ontology (they consider ontologies as a graph) to find the commonality in the structure of relations [133, 102]. They use the similarity of names, types, and structure of the relations between the entities. In this context, taxonomic (*is-a*) and mereologic (*part-of*) relations are the most usually used.

Techniques based on the use of external resources: These techniques use external resources to find or improve the matchings (*external* techniques). Usually, the external resources have a linguistic nature (e.g., lexicons, domain specific thesauri or terminologies) and the linguistic relations of the external resources (e.g., synonymy, hyponymy, hypernymy …) are used to map the terms [73]. An example of this kind of technique is the work of Aleksovski et al. [5] that match poorly structured resources using pre-existent upper formal ontologies (or formal domain ontologies if the area of interest is narrow enough).

Techniques based on previous alignments: These are also *external* techniques that, instead of using other ontology models to detect matchings, use previous available alignments between ontologies in the same area of knowledge [166]. For example, the work of Rahm et al. [167] proposes to reuse fragments of ontology alignments to detect more easily structural equivalences between the pre-existent matchings and the desired one. These ontology alignment fragments allow detecting subsets in the ontologies to match that are similar to other ones already matched in previous alignment processes.

Techniques based on semantic interpretation: These techniques require some semantic interpretation of the ontology. They usually apply a semantically compliant reasoner based on some formal semantics (model-theoretic semantics) to deduce the correspondences and perform the matching (*semantic* techniques). In this field, two entities are the same if they have the same semantic interpretation. Some examples are the techniques based on propositional satisfiability or description logics reasoning. Propositional satisfiability is based on deciding whether a formula of propositional logic is satisfiable or not. This is used to check exhaustively all possible matchings [64]. Description logics reasoning techniques are based on the use of a description logics language for representing structural meaning and any additional constraints (axioms) from the domain knowledge. The reasoning techniques use the language formalism to deduce the mappings [23].

Techniques based on data analysis: They are based on the use of data instances (i.e., a populated ontology) as input (*extensional* techniques). They use a representative sample of a population and analyze the similarity of the property values of the entity instances to find equivalences and discrepancies [182, 42]. For instance, FCA-Merge [182] uses a Formal Concept Analysis (FCA) based process to analyze the instances and perform the matching. An application of this merging schema is described by Nogueras-Iso et al. [153]. Another example is IF-Map [103] that shows a theory and method for automated ontology mapping based on channel theory, a mathematical theory of semantic information. It formalizes the notion of ontology, ontology morphism and ontology mapping linking them to the formal notions of local logic and logic info-morphism stemming from information-flow theory.

These matching approaches have been broadly used in alignment systems from areas such as schema translation and integration, knowledge representation, machine learning and information retrieval [166]. In these fields, there are many relevant works that use one or several of these matching techniques to generate an alignment between ontologies. Zeng and Chan [211] compile a detailed list of projects focused on the interrelation of terminological models and perform an analysis of the approaches used to interrelate them. Another relevant review of mapping works and interrelation approaches is the described by Tudhope et al. [193]. Focusing on the application of the matching techniques, Lim et al. [131] use linguistic and structure-based matchers as part of a data analysis process that deduces concept equivalences. In this same line of work it is SMART [159], a Protégé-2000 [158] plugin that looks for linguistically similar class names and the structure of relations to establish the mappings. Similarly, PROMPT [160] and Chimaera [136] search for linguistic similarities for classes and attributes, but focusing on human contribution as a vital element in the definition of the mappings. Faro et al. [49] presents another structure-based proposal that characterize the problem of Thesaurus Mapping as a problem of Information Retrieval. Working with semantic matchers there is the work of Compatangelo and Meisel [33] that use a description logic reasoner to find class equivalences, and linguistic and heuristic inferences to compare attributes. Somewhat related is the CROSI Mapping System [101] which integrates linguistic and semantic matchers to perform the alignment process. A completely different approach is the work of Prasad et al. [165] that analyzes the relations between classes using a Bayesian matcher. To finish, two works based on instances analysis can be highlighted. On the one hand, CAIMAN system [122] considers the concepts in an ontology implicitly represented by the documents assigned to each concept and provides these relations to a machine-learning process to generate the matchings. On the other hand, Doan et al. [42] present a system that uses probabilistic distribution based similarity measures on the ontology instances to find matchings.

1.5 Summary

This chapter has reviewed how the concept of terminological ontology is defined in the literature, the representation formats for this type of ontologies, and the possibilities of mapping between related terminological models. As part of this study, this chapter has introduced some terminology, elements, information structures, methodologies and processes that are used along the rest of the book, contextualizing them in the field of ontologies.

It has been shown that the term ontology covers a wide area of knowledge organization models, and there is still no whole consensus about an exact definition of what an ontology is and the models that can be considered as an ontology. This is due to the fact that different areas define the ontology concept in different ways, with definitions that range from the philosophical, logical, engineering and information retrieval perspectives among others. The classification of ontologies proposed by Lassila and MacGuinness [123] has been used as a basis to describe the main types of existent ontology models. It has been noted that the main difference between the different ontology models is their capacity to express semantics, being the main difference between them in the degree of formalism and semantics provided rather than in the kind of model.

Two big groups of ontology models have been studied: on the one hand, terminological ontologies, which are simpler and less expressive than full first-order predicate calculus; on the other hand, axiomatized or formal ontologies, which are much more complex to construct but they provide more semantics and their axioms and definitions can support more complex inferences and computations.

Information infrastructures usually require single access to heterogeneous data collections classified according to different ontologies. Therefore, there is need to relate the used ontologies to be able to jump from the terminology used in one system to the terminology used in the other one. Here, the issues related with ontology alignment and the different types of solutions that are usually used have been described.

Chapter 2
A representation framework for terminological ontologies

2.1 Introduction

From the different types of ontology models, terminological ontologies are intensively used by libraries, archives, museums and any other registry of information to facilitate the location of stored resources (classification and information retrieval). Historically, terminological models were printed and used as thematic indexes to locate associated resources. The development of new applications have translated them into the computers and made them to evolve quickly. They are domain or application models that contain the terminology required in an area of knowledge for a specific application and along the years, they have proven to be a useful tool to deal with ambiguity problems, providing inter-relation structure and semantics to the terminology used in these systems. Nowadays, there is a great deal of terminological models covering every area of interest and they have become a crucial part of the information retrieval systems of digital libraries, catalogues and any other system where information is searched or presented thematically.

The use of axiomatic models would be even better, because they provide additional semantics and formal specification of the relationships that could be used to improve the access to information. However, the great size of the required models (thousands of concepts) increases too much the complexity and cost involved in the creation of the model in comparison with the additional benefits obtained. Terminological models provide fewer semantics but they are simpler to create and bigger models are affordable. Additionally, depending on the purpose of an ontology, the level of granularity of the model has to be chosen carefully, because the use of a non-suitable model can reduce the usability and complicate the management of the whole system.

Focusing on terminological ontologies, one of the main problems they present with respect to their use in information systems is their heterogeneity (differences in structure, content and representation). The problem gets bigger when a set of systems using different terminological models have to be integrated. Then the used

J. Lacasta et al., *Terminological Ontologies: Design, Management and Practical Applications*, Semantic Web and Beyond 9, DOI 10.1007/978-1-4419-6981-1_2, © Springer Science+Business Media, LLC 2010

models must be matched to be able to jump from the terminology used in one system to the terminology used in another.

In this context, the first step needed in the process of harmonizing the management of terminological ontologies is the use of a common representation format. A common representation simplifies the construction of software having to manage multiple ontology models (only a single format has to be understood). This is required not only for the terminological ontologies, but also for the relationships defined between them. Relationships between ontology models are difficult to establish and must be properly represented to be able to reuse them when needed.

This chapter analyzes the most common representation models for ontologies and for relations between ontologies, and proposes a framework for its representation. This framework is based on SKOS as a common representation format for terminological models. It has been extended to fulfill some specific requirements, such as the need to represent additional concept properties and the selection of a suitable description model to identify and classify the used ontologies. With respect to the representation of mappings, given the lack of a suitable representation format, a new one based on BS-8723 terminology has been developed.

2.2 Related work in the representation of terminological ontologies

2.2.1 Representation of knowledge models

Along the years, specific adapted representation models have been created for different ontology types. Sections 1.3.7 and 1.3.8 have introduced some representation formats for the described formal ontology models. These representations formats are very complete and given that they can represent elaborated models, they can also be used for the simpler ones. However, a format that is not perfectly adapted to the model that tries to represent increases its difficulty of use. There are many primitives, properties and attributes that are not required and there are several ways to represent the same.

Focusing on terminological models, even simpler models such as controlled vocabularies or glossaries have some specific representation formats for them. Terminological Markup Framework (TMF) [83] is a meta-model that allows the definition of different Terminological Markup Languages for specific purposes. Two XML based formats created using this framework are the Geneter and the MSC (Machine-Readable Terminology Interchange Format with Specified Constraints) described both of them in the TMF standard. Geneter is a format to describe data categories and their relationships in a terminological data collection while MSC is designed to represent terminological data for the processes of analysis, dissemination, and exchange of information from human-oriented terminological databases (termbases). Another alternative representation framework is Term Base eXchange

(TBX) [91], an open XML-based standard for exchanging structured terminological data. In a similar way to TMF, it allows defining a variety of terminological markup languages. For other similar models, also specific representation formats exist. For example, the Lexical Markup Framework (LMF) [90] is an abstract meta-model that provides a common, standardized framework for the construction of computational lexicons that can be mapped to XML based representation. For authority files, the XML representation schema proposed by MARC-21 standard[1] can be considered.

Taxonomies and thesauri have also their own representation formats. Traditionally, each company has created their own ad-hoc formats to represent their taxonomies and thesauri. For example, the most popular thesauri used in geospatial science for classification of resources such as AGROVOC, EUROVOC or GEMET where initially generated in completely different formats.

Nowadays, some initiatives have tried to create homogeneous representation formats for thesauri. For example, the ADL thesaurus Protocol [97] defines an XML and HTTP based protocol for accessing thesauri that returns portions of the thesaurus contained encoded in XML. Another approach is the Thesaurus Interchange Format in RDF proposed by the Language Independent Metadata Browsing of European Resources (LIMBER) project [135]. Additionally, the California Environmental Resources Evaluation System (CERES) and the NBII Biological Resources Division collaborated in a Thesaurus Partnership project[2] for the development of an Integrated Environmental Thesaurus and a Thesaurus Networking ToolSet for Metadata Development and Keyword Searching. One of the deliverables of this project is another RDF format to represent thesauri.

For taxonomies, there are some general representation formats such as the one used in *Dewey Decimal Classification (DDC)*[3] [40] and *Universal Decimal Classification (UDC)*[4] [137, 138]. However, they are oriented to human visualization instead of computer processing and interchange. The existent computer oriented interchange formats are specific ad-hoc representations similar to the used for thesauri.

Finally, in the topic maps context, XML Topic Maps (XTM) format [163] is the most frequently used, being supported by many tools in quite different contexts.

All these formats have been designed to describe the terminological ontologies of a certain kind, but are not specifically adapted to be able to describe in a coherent way at least a common subset of different types of them. British standards BS-5723 [26], BS-6723 [25] and their international equivalent (ISO-2788 [81] and ISO-5964 [80]) propose models to manage monolingual and multilingual thesauri that can be also applied to simpler models but they lack a suitable representation format. The British Standards Institute IDT/2/2 Working Group has recently finished the 5th part of BS-8723 standard [27] that describes an exchange format and protocols for interoperability for terminological ontologies following the thesaurus model. It is

---

[1] http://www.loc.gov/standards/marcxml/

[2] http://ceres.ca.gov/ thesaurus

[3] http://www.oclc.org/dewey/

[4] http://www.udcc.org/about.htm

focused on thesauri, but it can be used to represent other terminological models. This format is based on XML, and has been promoted to ISO as part of the revision of the ISO-5964 standard (norm for multilingual thesauri) called ISO-25964 that is currently undergoing review by ISO-TC46/SC-9.

In the Semantic Web area, the Simple Knowledge Organization System (SKOS) project[5] [141, 139, 94] has become the reference to represent a broad set of terminological ontologies used for classification such as subject heading lists, taxonomies, classification schemes, thesaurus, folksonomies, controlled vocabularies, and also concept schemes embedded in glossaries and terminologies. SKOS was initially developed within the scope of the Semantic Web Advanced Development for Europe[6] (SWAD-E). SWAD-E was created to support W3C's Semantic Web initiative in Europe (part of the IST-7 programme). It is based on a generic RDF schema for thesauri that was initially produced by the DESIRE project [34], and further developed in the Limber project [135]. It has been developed as a draft of an RDF/OWL Schema for thesauri compatible with relevant ISO standards, and later adapted to support other types of terminological ontologies. SKOS is still under review but different drafts describing the structure already exists.

2.2.2 *Representation of mappings*

The representation of terminological ontologies is covered with the development of standards such as the previously described, but there are no works so advanced for mapping representation. The standards used to describe thesauri and similar models such as BS-5723 [26], BS-6723 [25] and their international equivalent (ISO-2788 [81] and ISO-5964 [80]) describe slightly the mapping needs but they do not provide a suitable representation. In a similar way, the Z39.19-2005 [9] (revision of Z39.19-1995) makes some more specific references to mapping between thesauri but does not provide either a mapping model nor representation format.

The most advanced proposal for mapping representation is the one developed in the context of the SKOS project [140, 141], where a draft version of a mapping model and interchange format (RDF based) called SKOS-Mapping has already been developed (see figure 2.1). However, the proposed representation format is still preliminary. It is under revision due to deficiencies such as the lack of structure in the mapping types and the types of connectors provided. SKOS-Mapping model proposes a set of mapping relations between concepts. Additionally, to provide 1:N relationships the concepts can be aggregated in a *rdf:Bag* structure by different composition functions. The meaning of each mapping relation and each composition function is described next in this section.

Given the lack of an established representation model and interchange format for mappings, it is needed to define one suitable for the context of this book (see

---

[5] http://www.w3.org/2004/02/skos/

[6] http://www.w3.org/2001/sw/Europe/reports/thes/

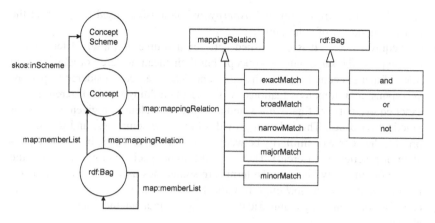

Fig. 2.1: SKOS-Mapping model

section 2.4.1). An initial step in this direction has been to analyze the representation requirements, describing the available alternatives in terms of structure, relations, and properties required to represent the mappings.

As previously indicated, a mapping is a representation of an alignment between ontologies. It represents the axioms that describe how to express concepts, relations or instances in terms of the second ontology [45]. Focusing on the thesaurus model as representative of terminological ontologies, ISO-5964 reduces the required types of inter-thesaurus relations to the following three: exact, inexact and partial equivalence. They correspond to the different types of alignment relations that can be considered in the matching process (see section 1.4). The top half of Venn diagrams in figure 2.2 show graphically their semantics. According to ISO-5964 they have the following meaning:

Exact equivalence: An exact equivalence is established between a source language term and a target language term when both of them have identical meanings. It is a bidirectional synonymy relation where the involved concepts can use different identifiers to represent the same concept. This inter-thesaurus relationship is a kind of generalization of the bidirectional intra-thesaurus synonymy relationship between the preferred and the alternative labels of a thesaurus concept, or between the different language dependent labels in a concept from a multilingual thesaurus.

Partial equivalence: It is the association between a source and a target term when both cannot be matched by an exact equivalence. One term has either a broader or a narrower meaning than the other one, but not both. That is, the meaning of one of the terms is completely contained within another one. This relation cannot be directly used because there is no way to distinguish which concept is the general one and which is the specific one. However, it can be expressed using two inverse relationships that show the directionality of the relation. It is equivalent to the *hyponymy* and *hypernymy* relationships used to construct the concept hierarchy of a thesaurus.

Inexact equivalence: It is established between a source and a target term when they express the same general concept, but their meanings are not identical and none of them is contained into the other one. They can be considered as partial-synonyms, and in many situations, two concepts holding subtle differences (inexact equivalent) are finally classified as exact equivalent in a given context for practical purposes. This relation provides quite few semantics, and it does not provide the degree of similarity between the concepts (they may be almost equivalent or practically different). Therefore, different specializations indicating the degree of similarity between the terms are sometimes used. For example, naming the relations as major/minor to indicate more or less similarity between the concepts, or even using a numerical percentage to indicate their degree of equivalence).

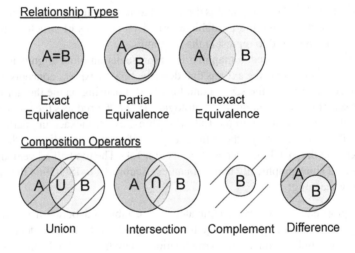

Fig. 2.2: Types of mapping relationships

In the draft of SKOS-Mapping (see figure 2.1), mapping relations have been represented by means of the *skos:mappingRelation*, a generic relation to indicate any kind of mapping. It specializes into *skos:exactMatch* for exact equivalences; *skos:broadMatch* and *skos:narrowMatch* for partial equivalence; and *skos: relatedMatch* for inexact mappings.

Having in mind the application of the defined mappings in the discovery process of an information retrieval system, and especially in query systems, Doerr [43] refines the definition of these relations and shows how they can be used to create a consistent set of mappings between ontologies. He indicates that the creation of an arbitrary set of equivalence expressions for correlation makes the replacement of terms in queries unpredictable. He proposes to provide a broader and a narrower relationship for each concept with the objective of improving automatic translation of queries. The mappings have to be created systematically by assigning to each source concept the nearest broader and narrower in the target model. For those concepts were finding a broader and a narrower cannot be possible, at least one should be provided.

The described mapping relationships allow defining 1:1 relationships between concepts. However, as Doerr [43] states, "the expressive power of the mapping should be at least equivalent to the expressiveness of the search paradigm, otherwise the user could express better queries in each target system than the mapping mechanism could provide". Greater cardinality such as 1:N (single to multiple equivalence) is then needed to deal with situations were exact mappings cannot be found, but a combination of the meaning of a set of concepts of one ontology is equivalent to a concept in another one.

If multiple equivalence relationships need to be defined, they also have to be properly represented. However, nowadays there is not a real consensus about which composition operators are needed. ISO-5964 does not define precisely the nature and types of composition. The technical specifications provided by the Z39.50 protocol use any combination of mathematical (logical) operators such as *intersection*, *union*, and *complement* to create combined concepts and map them [8]. Boolean algebra operators (AND, OR, NOT) are used indistinctly to *union*, *intersection* and *complement* operators, for example in SKOS-Mapping first draft [140] (see figure 2.1). BS-8723 remarks that only the *intersection* operator should be used since it is the only common composition operation. BS-8723 goes further completely rejecting the *complement* operator as a viable option for composition of concepts.

The *intersection* composition operator is accepted as it covers practical mapping requirements. It is used to create concepts whose meaning is restricted to the common elements of two (or more than two) other concepts. For example, the concepts *animal* and *biology* can be combined to create the *animal biology* concept of GEMET; then this concept can be used to classify the records that are about both of the original subjects. The set of records classified according this new concept would be the intersection of those classified with *animal* and those with *biology*.

With respect to the *union* operator, it is easy to imagine situations where it can be required. However, they are usually hypothetical applications with a low interest for the construction of real systems. For example, a composed concept equivalent to *tree* would be a set of concepts containing all the different tree species. However, it is not reasonable to think that the ontologies to mach, if are not specifically focused on that matter, would contain all those elements. A subset of them could be composed with *union*, but the associated mapping could not be considered as exact. Additionally, the semantic meaning of this possible equivalence would be the same as providing different partial equivalences for each concept (which is simpler). For mappings in contexts with very specific terminology it can be applicable, but is not a typical situation.

The use of the *complement* operator is even more limited. It has to be used in combination with other ones due to the extent of the result obtained (everything except the indicated concept). A suitable alternative is the *difference* operator (*A and not B*), which is commonly employed in information retrieval systems to reduce the possible senses of a concept used in a query. It is applicable for multilingual mappings where two terms can be considered as exactly equivalents if a part of the meaning of one of them is removed. For example, the Spanish term *pierna* is equivalent to English *leg* but it is only used for humans. Therefore, *pierna* can be seen as *exact equivalent* to the *difference* between *leg* and *animal leg*. However, it can be replaced many times by the intersection operator (e.g., *pierna* is also the intersection of *leg* and *human*).

The bottom half of the figure 2.2 describes the semantics of these operators by means of Venn diagrams.

2.3 Representation of terminological ontologies

Ontologies have to be properly represented to facilitate their interchange. Not only that, relations between two ontologies need to be represented if they want to be reused in other contexts. As this book is focused on the use of terminological ontologies, the analysis of the possible representation models has been centered on these models.

Each different ontology type provides different semantic expressiveness. As mentioned in section 1.2, the distinction between the different types of ontologies is one of degree rather than kind, where more complex models add new features to the "ones" provided by the simpler models. The representation of these models in a computer system is done through representations formats adapted to each model type. Until recently, the lack of standardized representation formats has produced the creation of a great variety of incompatible ad-hoc formats, created for specific ontologies and only used by the organizations that created them. Nowadays, the information community has reached agreements about the most suitable representation formats for some of the ontology models and it has standardized them. For other ontology models, there is still no complete consensus about their representation.

2.3.1 Knowledge model representation

From the different available representation alternatives, SKOS can be used to describe many different terminological models. This format is the most suitable for the desired classification and retrieval context where several ontology models are required. However, it is still under development and not all the needed characteristics are covered. Given this situation, it has been needed to extend it to deal with the situations not covered in the original SKOS format.

An advantage of using SKOS is that is it is becoming a de-facto standard for represent some types of terminological models. SKOS has been already used to represent some thesauri such as GEMET, AGROVOC, ADL Feature Types, or some parts of WordNet lexical database (see SKOS project web page[7]). Additionally, projects such as the OCLC Terminology Services[8] provide their terminological models in SKOS format.

As it is described in the SKOS reference document [139], the SKOS data model is formally defined as an OWL Full ontology. The "elements" of the SKOS data model are classes and properties, and the structure and integrity of the data model is defined by the logical characteristics of and interdependencies between those classes and properties. However, SKOS is not a formal knowledge representation language because terminological ontologies do not assert any axioms or facts, their structures do not have any formal semantics, and they cannot be reliably interpreted as either formal axioms or facts about the world. As mentioned by Miles and Bechhofer [139], SKOS is needed because OWL structure is not the most adequate for expressing terminological models, "It is not appropriate to express the concepts directly as classes of an ontology, or to express an informal (broader/narrower) hierarchy directly as a set of class subsumption axioms". Using SKOS data model, the "concepts" are modeled as individuals, and the informal descriptions and the links between those "concepts" are modeled as facts about those individuals.

SKOS is a collection of three different RDF-Schema application profiles:

SKOS-Core: It provides a model for expressing the basic structure and content of concept schemes, understanding them as a set of concepts, optionally including statements about semantic relationships between them. It is the basic profile used to define terminological ontologies and it provides a model to represent the common properties and relations shared by most of the terminological models.

SKOS-Extensions: They are a set of terms extending the SKOS Core vocabulary to support some features of specific knowledge organization systems, especially thesauri.

SKOS-Mapping: Its purpose is to describe relations between different ontologies. It is done providing mappings between concepts of different concept schemes. It is reviewed in section 2.4

It can be said that SKOS-Core contains the set of elements common to all terminological models and provide some guidelines to facilitate its extension with specific properties and relations existent in some particular models.

The structure of elements and relations of the SKOS-Core application profile is described in Figure 2.3. The model can be divided in two kinds of elements: firstly, those used to define the ontology structure; and secondly, those describing the lexical properties of each represented term.

The structure of the model is described by a small set of elements. The basic one is the *skos:concept*. It is used to represent an abstract or symbolic tag that attempts to model the reality (it is identified by an URI). A SKOS-Core file consists of a set of concepts grouped in a *skos:conceptScheme*. The *skos:conceptScheme* structure is the

---

[7] http://esw.w3.org/topic/SkosDev/DataZone

[8] http://www.oclc.org/research/projects/termservices/

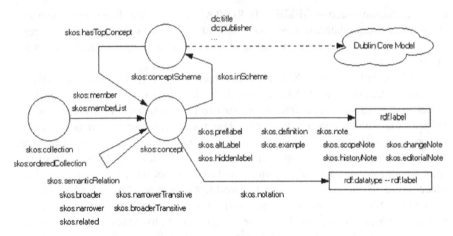

Fig. 2.3: SKOS-Core model

entry point to the ontology. It identifies the whole ontology with an URI and refers
to the upper concepts contained inside. Additionally, the *skos:conceptScheme* can
contain metadata describing its content to facilitate its use to the persons requiring
it.

To indicate that a *skos:concept* is part of a *skos:conceptScheme* (belongs to it),
the *skos: inScheme* relation is used. This relation allows a concept to be part of more
than a schema, making possible to create views of a model containing only certain
subsets of it by defining different concept schemes on the same set of concepts. The
relation of the *skos:conceptScheme* with the concepts of the ontology is defined by
the *skos:hasTopConcept* relation. This relation points to the *skos:concept*(s) which
are topmost (top concepts) in the hierarchical structure of concepts for that scheme.
If the represented model is flat (no hierarchy), there will be a *skos:hasTopConcept*
relation for each concept in the model.

To provide relations between concepts, SKOS defines a general relationship
called *skos:semanticRelation* that indicates that exist a link between two *skos:
concept* (the type is not indicated). All the different hierarchical and associative
relationship types defined by SKOS are specializations of it. *skos:broader* and
skos:narrower relations are inverse relations used to model the hierarchical characteristics of many terminological ontologies. They indicate that one concept is, in
some way, more general than the other. *skos:broader* is used to describe the relation
from the specific concept towards the general one and *skos:narrower* for the opposite. These two relations are not transitive, and therefore they can only be used to
assert an immediate hierarchical link between two *skos:concept*. Transitive equivalents for these relations are *skos:broaderTransitive* and *skos:narrowerTransitive*.
Associative relations between concepts are represented using *skos:related*. It indicates that two concepts are related in some way maintaining a symmetric relation

between them. Figure 2.4 contains a subset of EUROVOC thesaurus that shows how
some of these elements and relationships are represented in SKOS.

```
<rdf:Description rdf:about="http://europa.eu/eurovoc">
    <rdf:type rdf:resource=
        "http://www.w3.org/2004/02/skos/core#ConceptScheme"/>
    <dc:title>EUROVOC 4.1</dc:title>
    <skos:hasTopConcept rdf:resource="http://europa.eu/eurovoc/Domain04"/>
    <skos:hasTopConcept rdf:resource="http://europa.eu/eurovoc/Domain68"/>
    ...
</rdf:Description>
<rdf:Description rdf:about="http://europa.eu/eurovoc/Domain68">
    <rdf:type rdf:resource="http://www.w3.org/2004/02/skos/core#Concept"/>
    <skos:inScheme rdf:resource="http://europa.eu/eurovoc/eurovoc"/>
    <skos:prefLabel xml:lang="en">INDUSTRY</skos:prefLabel>
    ...
    <skos:narrower rdf:resource=
        "http://europa.eu/eurovoc/MicroThes6811"/>
    <skos:narrower rdf:resource=
        "http://europa.eu/eurovoc/MicroThes6821"/>
    ...
</rdf:Description> <rdf:Description
rdf:about="http://europa.eu/eurovoc/MicroThes6811">
    <rdf:type rdf:resource="http://www.w3.org/2004/02/skos/core#Concept"/>
    <skos:inScheme rdf:resource="http://europa.eu/eurovoc/eurovoc"/>
    <skos:prefLabel xml:lang="en">chemistry</skos:prefLabel>
    ...
    <skos:broader rdf:resource="http://europa.eu/eurovoc/Domain68"/>
    <skos:narrower rdf:resource="http://europa.eu/eurovoc/Concept3810"/>
    ...
</rdf:Description>
```

Fig. 2.4: Fragment of SKOS file from EUROVOC thesaurus

An additional characteristic included in the last version of SKOS model has been
the capacity to group concepts (for browsing, showing, printing...) that share something in common. To do this, the *skos:collection* and *skos:orderedCollection* are
used. They allow defining labeled and/or ordered groups of SKOS concepts that
share a property, when the value of this property can be used to group the concepts under different categories. *skos:collection* is used for general collections and
skos:orderedCollection for collections where the order of the elements is relevant
(e.g., for visualization). The relation between the collections and the *skos:concept*(s)
contained inside is done using the relationship *skos:member* for *skos:collection* and
skos:memberList for *skos:orderedCollection*.

The lexical properties of the terminological ontologies are directly included into
the *skos:concept*(s) structure. Since these properties are language dependent (they
contain terms that are part of a specific natural language), an attribute is used
to specify the language used in their content. The most relevant properties are
skos:preflabel and *skos:altLabel*, which provide the labels used for classification
and visualization. *skos:preflabel* contain the label that better identifies a concept (for
thesauri it must be unique). On the other hand, *skos:altLabel* contains synonyms or
spelling variations of the preferred label, and it is used to redirect to the preferred
label when required. *skos:hiddenlabel* is a kind of alternative label but containing

common misspellings of the preferred term. It can be used for comparison in search systems, but not for visualization by the user. The example shown in figure 2.5 shows the preferred and alternative labels of some concepts according to the SKOS format.

```
<rdf:Description rdf:about="http://europa.eu/eurovoc/Concept3810">
    <rdf:type rdf:resource="http://www.w3.org/2004/02/skos/core#Concept"/>
    <skos:inScheme rdf:resource="http://europa.eu/eurovoc/eurovoc"/>
    <skos:prefLabel xml:lang="en">chemical compound</skos:prefLabel>
    <skos:prefLabel xml:lang="es">compuesto químico</skos:prefLabel>
    ...
    <skos:altLabel xml:lang="en">compound, chemical</skos:altLabel>
    <skos:altLabel xml:lang="es">químico, compuesto</skos:altLabel>
    ...
    <skos:broader rdf:resource="http://europa.eu/eurovoc/MicroThes6811"/>
    <skos:narrower rdf:resource="http://europa.eu/eurovoc/Concept3817"/>
    ...
    <skos:related rdf:resource="http://europa.eu/eurovoc/Concept2739"/>
</rdf:Description>
```

Fig. 2.5: Fragment of SKOS concept from EUROVOC thesaurus

In addition to these properties, *skos:notation* has been defined to represent alternative identifiers, not recognizable as a word or sequence of words in any natural language, that identify uniquely a concept within the scope of a given concept scheme. Since they are not described in a natural language, they cannot be represented using the label properties. *skos:notation* is especially useful for classification schemes that provide multiple codes of terms. An example of this category is the ISO-639 [82] (ISO standard for coding of languages), which proposes different types of alphanumeric codes (e.g., 2 letter and 3 letter codes) to represent the existent languages. The need to represent models with this characteristic has required the definition of a representation able to manage notations of different types. The solution used has been to add inside the *skos:notation* an *rdf:datatype* containing the type of notation defined, with the objective of being able to distinguish between different identifiers created with different purposes. Figure 2.6 shows a fragment of the ISO-639 in SKOS using the *skos:notation* property, which distinguishes between the three code-sets for languages using notations with different *rdf:datatype*.

The last set of properties in the *skos:concept* model are those focused on documentation, which provide informal human-readable documentation to the user. SKOS provides a *skos:note* property for general documentation purposes and it is used to indicate additional information associated to the concept. To provide documentation elements with more specific semantic, some specializations of *skos:note* are defined. The main documentation properties are *skos:definition*, and *skos: example*. As it can be deduced by their name, *skos:definition* supplies a complete explanation of the intended meaning of a concept, and *skos:example* stores an example of the use of the concept. *skos:scopeNote* is also quite relevant; it provides information about the intended meaning of a concept in the specific context of the ontology. It is especially used as an indication of how the use of a concept is limited for indexing.

```
<rdf:Description rdf:about="http://www.iso.org/ISO639-3/eng">
    <skos:inScheme rdf:resource="http://www.iso.org/ISO639/ISO639"/>
    <rdf:type rdf:resource="http://www.w3.org/2004/02/skos/core#Concept"/>
    <skos:prefLabel xml:lang="en">English</skos:prefLabel>
    <skos:prefLabel xml:lang="es">inglés</skos:prefLabel>
    <skos:prefLabel xml:lang="fr">anglais</skos:prefLabel>
    <skos:prefLabel xml:lang="de">englisch</skos:prefLabel>
    <skos:scopeNote xml:lang="en">Living language</skos:scopeNote>
    <skos:notation rdf:datatype=
        "http://www.iso.org/ISO639-3/">eng</skos:notation>
    <skos:notation rdf:datatype=
        "http://www.iso.org/ISO639-2/">eng</skos:notation>
    <skos:notation rdf:datatype=
        "http://www.iso.org/ISO639-1/">en</skos:notation>
</rdf:Description>
```

Fig. 2.6: Fragment of SKOS file of ISO-639 classification scheme

Finally, *skos:historyNote* describes significant changes to the meaning or the form of a concept.

Other *skos:note* specializations also exist, but they are oriented to be used as part of the management process of the terminological ontology, and not to be provided to the final user. *skos:editorialNote* supplies management information (e.g., reminders of editorial work still to be done), and *skos:changeNote* documents fine-grained changes to a concept for the purposes of administration and maintenance.

2.3.2 Metadata for ontology description

A terminological ontology, independently of the representation, has to be properly described to be able to identify its content. A user has to know what each terminological model is about to be able to decide which one suits better to his requirements.

In order to describe general ontologies the Ontology Metadata Vocabulary[9] (OMV) developed in OWL can be used. This is a metadata vocabulary to describe any type of ontology, and it is quite complete. However, to describe the content of a SKOS terminological ontology, a simpler metadata model adapted to the description requirements of terminological models is preferred. A suitable alternative is Dublin Core [85] because it is a standard for representing metadata. Additionally, it is extensively used in the digital library area to classify resources and there is a lot of experience in its use in different contexts. It provides a simple way to describe a resource using general metadata terms, which can be easily matched with complex domain-specific metadata standards. Although Dublin Core metadata vocabulary is general, this is not a problem since it can be extended to define application profiles for specific types of resources such as terminological ontologies. Other metadata approaches are reviewed by the Terminology Registry Scoping Study as part of its

---

[9] http://ontoware.org/projects/omv

study[10]. Additionally, this study proposes a specific metadata profile based on the reviewed metadata schema.

In the defined representation framework, it has been decided to follow the metadata profile hierarchy described in Tolosana-Calasanz et al. [187] to propose an application profile for the description of ontologies that refines the definition and domains of Dublin Core elements (see table 2.1). To represent this metadata profile, the IEMSR format[11] [75] has been used.

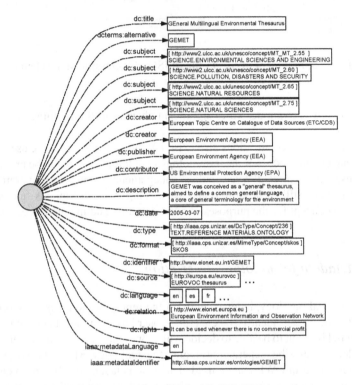

Fig. 2.7: Metadata describing the GEMET thesaurus

The metadata profile includes a subset of the basic Dublin Core elements adding the *applied in* field for describing the thematic context in which the ontology can be used. Besides, it also includes the following metadata management fields extracted from ISO-19115 standard [84]: *metadata language* to indicate the language of the metadata, *metadata identifier* to identify the metadata record, *metadata creation date* to store the date when the metadata was created and *metadata point of contact* to indicate who created the metadata. Table 2.1 contains all the metadata elements

---

[10] http://www.ukoln.ac.uk/projects/trss/dissemination/metadata.pdf

[11] IEMSR is an RDF based format created by the JISC IE Metadata Schema Registry project to define metadata application profiles

included in the metadata profile, together with their identifiers, the label used to describe them, their obligation, their cardinality, and a description of the element.

Resource	Label	Obligation	Cardinality	Description
http://purl.org/dc/elements/1.1/title	Name	Mandatory	Unbounded	A name given to the ontology
http://purl.org/dc/terms/alternative	Short name	Mandatory	Unbounded	Any form of the title used as a substitute or alternative to the formal title of the ontology
http://purl.org/dc/elements/1.1/creator	Creator	Mandatory	Unbounded	An entity primarily responsible for making the content of the ontology
http://purl.org/dc/elements/1.1/subject	Subject	Mandatory	Unbounded	The topic of the content of the ontology
http://iaaa.cps.unizar.es/iaaaterms/AppliedIn	Applied in	Mandatory	Unbounded	Field in which the ontology can be used
http://purl.org/dc/elements/1.1/description	Description	Optional	Unbounded	An account of the content of the ontology
http://purl.org/dc/elements/1.1/publisher	Publisher	Optional	Unbounded	An entity responsible for making the ontology available
http://purl.org/dc/elements/1.1/contributor	Contributor	Optional	Unbounded	An entity responsible for making contributions to the content of the ontology
http://purl.org/dc/terms/created	Date of creation	Mandatory	Unbounded	Date of creation of the ontology
http://purl.org/dc/terms/issued	Date of publication	Optional	Unbounded	Date of formal issuance (e.g., publication) of the ontology
http://purl.org/dc/terms/modified	Date of modification	Optional	Unbounded	Date on which the ontology was changed
http://purl.org/dc/elements/1.1/type	Type	Mandatory	Unbounded	The nature or genre of the content of the ontology
http://purl.org/dc/elements/1.1/format	Format	Optional	Unbounded	The physical or digital manifestation of the resource
http://purl.org/dc/elements/1.1/identifier	Ontology identifier	Mandatory	Unbounded	An unambiguous reference to the ontology within a given context
http://purl.org/dc/elements/1.1/source	Source	Optional	Unbounded	A reference to a resource from which the present ontology is derived
http://purl.org/dc/elements/1.1/language	Ontology language	Mandatory	Unbounded	A language of the intellectual content of the ontology
http://purl.org/dc/elements/1.1/relation	Relation	Optional	Unbounded	A reference to a related ontology or resource
http://purl.org/dc/terms/conformsTo	Conforms to	Optional	Unbounded	A reference to an established standard to which the ontology conforms
http://purl.org/dc/terms/isVersionOf	Is version of	Optional	Unbounded	The described ontology is a version, edition, or adaptation of the referenced ontology. Changes in version imply substantive changes in content rather than differences in format
http://purl.org/dc/terms/isReplacedBy	Is replaced by	Optional	Unbounded	The described ontology is supplanted, displaced, or superseded by the referenced resource
http://purl.org/dc/terms/replaces	Replaces	Optional	Unbounded	The described ontology supplants, displaces, or supersedes the referenced resource
http://purl.org/dc/terms/hasVersion	Has version	Optional	Unbounded	The described ontology has a version, edition, or adaptation, namely, the referenced resource
http://purl.org/dc/elements/1.1/coverage	Coverage	Optional	Unbounded	Place covered by the ontology (if it is the case)
http://purl.org/dc/terms/spatial	Spatial characteristics	Optional	Unbounded	Spatial characteristics of the intellectual content of the ontology
http://purl.org/dc/terms/temporal	Temporal	Optional	Unbounded	Temporal characteristics of the intellectual content of the ontology
http://purl.org/dc/elements/1.1/rights	Rights	Mandatory	Unbounded	Information about rights held in and over the ontology
http://purl.org/dc/terms/accessRights	Access rights	Optional	Unbounded	Information about who can access the ontology or an indication of its security status
http://purl.org/dc/terms/license	License	Optional	Unbounded	A legal document giving official permission to do something with the ontology
http://purl.org/dc/terms/audience	Audience	Optional	Unbounded	A class of entity for whom the ontology is intended or useful
http://purl.org/dc/terms/mediator	Mediator	Optional	Unbounded	A class of entity that mediates access to the ontology and for whom the ontology is intended or useful
http://www.isotc211.org/19115/MD_Metadata.dateStamp	Metadata creation date	Mandatory	Unbounded	Date in which the metadata has been created
http://www.isotc211.org/19115/MD_Metadata.contact	Metadata point of contact	Mandatory	Unbounded	Person who has created the metadata
http://www.isotc211.org/19115/MD_Metadata.language	Metadata language	Mandatory	Unbounded	Language used for documenting the metadata record
http://www.isotc211.org/19115/MD_Metadata.fileIdentifier	Metadata identifier	Mandatory	Unbounded	Unique identifier for the metadata record

Table 2.1: Terminological ontology metadata application profile

Figure 2.7 shows an example of ontology metadata describing the GEMET thesaurus. The RDF metadata is displayed as a hedgehog graph (reinterpretation of RDF triplets: resources, named properties and values). The purpose of these metadata is not only to simplify discovery, but also to identify which ontologies are useful for a specific task in a peer-to-peer communication (e.g., ontologies that cover a restricted geographical area or about a specific theme).

2.4 Representation of ontology mappings

Creating a good alignment between two terminological ontologies is an expensive task (in time and cost). Even using automated matching processes, the results have to be manually revised and updated to remove inconsistencies. Due to the difficulty to reduce these costs, at least the obtained mappings should be represented in a way that facilitates their reuse. This section focuses on how to perform this representation and how to describe it to facilitate its reuse.

2.4.1 Mapping representation

As described in section 2.2.2, the most advanced representation model for terminological ontologies is SKOS-Mapping. However, it lacks some necessary characteristics such as the possibility to store the reliability of the mappings when they are generated by an automatic system, and the representation of the inverse relationships of the mappings (given a concept, to know which other concepts consider it as equivalent according to certain type of mapping function).

The first step to define the mapping representation format was to select an appropriate terminology for the elements that should be represented. In this area, the existent nomenclature is quite heterogeneous. Each standard and model that takes into account mappings needs use its own terminology. For example, an exact mapping is described in the ISO and the BS standards as *exact equivalence*, but in the SKOS-Mapping is called *exact match* or *equivalent concept* depending on the version of the standard, and in the Getty Art & Architecture thesaurus [93] it is represented using mathematical notation ("=" symbol).

The notation that has been selected is the one used in the BS-8723 standard. BS-8723 standard does not propose a representation model for relations between thesauri but it reviews the mapping requirements.

Using the BS-8723 nomenclature as base, the representation model shown in figure 2.8 is proposed. It is based on the BS-8723 notation, but it has been adapted to be used in mappings between terminological ontologies different from thesauri.

The *Concept* class shown in the model is equivalent to the *ThesaurusConcept* used in the BS standard to represent each concept in a thesaurus. Its name has been generalized to use it in terminological models different from thesauri, and it can

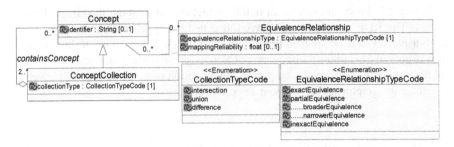

Fig. 2.8: Proposed mapping model

be identified with the *skos:Concept* defined in SKOS where the identifier field is the URI of the *skos:Concept*. The mapping model adds to the *Concept* class the *EquivalenceRelationship* to indicate the equivalence between two concepts of different terminological ontologies. The type of equivalence (exact, inexact or partial) is described by the *EquivalenceRelationshipType*. The way in which this property is defined is based on the one used in the BS-8723 model to represent relations between concepts. It facilitates the creation of a parallel hierarchical vocabulary of types of relationships for *EquivalenceRelationshipType* with specializations of the basic mapping relationships. The hierarchy of mapping relations could have been included in the model as different classes inheriting from *EquivalenceRelationship-Type*. However, it would create the need of defining extensions of the model each time a new relationship is used. The other property of an *EquivalenceRelationship* is the *mappingReliability*, which contains, if it is required, the quality of the defined mapping (value between 1 and 100).

As commented previously, the representation of composed concepts is needed to be able to provide the same expressivity as the one in the search paradigm. In the proposed model, the *ConceptCollection* class is used to define composed concepts. It is a specialization of the *Concept* class that aggregates several concepts through a collection type such as *intersection, union* or *difference*. The possible composition values are indicated as a controlled list in an equivalent way to the types of equivalence relationships. This facilitates the addition or elimination of different composition types, allowing the customization to the needs of each system. Since *ConceptCollection* extends *Concept*, a *ConceptCollection* can be part of another one providing a constructor for the nesting of several levels of composed concepts, e.g. *(A intersection B intersection (C union (D intersection F))) exact equivalent to G.*

The representation of direct mappings (a single concept related to another one) is quite simple: an *EquivalenceRelationship* must be defined with a specific type between the two desired *Concepts*. The representation of composed concepts increases the complexity of the mapping representation, but this increase is proportional to the composition complexity. For instance, one level of composition requires: the definition of a *ConceptCollection* with a set of *Concept* associated to it; and the relation of the collection with the equivalent *Concept* in the same way as it is done for direct mappings.

The mapping model has to be represented in a suitable interchange format. In this context, it is important to represent the mappings independently of the related terminological models to avoid modifying them in any way. This is required to allow the use of the mapped ontologies independently of the mapping developed between them. As the developed mapping model is inspired on BS-8723 terminology, the first approach for the mapping representation format was to base it on the XML based format of BS-8723[12]. However, basic XML representation is not appropriate for the mapping structure where each mapping relation is independent from the rest and there is not a deep hierarchical structure of properties.

More suitable XML based alternatives are RDF and OWL. They are languages that have been designed in the Semantic Web context to define relations between any two concepts. The use of any of them has the additional advantage of facilitating their integration with other RDF/OWL representations for terminological models such as SKOS. The solution adopted has been to define an RDF-Schema with the structure defined in the model, using OWL to express the characteristics that cannot be expressed using RDF (e.g., cardinality).

Figure 2.9 presents an example of representation of a direct mapping between two concepts from different thesauri. The *Concept* class is defined as an RDF resource with the identifier field transformed into a URI resource. The use of URIs makes the defined mapping very easy to relate with the original source and the destination concepts because modern terminological ontology representation formats use URIs, instead of labels, to identify univocally the defined concepts. That is to say, independently of the format used by the terminological ontologies involved in the mapping (e.g., BS-8723 format or SKOS Core), the mapped concepts can be located in the original structures since they share the URIs with the *Concept* classes used in the mapping (they refer to the same entity).

The equivalence relationship shown in figure 2.8 cannot be directly represented using RDF-Schema because it contains attributes. Therefore, the solution adopted has been to model it with an additional *Equivalence* class that contains the attributes and relates the source and the destination concept of the mapping. Each *Concept* conforming the mapping is related to an *Equivalence* instance through an *equivalenceRelationship*. Additionally, each *Equivalence* contains a *mappingOrigin* relation and a *mappingDestination* relation to the source and destination concepts involved in the mapping. Finally, the *Equivalence* class contains as attributes the *equivalenceRelationshipType* with the type of relation between the concepts, and the optional *mappingReliability* to describe the mapping quality. If in a specific application context it is not required to know which concepts describe to the selected one as an equivalent, the *equivalenceRelationship* of the destination concept and the *mappingOrigin* relation in its associated *Equivalence* instance can be omitted.

The representation of composed concepts and their mapping is described in figure 2.10. The equivalence relationship, instead of relating two concepts, relates a

---

[12] http://schemas.bs8723.org/2007-06-01/Documentation/Home.html

```
<rdfs:Class rdf:ID="Concept"/>
<rdfs:Class rdf:ID="Equivalence"/>
<rdf:Property rdf:ID="equivalenceRelationship">
    <rdfs:domain rdf:resource="#Concept"/>
    <rdfs:range rdf:resource="#Equivalence"/>
</rdf:Property>
<rdf:Property rdf:ID="equivalenceRelationshipType">
    <rdfs:domain rdf:resource="#Equivalence"/>
    <rdfs:range rdf:resource=
        "http://iaaa.cps.unizar.es/schemas/mapping#
        equivalenceRelationshipTypeCode"/>
    <owl:cardinality rdf:datatype=
        "http://www.w3.org/2001/XMLSchema#int">1</owl:cardinality>
</rdf:Property>
<rdf:Property rdf:ID="mappingReliability">
    <rdfs:domain rdf:resource="#Equivalence"/>
    <rdfs:range rdf:resource=
        "http://www.w3.org/2001/XMLSchema#float"/>
    <owl:maxCardinality rdf:datatype=
        "http://www.w3.org/2001/XMLSchema#int">1
    </owl:maxCardinality>
</rdf:Property>
<rdf:Property rdf:ID="mapping">
    <rdfs:domain rdf:resource="#Equivalence"/>
    <rdfs:range rdf:resource="#Concept"/>
    <owl:cardinality rdf:datatype=
        "http://www.w3.org/2001/XMLSchema#int">1</owl:cardinality>
</rdf:Property>
<rdf:Property rdf:ID="mappingOrigin">
    <rdfs:subPropertyOf rdf:resource="#mapping"/>
</rdf:Property>
<rdf:Property rdf:ID="mappingDestination">
    <rdfs:subPropertyOf rdf:resource="#mapping"/>
</rdf:Property>
```

(a) RDF-Schema elements needed for direct mappings

```
<map:Concept rdf:about="http:/T1/HealthCare">
    <map:equivalenceRelationship rdf:nodeID="A28660"/>
</map:Concept>
<map:Equivalence rdf:nodeID="A28660">
    <map:mappingOrigin rdf:resource="http:/T1/HealthCare"/>
    <map:mappingDestination rdf:resource="http:/T2/HealthCare"/>
    <map:equivalenceRelationshipType
        rdf:dataType="map:equivalenceRelationshipTypeCode">
        exactEquivalence <map:equivalenceRelationshipType/>
    <map:mappingReliability rdf:dataType="xsd:float">
        90<map:mappingReliability/>
</map:Equivalence>
<map:Concept rdf:about="http:/T2/HealthCare">
    <map:equivalenceRelationship rdf:nodeID="A28660"/>
</map:Concept>
```

(b) RDF example of a direct mapping

Fig. 2.9: RDF-Schema section required for a direct mapping and example of use

Concept with a *ConceptCollection* containing a set of *Concepts* grouped by a com-position type (e.g., union, intersection or difference). Thanks to the fact that a *Con-ceptCollection* is a *Concept*, an *EquivalenceRelationship* can be directly defined between them. This approach is flexible in the sense that allows the definition of more general mappings than the required ones, such as the aggregation of concepts from different terminological ontologies (described by their URIS) in a *Concept-Collections* or the mapping between two *ConceptCollections*.

The set of mappings between two terminological ontologies has to be managed as a whole to be able to integrate them in systems where they are required (e.g., a query expansion system). Each mapping is generated following specific matching criteria being only consistent with respect to the others in the same set. The combination of mappings from different sources without knowing if they are compatible can lead to misinterpretations in the meaning of the associated concepts.

To be able to identify properly the origin of each mapping, a mapping scheme similar to the one used in SKOS-Core for concepts has been defined (see figure 2.11). Each mapping contains a reference to its associate mapping scheme to fa-cilitate its identification (*inMappingScheme* relation). Given the large amount of mappings that can be defined between two terminological models, a relation be-tween the scheme and all the mappings contained in the scheme (inverse of *inMap-pingScheme*) would increase greatly the size of the scheme. In addition, since this relation can be deduced from the existent *inMappingScheme* relations, it has not been defined.

Terminological ontologies are designed as discrete entities intended to be domain consistent. Mappings between them do not have to affect the integrity of their con-cepts/relations. Integrating a set of mappings into the files of the original ontologies is discouraged because it would add many relations non relevant in most of the con-texts and reduce the generality of the ontology model. Additionally, the independent storage of mappings reduces the cost of performing changes to the models. If a new alignment between the ontologies is provided, it only has to replace the older ver-sion of the mapping, without any change in the involved ontologies. If one of the ontologies changes, only the mapping has to be updated (it does not affect the other ontology).

2.4.2 Metadata for mapping description

In the same way that it is required to describe the content of each terminological ontology to identify its purpose, function, and origin; each set of mappings between two terminological models must be also properly described to facilitate its identi-fication and simplify its reuse. The use of metadata to describe mappings enables a user to locate all the mappings generated between two terminological ontologies for a specific use, and it makes possible to compare different approaches defined in different contexts.

```
<rdfs:Class rdf:ID="ConceptCollection">
    <rdfs:subClassOf rdf:resource="#Concept"/>
</rdfs:Class>
<rdf:Property rdf:ID="containsConcept">
    <rdfs:domain rdf:resource="#ConceptCollection"/>
    <rdfs:range rdf:resource="#Concept"/>
    <owl:minCardinality rdf:datatype=
        "http://www.w3.org/2001/XMLSchema#int">2
    </owl:minCardinality>
</rdf:Property>
<rdf:Property rdf:ID="collectionType">
    <rdfs:domain rdf:resource="#ConceptCollection"/>
    <rdfs:range rdf:resource=
        "http://iaaa.cps.unizar.es/schemas/mapping#
        CollectionTypeCode"/>
    <owl:cardinality rdf:datatype=
        "http://www.w3.org/2001/XMLSchema#int">1</owl:cardinality>
</rdf:Property>
<rdf:Property rdf:ID="containedInCollection">
    <rdfs:domain rdf:resource="#Concept"/>
    <rdfs:range rdf:resource="#ConceptCollection"/>
</rdf:Property>
```

(a) Additional RDF-Schema elements for composed mapping

```
<map:Concept rdf:about="http:/T1/DentalHealthCare">
    <map:equivalenceRelationship rdf:nodeID="A28661"/>
</map:Concept>
<map:Equivalence rdf:nodeID="A28661">
    <map:mappingOrigin rdf:resource="http:/T1/DentalHealthCare"/>
    <map:mappingDestination rdf:nodeID="C3456"/>
    <map:equivalenceRelationshipType
        rdf:dataType="map:equivalenceRelationshipTypeCode">
        exactEquivalence<map:equivalenceRelationshipType/>
    <map:mappingReliability rdf:dataType="xsd:float">
        90<map:mappingLiability/>
</map:Equivalence>
<map:ConceptCollection rdf:nodeID="C3456>
    <map:collectionType rdf:datatype=
        "map:collectionTypeCode">intersection</map:CollectionType>
    <map:containsConcept rdf:about="http:/T2/HealthCare">
    <map:containsConcept rdf:about="http:/T2/DentalHealth">
    <map:equivalenceRelationship rdf:nodeID="A28661"/>
</map:ConceptCollection>
<map:Concept rdf:about="http:/T2/HealthCare">
    <map:containedInCollection rdf:nodeID="C3456"/>
</map:Concept>
<map:Concept rdf:about="http:/T2/DentalHealth">
    <map:containedInCollection rdf:nodeID="C3456"/>
</map:Concept>
```

(b) RDF example of a composed mapping

Fig. 2.10: RDF-Schema section required for a composed mapping and example of
use

```
<rdfs:Class rdf:ID="MappingScheme"/>
<rdf:Property rdf:ID="inMappingScheme">
    <rdfs:domain rdf:resource="#Equivalence"/>
    <rdfs:range rdf:resource="#MappingScheme"/>
</rdf:Property>
```

(a) RDF-Schema elements needed for mapping schemes

```
<map:MappingScheme rdf:about="http:/Mapping1">
    <dc:title>
        Mapping between AGROVOC and EUROVOC
    </dc:Title>
    <dc:creator>Javier Lacasta<dc:Creator>
    ...
</map:MappingScheme>
<map:Equivalence rdf:nodeID="A28661">
    <map:inMappingScheme rdf:resource=http:/Mapping1>
    ...
</map:Equivalence>
```

(b) RDF example of a mapping scheme

Fig. 2.11: RDF-Schema section required for a mapping scheme and example of use

In parallel to the work shown in section 2.3.1 for the description of terminological ontologies, a metadata application for ontology mappings based on the Dublin Core Metadata Element Set [85] has been defined (see table 2.2). The metadata profile is similar to the one described in section 2.3.1 for terminological ontologies, but changing some metadata elements and redefining the use of the common ones. The specific metadata fields related to ontology mapping features are: *source of mapping* and *destination of mapping*, which are used to identify the ontologies that the mapping relates; *generation process*, which is used to indicate the alignment techniques and processes used in the generation of the mapping; and *quality*, which is thought to contain the measure of the average mapping quality obtained in the alignment process.

Resource	Label	Obligation	Cardinality	Description
http://purl.org/dc/elements/1.1/title	Name	Mandatory	Unbounded	A name given to the mapping
http://purl.org/dc/elements/1.1/alternative	Short name	Mandatory	Unbounded	Any form of the title used as a substitute or alternative to the formal title of the mapping
http://purl.org/dc/elements/1.1/creator	Creator	Mandatory	Unbounded	An entity primarily responsible for making the content of the mapping
http://purl.org/dc/elements/1.1/description	Description	Optional	Unbounded	An account of the content of the mapping
http://purl.org/dc/elements/1.1/publisher	Publisher	Optional	Unbounded	An entity responsible for making the mapping available
http://purl.org/dc/elements/1.1/contributor	Contributor	Optional	Unbounded	An entity responsible for making contributions to the content of the mapping
http://purl.org/dc/terms/created	Date of creation	Mandatory	Unbounded	Date of creation of the mapping
http://purl.org/dc/terms/issued	Date of publication	Optional	Unbounded	Date of formal issuance (e.g., publication) of the mapping
http://purl.org/dc/terms/modified	Date of modification	Optional	Unbounded	Date on which the mapping was changed
http://purl.org/dc/elements/1.1/type	Type	Mandatory	Unbounded	The nature or genre of the content of the mapping
http://purl.org/dc/elements/1.1/format	Format	Optional	Unbounded	The physical or digital manifestation of the mapping
http://purl.org/dc/elements/1.1/identifier	Mapping identifier	Mandatory	Unbounded	An unambiguous reference to the mapping within a given context
http://purl.org/dc/elements/1.1/source	Source	Optional	Unbounded	A reference to a resource from which the present mapping is derived
http://purl.org/dc/terms/conformsTo	Conforms to	Optional	Unbounded	A reference to an established standard to which the mapping conforms
http://purl.org/dc/terms/isVersionOf	Is version of	Optional	Unbounded	The described mapping is a version, edition, or adaptation of the referenced resource. Changes in version imply substantive changes in content rather than differences in format
http://purl.org/dc/terms/isReplacedBy	Is replaced by	Optional	Unbounded	The described mapping is supplanted, displaced, or superseded by the referenced resource
http://purl.org/dc/terms/replaces	Replaces	Optional	Unbounded	The described mapping supplants, displaces, or supersedes the referenced resource
http://purl.org/dc/terms/hasVersion	Has version	Optional	Unbounded	The described mapping has a version, edition, or adaptation, namely, the referenced resource
http://purl.org/dc/elements/1.1/rights	Rights	Mandatory	Unbounded	Information about rights held in and over the mapping
http://purl.org/dc/terms/accessRights	Access rights	Optional	Unbounded	Information about who can access the mapping or an indication of its security status
http://purl.org/dc/terms/license	License	Optional	Unbounded	A legal document giving official permission to do something with the mapping
http://purl.org/dc/terms/audience	Audience	Optional	Unbounded	A class of entity for whom the mapping is intended or useful
http://purl.org/dc/terms/mediator	Mediator	Optional	Unbounded	A class of entity that mediates access to the mapping and for whom the mapping is intended or useful
http://iaaa.cps.unizar.es/mapping/source	Source of mapping	Mandatory	Unbounded	An unambiguous reference to the ontology source of the mapping
http://iaaa.cps.unizar.es/mapping/destination	Destination of mapping	Mandatory	Unbounded	An unambiguous reference to the ontology destination of the mapping
http://iaaa.cps.unizar.es/mapping/process	Generation process	Mandatory	Unbounded	Description of the process used to generate the mapping
http://iaaa.cps.unizar.es/mapping/quality	Quality	Mandatory	Unbounded	Measure of the quality of the mapping
http://www.isotc211.org/19115/MD_Metadata.dateStamp	Metadata creation date	Mandatory	Unbounded	Date in which the metadata has been created
http://www.isotc211.org/19115/MD_Metadata.contact	Metadata point of contact	Mandatory	Unbounded	Person who has created the metadata
http://www.isotc211.org/19115/MD_Metadata/language	Metadata language	Mandatory	Unbounded	Language used for documenting the metadata record
http://www.isotc211.org/19115/MD_Metadata/fileIdentifier	Metadata identifier	Mandatory	Unbounded	Unique identifier for the metadata record

Table 2.2: Ontology mapping metadata application profile

2.5 Case of study: Mapping of terminological ontologies to an upper level ontology

In order to test the feasibility of this representation framework, we decided to align a terminological ontology with an upper level ontology. For this purpose, it was decided to use the alignment method described by Nogueras-Iso et al. [156]. This process is focused on relating a terminological ontology with respect to WordNet lexical database and it is similar to the methods described in Sussna [184], Agirre and Rigau [1], and Resnik [169]. However, this process does not require a training corpus to estimate probabilities for calculating the semantic similarity. It identifies the similarity using the thesaurus hierarchical structure as the context to evaluate each particular term.

Following the classification of matching algorithms described in section 1.4, this matching algorithm can be considered as a *Relational* technique because it is based on the analysis of the entities structure using the relations between the concepts in the source ontology and in the lexical database. In addition, to match the labels from the ontologies they are processed using *Linguistic* techniques, such as lemmatization (to reduce the terms to their original forms) and term extraction (to obtain the different words contained in each term). Additionally, as this technique has as final objective to use the lexical database as a pivot to relate a set of terminological ontologies between them, it can be viewed as an *external* matching process.

As commented in section 1.4, the problem of ontology alignment consists in finding equivalences between concepts from different models. To do so, it is needed to determine for each term which of its possible senses is the used in the analyzed terminological model. In this case, in the same way that the sense of a word in a natural language text can be determined by the context of the word (the other words in the same phrase or paragraph), the sense of a concept in a terminological ontology can be determined by analyzing the concepts that are related to it (in a thesaurus, the broader and narrowers).

The work proposed in Nogueras-Iso et al. [156] uses this context information to determine which of the senses of WordNet lexical database concepts fits better with the intended meaning of each concept in the source thesaurus. The objective of establishing the mapping between different thesauri and WordNet is to use it as a kernel to unify, at least, the broader concepts included in distinct thesauri. The proposed alignment method can be classified as an unsupervised disambiguation method. It applies a heuristic voting algorithm that makes profit of the hierarchical structure of both WordNet and the thesauri. Whereas the thesaurus hierarchical structure provides the disambiguation context for terms, the hierarchical structure of WordNet enables the comparison of senses from two related thesaurus terms.

The initial step of the disambiguation process divides the thesaurus into branches (a branch corresponds to a tree composed by a top term and all the descendants in the *broader/narrower* hierarchy). The branch provides the disambiguation context for each term in the branch. Secondly, the disambiguation method finds all the possible WordNet synsets (WordNet is structured in a hierarchy of synsets which represent a set of synonyms or equivalent terms) that may be associated with the terms in a thesaurus branch. If a term is compound (more than one word) and it is not included in WordNet, the senses for each word are extracted. Finally, a voting algorithm where each synset related to a thesaurus term votes for the synsets related to the rest of terms in the branch is applied. This method uses the hierarchical structure of WordNet on the assumption that: "the more similar two senses are, the more hypernyms they share". Given a synset path (i.e., a possible sense) of a term, the voting system compares it with the rest of synset of the other terms in the same branch (i.e., the context). Additionally, in the case of having a compound term, a synset path of a subterm would also vote for the synset paths associated with the rest of subterms of this compound term. For each pair of synset paths, the system counts the number of hypernyms (WordNet synsets) that subsume both of them, giving an accumulated result for the initial synset path. The main factor of this score is the number of subsumers in synset paths (the synset and its ancestors in WordNet). The synset with the highest score for each term is elected as the disambiguated synset.

Table 2.3 shows as a disambiguation example the final score of synsets for the branch accident of the GEMET thesaurus. For the sake of clarity, some terms and their corresponding synsets have not been shown.

Regarding the score given by one synset path to another, the initial idea was to assign each other the total number of shared hypernyms. For instance, the two synset paths for the term *accident* would assign each other two votes because they share the synsets *event* and *happening*. Let us observe that they would not receive the third vote by the synset *accident* because the depth is different:

- synset path 1: *event→happening→trouble→misfortune→mishap→accident*
- synset path 2: *event→happening→accident*

In this algorithm, three criteria have been applied to correct this score (the length of a path of concepts in WordNet, the hierarchy, and the density depth). These criteria are slightly related to the aspects that Agirre and Rigau [1] uses to define the conceptual distance. In order to facilitate the understanding of these criteria, they will be explained in parallel with the example in table 2.3 that shows the scores given by synset paths in the branch *accident* to the synset path *event→happening→trouble→misfortune→mishap→accident* of the term *accident*. The column *sco* shows the final score given by each synset path after applying the three criteria. The total score for the voted synset is marked on the right of this synset path.

1. Firstly, lower level WordNet concepts (synsets) have longer paths and then, share more sub-hierarchies. Therefore, the number of shared hypernyms (*sub* column in table 2.3) is divided by the length of the path, i.e. the depth of the WordNet concept. For instance, synset path *event → happening → trouble → misfortune → mishap → accident* (depth=6) is likely to receive more votes than synset path *event→happening→accident* (depth=3) if this restriction is not applied. In table 2.3, the depth of every synset path is shown in column *dep*.
2. Secondly, not all the terms in the context should be valued in the same way. The number of votes provided by the synset paths of a term A to a synset path of a term

Term	Subterm	Synset path	sub	dep	dis	pol	sco
accident							
		event→happening→trouble→misfortune→mishap →accident	**total score = 3.143**				
		event→happening→accident	*it doesn't vote*				
accident→accident source							
	accident	event→happening→trouble→misfortune→mishap →accident	6	6	1	4	0.250
		event→happening→accident	2	3	1	4	0.167
	source	*7 synsets without subsumers*					
accident→accident source→oil slick							
		entity→object→film→oil_slick	0	4	2	1	0.000
accident→environmental accident							
	accident	event→happening→trouble→misfortune→mishap →accident	6	6	1	4	0.250
		event→happening→accident	2	3	1	4	0.167
	environmental	*2 synsets without subsumers*					
accident→environmental accident→explosion							
		event→happening→discharge→explosion	2	4	2	3	0.083
		act→action→change→change_of_integrity→explosion	0	5	2	3	0.000
		act→action→change→change_of_state→termination →release→plosion	0	7	2	3	0.000
accident→environmental accident→leakage							
		event→happening→movement→change_of_location →flow→discharge→escape	2	7	2	1	0.143
accident→major accident							
	accident	event→happening→trouble→misfortune→mishap →accident	6	6	1	4	0.250
		event→happening→accident	2	3	1	4	0.167
	major	*1 synset without subsumers*					
accident→major accident→nuclear accident							
	accident	event→happening→trouble→misfortune→mishap →accident	6	6	2	4	0.125
		event→happening→accident	2	3	2	4	0.083
	nuclear	*2 synsets without subsumers*					
accident→major accident→nuclear accident→core meltdown							
	core	*8 synsets without subsumers*					
	meltdown	*no synsets in WordNet*					
accident→traffic accident							
	accident	event→happening→trouble→misfortune→mishap →accident	6	6	1	4	0.250
		event→happening→accident	2	3	1	4	0.167
	traffic	*3 synsets without subsumers*					
accident→traffic accident→shipping accident							
	accident	event→happening→trouble→misfortune→mishap →accident	6	6	2	4	0.125
		event→happening→accident	2	3	2	4	0.083
	shipping	*2 synsets without subsumers*					
accident→work accident							
	accident	event→happening→trouble→misfortune→mishap →accident	6	6	1	4	0.250
		event→happening→accident	2	3	1	4	0.167
	work	*7 synsets without subsumers*					
accident→technological accident							
	accident	event→happening→trouble→misfortune→mishap →accident	6	6	1	4	0.250
		event→happening→accident	2	3	1	4	0.167
	technological	*2 synsets without subsumers*					

Table 2.3: Voting for synset path *event → happening → trouble → misfortune → mishap → accident* of term accident

B are divided by the distance between the two terms (A and B) in the thesaurus. For instance, obtaining the scores for the synsets of the term *accident*, the term *environmental accident* is more important than the term *explosion* because it is closer in the hierarchy. In table 2.3, the distance of every synset path is shown in *dis* column.

3. And thirdly, the most polysemic terms in the context vote more times since each one of their senses has the opportunity to vote. Therefore, the number of votes

provided by a synset path is divided by the number of senses of the term to which it belongs. For instance, term *accident source* votes with its nine synset paths, meanwhile term *leakage* only votes with one synset path. In table 2.3, the polysemic value of every synset path is shown in *pol* column.

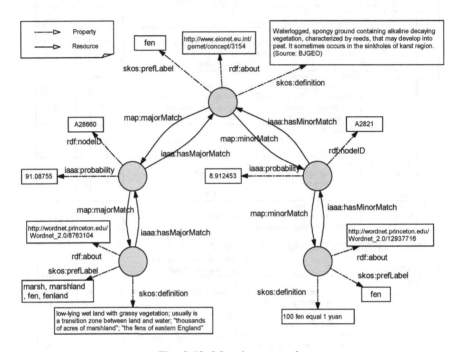

Fig. 2.12: Mapping example

Since the disambiguation algorithm cannot assure a 100% exact mapping, the identified relationships have been marked as inexact equivalences with the reliability factor showing the probability of equivalence. The mapping with the highest reliability may have been marked as exact equivalence. However, since an exact equivalence cannot be assured without a manual revision the mappings are left as inexact. An example of a mapping found with the algorithm used is shown in figure 2.12. There, the concept *3154 (fen)* of GEMET is correctly mapped to the WordNet concept *8763104 (marsh, marshland, fen, fenland)* with a probability of 91.08755%. In addition, another unrelated mapping is found, but it is given a low probability (8.912453%).

2.6 Summary

This chapter has presented the terminological ontologies as the most suitable alternative for classification and information retrieval. However, it has been remarked that there is a heterogeneity problem in the representation of terminological models that makes difficult their use by different communities (different groups and organizations have created their own ad-hoc representation models).

With the objective of reducing these heterogeneity problems, this chapter has presented a framework for the representation of terminological ontologies that focus on the harmonization of the representation formats of terminological models and the relations between them. As a first step in this harmonization process, this chapter has reviewed the different existent representation approaches and how suitable they are to represent the different used terminological models. From the analyzed models, SKOS has been selected as the most suitable one, but it has been adapted to include some additional elements that were required. Besides a suitable metadata application profile to describe the terminological models has been proposed.

Additionally, the interrelation needs of terminological ontologies has make us define a representation model for mapping between terminological models. It has as objective to facilitate the reuse of the mappings. The developed format has been based on the thesaurus model and in the mapping nomenclature and definitions described in the BS-8723 standard, but adapted to be applicable to different terminological models.

2.6 Summary

Chapter 3
Ontology learning for terminological ontologies

3.1 Introduction

The use of suitable terminological ontologies is vital in classification and information retrieval to obtain high quality results. For example, in a discovery system, if
the resources are annotated using a vocabulary that does not contain all the required
terms to describe the collection, the construction of an effective search system becomes much more difficult.

However, the creation of a suitable model for a certain collection from scratch
is quite costly. It is a long and difficult task that requires a deep knowledge of the
domain vocabulary and the nature of the relations holding between them. In this
context, the activity of knowledge acquisition constitutes one of the most important
steps at the beginning of the ontology development process. This activity is essential in all the different methodologies for ontology design as a previous step to the
conceptualization and formalization phases. As its name indicates, this activity is
devoted to gather all available knowledge resources describing the domain of the
ontology and identify the most important terms in the domain [171].

This chapter is focused on the study of methods and techniques for the (semi-)
automatic processing of knowledge resources that may alleviate the work of knowledge acquisition. This task is known as ontology learning in the literature of ontological engineering [65, 10]. The aim of ontology learning is to apply the most appropriate methods to transform unstructured (e.g., text corpora), semi-structured (e.g.,
folksonomies, HTML pages) and structured data sources (e.g., databases, thesauri)
into conceptual structures. The methods of ontology learning are usually connected
with the activity of ontology population which also relies on (semi-)automatic methods to transform unstructured, semi-structured and structured data sources into instance data (i.e., instances of ontology concepts).

This chapter reviews the state of the art in ontology learning and population from
different types of source data, showing how these techniques can be applied. It focuses on four different types of source data: corpora, dictionaries, schemata and
thesauri. In the first one, the objective is to use a resource collection (corpora) to

J. Lacasta et al., *Terminological Ontologies: Design, Management and Practical
Applications*, Semantic Web and Beyond 9, DOI 10.1007/978-1-4419-6981-1_3,
© Springer Science+Business Media, LLC 2010

generate the knowledge model that better fits with the collection. In the other three, the objective is to use one or several knowledge models to create a new one more fitted to the intended purpose, the difference lies in the structure of the source data, and the process used to generate the new one. As example of applicability, it describes two use cases. The fist one, focused on solving model heterogeneity problems, and the second one in providing a mostly automatic leaning process.

3.2 Ontology learning from corpora

The task of identifying, defining, and entering the concept definitions in large and complex application domains can be lengthy, costly, and controversial, since different persons may have different points of view about the same concept [201]. In order to save resources, ontologists recommend referring, in constructing or updating an ontology, to the documents available in the field. As stated in Velardi et al. [201], although concept names do not always have a lexical correspondent in natural language, especially at the top most levels of the ontology, often a correspondence may be naturally drawn among certain domain concepts and domain-specific terms like: domain named entities (e.g., proper names), domain-specific multiword terms (e.g., travel agent, reservation list, ...), or domain-specific singleton words (e.g., hotel, reservation).

Because of the accessibility and availability of corpora in different domains, there are many works in the literature of ontology engineering describing ontology learning methods using as input a corpus of texts that are representative in the domain. These methods are mostly based on the use of natural language processing, clustering techniques, machine learning and statistical analysis [66].

Without entering into the details of the different approaches, it is worth mentioning the contribution of Cimiano [30] as regards the formalization of subtasks involved in the ontology development. These subtasks are the following: acquisition of the relevant terminology; identification of synonym terms and linguistic variants (possibly across languages); formation of concepts; hierarchical organization of the concepts; learning relations, properties or attributes, together with the appropriate domain and range; hierarchical organization of the relations; instantiation of axiom schemata; and definition of arbitrary axioms.

A good example of an ontology learning method facing the first 4 subtasks defined by Cimiano [30] is the OntoLearn system [201, 144, 146]. OntoLearn is a text-mining system that extracts prominent domain concepts from the related literature and detects the semantic relations among them. To mine texts, they use a corpus processor named ARIOSTO, whose performance has been improved with the addition of a Named Entity recognizer and a chunk parser called CHAOS. As proper names are pervasive and they may represent more than 20% of the total occurring words, they used a module for Named Entity recognition, which is based on a set of contextual rules (e.g., a complex or simple proper name followed by the trigger word *authority* is a organization named entity). For the rest of terminology extraction, the proposed method exploits both linguistic and statistical properties to build a domain specific terminological glossary. They use the chunk parser CHAOS (part of speech tagging, chunking, verb argument structure matching, and shallow grammatical analysis), and statistical methods to identify the terminology that is really relevant in the domain. They propose a metric to estimate the relevance of a term with respect to a domain and compare the value of this metric in different domains. Additionally, it uses inductive machine learning for extracting semantic relationships between the headword and its modifier in compound nouns.

For a more detailed review of approaches and methods we refer the reader to Cimiano [30], chap. 3 and Gómez-Pérez and Manzano-Macho [66], chap. 3. Cimiano [30] identifies different algorithms and techniques for each subtask of the process. Gómez-Pérez and Manzano-Macho [66] offers a detailed description of methods and their associated tools.

3.3 Ontology learning from dictionaries

Dictionaries are semi-structured resources that are infrequently updated; domain dictionaries, in particular, are suitable for extracting terms and their relationships (e.g., hyponyms, meronyms, and synonyms) as well as their definitions [176]. Dictionary definitions form a closed domain in the sense that the set of words used in definitions are defined elsewhere in the dictionary [98].

There are different works on ontology construction that use dictionaries as primary sources. Usually, these methods are usually based on the use of natural language processing and statistical analysis.

For instance, Jannink [98] describes a method for converting a dictionary into a directed graph, which could be considered as an initial ontology draft. For the graph extraction, each word and definition grouping is transformed to a node, and each word in a definition node is transformed into an arc to the node having that headword. Additionally, this work proposes an algorithm, called ArcRank, for ranking the importance of relationships between headwords. As a first step, the algorithm computes the importance of each node following a PageRank-based method. And as a second step, the algorithm ranks the relative importance of the output arcs of a node taking into account the importance of the target node. Thus the most representative relationships of a headword are those arcs with higher rank.

Kietz et al. [110] provides a generic architecture, an acquisition methodology and several new approaches for acquiring concepts and relations from intranet resources, being domain dictionaries one of these resources. The acquisition approach has three main steps. First, a generic core ontology is used as a top level structure for the domain-specific goal ontology. Secondly, domain-specific concepts are acquired from a dictionary that contains important corporate terms described in natural language. After resolving some naming conflicts between the concepts of the core ontology and the dictionary concepts (e.g., acronyms), the dictionary concepts are linked to the core ontology. Additionally, this work proposes several natural language processing heuristics (analysis of noun-phrases and compound terms together with the identification of patterns inducing hyponym relationships) to establish a taxonomy of dictionary concepts. Finally, this work proposes a third step where a domain-specific and a general corpus of texts are used to remove concepts that were domain unspecific.

Rigau et al. [170] presents a method for learning lexical ontologies from dictionaries, which is supported by a tool called SEISD. The input data of this method is extracted from monolingual machine-readable dictionaries. In this method, each dictionary definition is analyzed in order to find a hypernym (called genus) of the word being defined. Later, a Word-Sense Disambiguation (WSD) algorithm is applied on the genus word to find the correct corresponding meaning from a range of semantic primitives, which are top concepts in an upper-level lexical ontology such as WordNet.

3.4 Ontology learning from schemata

Schemata such as database models, Entity/Relationship (ER) models, object-oriented models or even unstructured schemata (e.g., XML documents) are directly considered in the literature of ontology engineering as model-driven ontologies [21] or information ontologies [200]. Thus, it is very usual to find methods that based on mapping techniques enable the reverse engineering of schemata to derive ontologies. Volz et al. [202] use the term lifting for this type of ontology learning as it mainly consists in lifting or mapping definitions from the schema to corresponding ontological definitions.

As far as reverse engineering of relational databases is concerned, Astrova and Stantic [12] classifies the different approaches in three categories: approaches based on the analysis of relational schema; approaches based on the analysis of tuples; and approaches on the analysis of user queries. We could generalize this classification for schemata, including as well semi-structured schemata such as XML, in the following categories: approaches based on the analysis of schemas; approaches based on the analysis of instances; and approaches on the analysis of user queries.

Approaches based on the analysis of schemas establish a set of rules for mapping the constructs in a source schema (i.e., for a relational schema the constructs would be relations, attributes, tuples and constraints) into semantically equivalent constructs in the ontology (i.e., classes, attributes, instances and axioms). A seminal work of these approaches is Johannesson [99], which presents a method for translating a schema in the relational model into a schema in a conceptual model. The conceptual model used is a formalization of an extended ER model, which also includes the subtype concept. A more recent approach in the context of the Semantic Web is the work of Stojanovic et al. [181], which describes a method for migrating the contents of a database into RDF data. The objective of this work was to convert a database-driven web site into a machine-understandable and visible web. This type of approaches giving visibility to back-end data on the Web are acquiring great acceptance nowadays. Some researchers have coined the term Semantic Deep Web to address the problems associated with accessing rich, structured back-end data as well as ontology construction and use [60].

With respect to the existent tools implementing this transformation from databases to ontologies, we must mention OntoStudio [1] and KaOn Reverse [2]. OntoStudio is a commercial modeling environment for the creation and maintenance of ontologies, which allows importing structures, schemas and models. OntoStudio includes a mapping tool with which heterogeneous structures can be mapped onto each other. KAON Reverse is a prototype for mapping relational database content to ontologies, enabling both storage of instance data in such databases and querying the database through the conceptualisation of the database.

Finally, also within this first category but considering XML data as primary resources, we must mention the work of Volz et al. [202]. This method transforms XML Schemas (also DTDs and XML documents are allowed as input) into regular tree grammars, where non-terminal and terminal symbols are matched later with concepts and roles in the output ontology.

Within the category of approaches based on the analysis of instances, we include methods that, in addition to the analysis of schemas, also analyze instance data of those schemas to discover additional hidden semantics. For instance, the method proposed by Astrova [11] analyzes key, data and attribute correlations to identify hidden semantics in relational databases. There are also works that apply strategies of Formal Concept Analysis to derive an ontology from instance data [153]. FCA analyzes similarities and dissimilarities among attribute values of database tuples to generate an output concept lattice.

Within the third category, approaches based on the analysis of user queries, user queries enable the refinement of ontologies. This is the case of the work described by Kashyap [107]. User queries may suggest different refinements: create new entities and attributes; drop entities and attributes not referenced in the queries; or suggest subclass relationships. Another approach related to this category is the work of Astrova and Stantic [12], which extracts the semantics by analyzing HTML forms. HTML forms are the most popular interface to communicate with relational databases for data entry and display on the Web.

3.5 Ontology learning from thesauri

As it has been shown in chapter 2, hierarchical terminological ontologies such as taxonomies, or thesauri are widely used in the context of resource classification and information retrieval to provide a uniform way to describe the resource contents and improve discovery systems. Nowadays, there is a great deal of terminological models covering each area of interest. Therefore, in the case of constructing a new

---

[1] http://www.ontoprise.de/de/en/home/products/ontostudio.html

[2] http://kaon.semanticweb.org/alphaworld/reverse/

system, it is usually possible to find a model (or a small set of models) that fit in a great extent to the required terminology. Here, two problems arise. On the one hand, the great heterogeneity of representation models makes its integration in a new system a complex task. Ad-hoc formats are frequent, and extensions to the general models are common. On the other hand, it is not always possible to find another model that perfectly match the desired ontology. In this context, the solution reside in translating existing models to a common format and adapting them, if the required changes are minimum, or using them to create a new model.

The heterogeneity of the used ontology formats increases the cost of translation. Each translation process requires a deep knowledge of the models involved in the transformation and the development of specific translation software. Therefore, if the number of terminological models to translate is high (as happens in the context of this book), it is important to define the translation processes as similar as possible, and to reuse as much created software as possible to save development efforts.

Translation of models (from one format to another one) is required in contexts where it is needed to integrate external information or update existent information. In the context of terminological ontologies there are many different ad-hoc translation approaches to change the format of the selected models. For example, Golbeck et al. [67] describe the transformation to OWL of the National Cancer Institute Thesaurus[3]. Soualmia et al. [177] do the same with the Medical Subject Headings[4].

An ad-hoc solution solves the problem of how to transform a specific model into another one, but it is not applicable to other translation processes. If a new transformation is needed, it has to be constructed from scratch without the possibility of using previous works as help or guideline. To simplify and reduce the creation cost of new translation processes, some approaches focus on establishing a methodology that can be applied to different situations. Following the methodology, all the translation processes are constructed in a harmonized way, using the same structure, creating the same documentation and following the same steps. They focus on performing in the same way those steps that are common in the different translation processes such as the need to define the source and target model, and the establishing of mappings between them. Internally they are different but follow the same construction patterns. Therefore, they are easier to create, understand, and update.

An example of methodology to create translation processes is described by van Assem et al. [198]. It provides a guideline and some recommendations about how to perform the transformation of thesauri into RDF/OWL. The first step is an analysis of the thesaurus model and related documentation. Then, it is converted to a basic RDF version and enriched with properties and attributes. Finally, the RDF/OWL meta-model developed is mapped to SKOS. The methodology is applied to create the software needed to translate to RDF/OWL the Medical Subject Headings and WordNet [52]. van Assem et al. [197] describes an upgraded version of this methodology that simplifies the steps to perform to only two: the analysis of the thesaurus model, and the mapping to SKOS model. The upgraded methodology is more de-

---

[3] http://www.cancer.gov/cancertopics/terminologyresources

[4] http://www.nlm.nih.gov/mesh/

tailed, and the matching between model properties and relations is represented more formally. Additionally, while in the first process the construction of the software is almost secondary, this latter one includes a specific stage for its construction. This improved methodology is applied to translate to SKOS the previously commented Medical Subject Headings, the Integrated Public Sector Vocabulary[5] and the Common Thesaurus for Audiovisual Archives[6].

Another translation methodology is the one proposed by Miles et al. [142]. The proposed translation process consists of three steps: generation of the RDF encoding, error checking, and validation and publishing of the encoding on the web. It provides a specific guideline to transform thesauri following standard structure; additionally, it comments how some non-standard structure such as groups, themes, and supergroups present in GEMET thesaurus could be mapped. The methodology is applied to: the Australian Public Affairs Information Service Thesaurus[7], represented in XML following a model based on the Z39.50 profile for thesaurus; the English Heritage Aircraft Type Thesaurus[8], defined by comma delimited files; and GEMET, described in XML using a non-standard model.

3.6 Cases of study

With the objective of reducing costs and providing reusability objective, and as an example of applicability, this section describes two cases of study. The fist one, is focused on solving model heterogeneity problems, and the second one describes a semi-automatic learning process.

Subsection 3.6.1 shows a methodology for the creation of translation systems. It defines a methodology to create a new translation process, and the architectural pattern to follow when constructing new translation tools (to reduce the creation effort). It focuses on translating terminological models to SKOS given that, as it has been shown in section 2.3, it seems the most suitable format for representing terminological models. In any case, following the same methodology, an equivalent process could be used to generate other different interchange format.

Subsection 3.6.2 describes a method for the construction of ontologies based on combining the knowledge provided by different knowledge models. It shows a method that extracts from a set of terminological ontologies (following a multilingual thesaurus structure) the common elements and relations about the desired theme and combines them to generate a new single model. The different views of the same knowledge provided by each ontology are merged to obtain a better definition of the vocabulary and the relation structure.

---

[5] http://www.esd.org.uk/standards/ipsv/index.html

[6] http://www.beeldengeluid.nl/index.jsp

[7] http://www.nla.gov.au/apais/thesaurus/

[8] http://www.english-heritage.org.uk/thesaurus/aircraft/

3.6.1 Transformation of heterogeneous thesaurus representations into terminological ontologies

For decades, the evolution of digital libraries has encouraged the use of terminological ontologies describing the vocabulary of an area of knowledge (in the form of taxonomies, classification schemes or thesauri), promoting in that way the creation and diffusion of well-established collections in different domains. However, the lack of standardization has produced a huge variety of incompatible formats that make difficult their manage and use. To be able to manage the different ontologies we need to harmonize their representation, transforming all the used terminological ontologies to the same interchange format.

As proposed in section 2.3, the most adequate alternative to represent terminological ontologies is the Simple Knowledge Organization System (SKOS) format [141]. The creation of terminological models following this format must be based on the SKOS model documents[9], but other complementary documents such as the guide created by the Porting Thesauri Task Force PORT[10] (subgroup of the W3Cs Semantic Web Best Practices and Deployment Working Group[11]) to facilitate the creation of terminological models in SKOS can be used.

Once the terminological ontologies have been translated to SKOS, they can be commonly managed by the required software components. Additionally, since the selected interchange format is becoming very common for different organizations and research groups, the translated ontologies can be provided to the public.

The translation of a terminological ontology from one format to another one requires the construction of some kind of translation software to perform this task. Information translation processes are usually ad-hoc systems specifically created for a required transformation and discarded after that (two translations processes with different source and target models have very few characteristics in common). However, when the number of terminological models to translate is high, creating completely different translation processes for each model is too costly.

This problem has been tackled by developing a general process to help to identify equivalences between the source and target models. It has as objective to harmonize the structure and content of the different translation processes, to reduce the cost of creation a new one, and to make them easier to understand. The process defines the steps to follow, techniques to apply and documentation to define. Additionally, to simplify the construction of the translation software, a library providing the common functionality required for the different translation processes has been created.

---

[9] http://www.w3.org/2004/02/skos/

[10] http://www.w3.org/2004/03/thes-tf/mission

[11] http://www.w3.org/2001/sw/BestPractices/

3.6.1.1 Description of the method

One of the main drawbacks of existent approaches is the lack of harmonized description of the source (and also the target) models. Ontologies should be ideally described using graphical models, but most of the times only a list of entities, properties, and relations described in natural language is available as documentation. A formal representation of the models simplifies the identification of matchings because it gives a detailed semantic to each element of the model and additionally it facilitates the use of automatic matching techniques. However, even when a formal model is available, if each time it follows a different notation and/or representation, the way to define the mappings must be redesigned for each particular case. This is a problem in the sense that it implies additional learning effort in each performed alignment.

Another relevant problem is concerned with the conversion of data types. The reviewed techniques seem to consider that the data-type of the properties in the source format is the same as in the target one. However, this is not always true. For instance, the identifier of the concepts can be a number in the source format and an URI in the target one. When a data-type changes, a transformation pattern has to be provided.

The last identified problem is the lack of a homogeneous policy for the construction of translation tools. In the analyzed proposals, each translation tool has been created independently from the rest, using different languages and tools. This is a waste of effort. The cost of new developments should be minimized by reusing software of previous transformations.

This section proposes a new methodology to define translation processes between terminological ontology models that focus on the problems previously described. The proposed methodology consists of the following four steps (see figure 3.1):

- First, the analysis of the source and target format models. The two models have to be properly reviewed and described to simplify the later translation process.
- Second, the matching of each entity, property, and relation of the source model with the equivalent one (if it exists) in the target model. The mappings obtained between the elements of the two models have to be described in a way that facilitates the automation of the translation process.
- Third, the development of the translation tool. In this step the objective is to reuse previous translation works and implement as few new software as possible.
- Fourth, the validation of the generated result. Once the translation software has been created, it is needed to check whether the transformation performed is valid.

Analysis of the source and target formats

The first step to translate a terminological ontology into SKOS format is to understand the structure of the source and target models. In the developed work, the

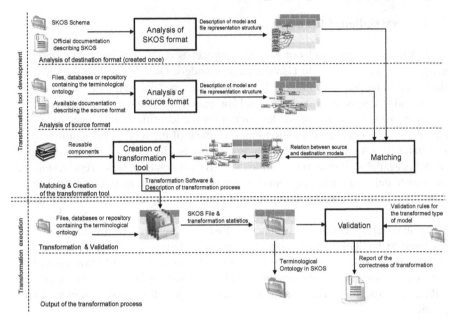

Fig. 3.1: Process to develop SKOS translation tools

different representation formats for the source models that have been found can be grouped in the following categories:

- Databases: The terminological ontology is stored in a database where the different entity types are represented as tables, the concepts as elements stored in a table, and the relationships are managed as foreign keys between elements of the table model.
- XML files: The content ontology is described in XML following a specific XML schema. Other approaches use RDF instead of plain XML, and use an RDF-Schema to describe the model (e.g., SKOS).
- HTML files: Some terminological ontologies are only accessible on the web. Therefore, they must be downloaded as HTML files which have to be processed to extract the elements and structure of the terminological ontology.
- Plain text: The most basic representation is directly using text, where the structure has to be deduced by the documentation. For example, the NT relationship can be indicated by the use of tabulation between two different lines of the text.

The main problem identified to process the source formats has been the heterogeneity in their structure and the low quality of the documentation. In many cases, the structure of the model had to be deduced from the data since there was no documentation. In other cases, textual descriptions of the model existed, but they were full of ambiguities and inconsistencies. Only one of all the translated terminological ontologies (see section 3.6.1.2) provided a graphical representation of its model.

Therefore, in order to facilitate the automation of the translation process, each element, property and relation has to be identified and described using a common conceptual schema language (or common description language).

On the one hand, to perform the translation it is required to understand the structure and purpose of each element contained in analyzed model (source and target). This can only be done if it is properly described. On the other hand, to be able to access to the content of the analyzed model (source and target), the storage organization structure (e.g., files or databases) has also to be perfectly known (e.g., name and format of the files, part of the model they contain . . .). As in the previous case, this is only possible if it has been properly described.

To facilitate the use and management of these model descriptions (content and structure), they have been harmonized by using specific models created for this purpose.

The model created for the description of the content structure is shown in figure 3.2. In this model, the main element to take into account is the *Entity* class. Each element of the analyzed model is registered as a new *Entity* with an identifier, a description, and its cardinality. The different *Entities* of the same model are related (through the *relation* relationship) to indicate which structural elements are contained inside the others. Additionally, the entities of the same model are grouped as a terminological *Model* through the *composedOf* relation. To facilitate its identification, the *Model* class contains the name and a description of the format model of the ontology to translate.

As it can be seen in figure 3.2, two different subtypes of entities have been identified. On the one hand, the *Registry* class is used to represent those entities that are information containers of collections of other entities; that is, they provide the organization of the ontology content. On the other hand, the *Field* class is used to represent those entities in the model that really contain the data of the terminological ontology. The type of the contained value is represented through the *ValueType* class that contains the type name and the range of values. Each type used in the analyzed terminological ontology is created once and related to the elements in the model that use them through the *contentType* relationship. Additionally, the *Field* class contains a *type* element that indicates the structural purpose of the *Field*. In this context, two purposes have been considered: as *properties* that contain the value associated with a relation; and as *attributes* whose value qualifies the relation itself.

The model created for the description of the storage organization structure is shown in figure 3.3. This schema relates a terminological model (*Model* class of figure 3.2) with the storage items used to store it. These storage items are described through the *Resource* class. Its objective is to provide enough information to identify each storage item used for a model. The defined fields of the *resource* class are detailed in table 3.1. The fields included in this class are based on a subset of the core elements of the Dublin Core metadata standard [85].

The storage resources can be divided into two groups: those containing a section or the whole analyzed model, and those describing the structure of the elements in the previous category (e.g., an XML schema of the XML files containing the model). With respect to the first group, to indicate which model elements are stored

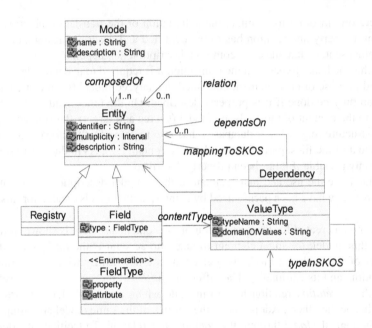

Fig. 3.2: Meta model for describing the source, target model, and translation rules

in each resource, the *source* relation between the *entity* class of figure 3.2 and the *resource* class has been defined. With respect to the second group, to indicate in which *resource* the structure of each *entity* is described, the *descriptiveModel* relation is provided. Additionally, it has been needed to indicate the relation between the *resources* containing the terminological model and the *resources* describing their structure. This has been done with the *relation* relationship shown in figure 3.3. To indicate the type of relation between these resources the *relation* relationship is qualified with a description through the *relationDescription* class.

ID	DESCRIPTION
Identifer	Name/URL of a resource containing part of the terminological ontology
Type	Type of resource (e.g., file, database, web page)
Format	Specific structure of the resource, (e.g., SKOS, OWL, HTML, Access 2000)
Language	Languages in which the content of the resource has been created. For example, it indicates that the tags used in XML labels are French based or that the comments included in the file are in English.
Description	Small description of the subsection of the model contained in the resource
Comments	Additional relevant information about the content

Table 3.1: Fields in the *Resource* class

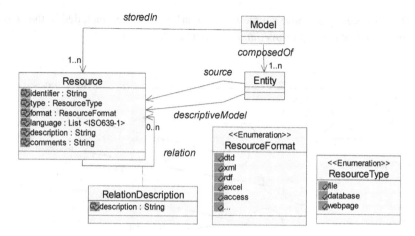

Fig. 3.3: Meta model for describing the storage characteristics

Mapping between source and target model

Having completely described the source and target models, the next step in the trans-lation process consists in matching them (classes, properties and relations).

In a first step, the models of source and target formats are manually matched. The matching is performed by analyzing both models and the descriptions of the format structure created following the model described in figure 3.2 to find equivalences.

Figure 3.4 shows as example of matching the established between a traditional thesaurus model and the SKOS model (represented both of them using UML nota-tion). As it can be observed in the figure, the following transformations are applied:

- Each *term* in the source model that is selected to be used for classification (it has not a USE relationship with another one) is translated into a *skos:concept*.
- The URI required for each *skos:concept* is generated by converting the *term* value into a URI through the addition of an *http://* prefix.
- The *translation* instances related to the previous *term* are transformed into *skos:prefLabel* of the newly generated *skos:concept*.
- The *terms* related to the converted one through an USE relationship are converted into *skos:altLabel* of the generated *skos:concept*.
- The *description* of a term (related through the *SN* relationship) is converted into the *skos:definition* of the generated *skos:concept*.
- The *RT* relationships between *terms* are converted into *skos:related* relations be-tween the corresponding *skos:concept*(s). With respect to the *BT* and *NT* rela-tionships they are converted into *skos:broader* and *skos:narrower* relationships respectively.
- A model in SKOS format requires of a *skos:conceptScheme*. Because nothing equivalent exists in the source model, a *skos:conceptScheme* is created using an URI based on the available information of the source model.

- The *skos:concepts* whose source *term* is marked as *TT* are included in the *skos: conceptScheme* as top terms (*hasTopConcept* relationship).

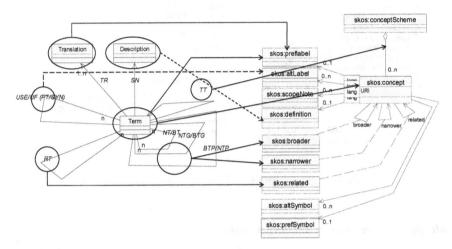

Fig. 3.4: Mappings between a traditional thesaurus model and the SKOS-Core model

The obtained matchings are stored in the model described in figure 3.2 to facilitate its latter processing. They are represented through the *mappingToSKOS* and the *typeInSKOS* relationships.

The *mappingToSKOS* relationship is used to establish an equivalence relationship between an *entity* of the source model and another one of the target model (SKOS model). In general the conversion is direct (an *entity* is converted in another one). However, in some situations the conversion is more complex and depends on other elements in the model. For those cases, the *mappingToSKOS* relationship can be qualified with other *entities* through the *dependsOn* relationship.

In addition to the transformations in the structure (conversion of *entities*), the types of the content must be also converted if they are different. This task is performed by the *typeInSKOS* relationship, which describes the equivalences in the types of the source and target model. In the translation process described in the following steps, for each *typeInSKOS* relationship, a procedure to transform the data from the source type to the destination type has to be provided. For example, in the matching example described in figure 3.4. the label of a *term* has to be transformed into an URI, i.e., a transformation method from a type string into a type URI is required (it is done by adding an *http://* prefix to the string).

Creation of the translation tool

The uniform representation of the source format, the target format, and the transformation rules simplifies the management of different translation requirements and it facilitates the creation and automation of a new translation process.

The creation of a new translation tool may not seem a very costly process because the structure of source and target models is usually small. However, many translations are required, the cost of creating a new translator becomes a factor to take into account. The solution adopted to reduce the needs of new software has been to define an architectural pattern based on the harmonized description of the models that allows reusing a set of common elements in the different translation processes. Figures 3.5 and 3.6 show this architectural pattern with different levels of detail.

Figure 3.5 shows that each translator tool consists of three different components: a reader of the source format, a matcher of the source model to the SKOS model, and a writer of the SKOS model to RDF. As the target format is always SKOS, the writer component is directly reusable in all the different translation processes. On the other hand, the reader and the matcher have to be adapted to each specific translation, but they share a common part that can be reused.

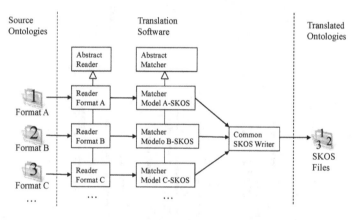

Fig. 3.5: Architectural pattern for the format translator

Additionally, figure 3.6 shows a detailed view of this architectural pattern. On the one hand, it provides a set of common elements that can be reused in different translation processes. On the other hand, it defines a set of abstract components (and the required methods) that each new translator tool has to implement with the non-reusable functionality required for the translation. Using the components provided by the library the construction of a new translation tool is reduced to the following two steps: definition of a new reader for the source format that implements the *AbstractReader* class, and creation of a matcher that implements the abstract functions provided by the *AbstractMatcher*.

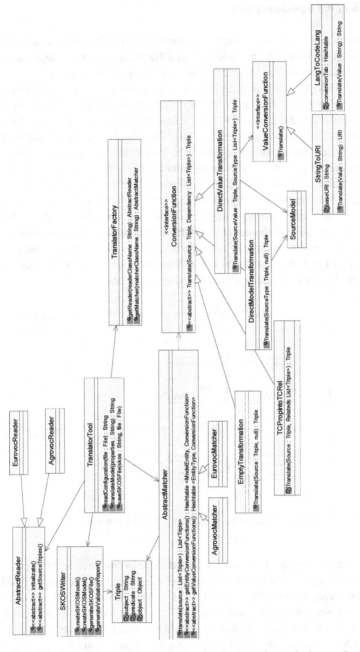

Fig. 3.6: An architectural pattern for the design of translation tools

The translation components described in figure 3.6 use a triples based model <element, property, value> as a common model for processing. In this context, the reader task is to retrieve the entire source model content, to construct the triples model required for the rest of the translator components (specially the matcher), and to return it through the *getSourceTriples* method. This component is different in each translation process because it has to access to different source format in each translation. The definition of the source format created previously facilitates the work of the programmer to implement the reader.

The generated triple model contains the information about the structure of the source model and about their content. Each entity in the source model (registry, field, or attribute) is marked with a unique identifier, and its type. For example, a narrower relationship that in the description model (figure 3.2) is labeled as type *"CONCEPT.RECORD.NT"* would be identified with the triple <ID@1546, *type*, CONCEPT.RECORD.NT>. In this context, if two concepts are identified as ID@196 and ID@15, the triple <ID@196, ID@1546, ID@15> indicates a narrower relation between them.

The purpose of the matcher is to take the set of triples provided by the reader according to the source model and to transform it into another set of tipples according to the target model (SKOS model). This matcher can be implemented manually, analyzing the mappings between the source and target model, and creating the required translation code. However, the harmonization of the source model, the target model, and the matchings between them (described through the model shown in figure 3.2) facilitates the automation of the matcher.

The most usual matchings between the models are 1:1 equivalences; that is to say, an entity in the source model is converted into one entity in the SKOS model. In these cases it is required to change the type of the entity and to perform a transformation in the value. In addition to these 1:1 equivalences, there are some specific situations where the translation of an entity depends on the value of another one (N:1 equivalences). Fortunately, this kind of dependencies have been found to be not very complex (the most complex one has been to translate a property value into a relation of the concept associated to the property) and it has been possible to accommodate them to the general system.

The matcher performs the transformation of the triples by applying a conversion function for each type of element and type of value. For general transformations, the conversion functions *DirectModelTransformation* and *DirectValueTransformation* shown in figure 3.6 are used. These translators use the descriptions of the mappings between the source and target models created previously (figure 3.2) to perform the translation. For more specific transformations, ad-hoc translators must be developed. The outcome of these translations depends on additional entities of the source model that have to be provided to the translator to perform its task. In addition to the changes in the structure, the values of the model have to be sometimes converted (changes in data types). These conversions are managed through the creation of *ValueConversionFunctions* that indicate how to translate the value associated to an element into the type required in the target model. For instance, a string may have to be converted into a URI by adding to it an http prefix.

The output of the matcher is a set of triples following the SKOS model. The task of the writer is to take these triples and generate the target SKOS file. Thanks to the fact that the output of the matcher is always a set of triples following the SKOS model, the writer can be reused in all the constructed translation tools. Figure 3.7 describes the writer structure. The set of triples provided as input are used to fill the SKOS-RDF model constructed by the *SKOSModel* class through the use of a library for RDF management such as Jena.

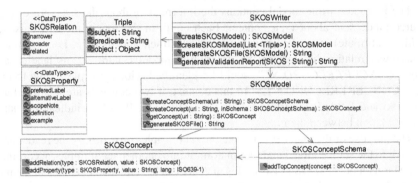

Fig. 3.7: Structure of the writer component

Validation of the translated terminological ontology

Once the target SKOS file has been generated, its structure must be checked to verify whether it is correct (no errors have been introduced by the translator tool) and consistent (it follows the terminological ontology model that it is supposed to follow). This verification can be manually done by reviewing the obtained model. However, it may require quite a lot of time and effort.

To facilitate the validation of the correctness, an implementation of the components proposed in the previous step may also provide different statistics. Specifically, the following data would be necessary: the number of concepts, number of relations of each type, and number and type of the properties. In this context, given the heterogeneity of the source models, some of the source element may be lost in the translation (for these, no conversion function is defined) due to they do not have correspondence in the target SKOS model. In this situation, the alternatives are to use a descriptive field of SKOS (e.g., *skos:note*) to store the non-compatible fields or directly to discard them.

In the generated translation processes it has been found that most of the managed thesauri have extensions that cannot be matched to SKOS. Therefore, to maintain the resulting model adjusted to SKOS specification and since the additional elements are not always concept properties that can be stored as notes (e.g., the extended set of relationships of AGROVOC) and given that they only affects to not vital areas in the model, it has been decided to discard them. However, it is important to take into account the elements that are lost in the translation to be able to validate that their loss is not a translation mistake. To facilitate this task, a report with the elements from the source model that have not equivalence in the target one is generated.

With respect to the validation of the consistency of the generated model, for each different type of terminological model generated a set of rules indicating the structural conditions to validate must be defined. For example, to validate that a thesaurus represented in SKOS format is valid the following restrictions have to be checked:

- A single *ConceptScheme* must exist. All the concepts contained in the SKOS file must refer to this *ConceptScheme*.
- Every concept must have a single *broader* concept except when it is a top concept. Top concepts do not have any *broader* concept and must be referenced in the *ConceptScheme* structure.
- Each concept must have one and only one preferred label for each available language. Additionally, that label must be unique throughout the thesaurus.
- All the relations between concepts must reference to existent concepts (orphan relations are not allowed).
- The structure of *broader/narrower* relationships must not contain cycles.
- The *related* relation is symmetric; therefore, if "A" is *related* with "B", then "B" must be *related* with "A".
- The *broader* relation is the inverse of the *narrower* one; therefore, if "A" is the *broader* of "B", then "B" must be *narrower* of "A".

Each different type of terminological ontology requires their specific set of validation rules. For example, dictionaries do not have broader/narrower relationships but it is mandatory that they have a definition associated to each concept. The application of the validation rules corresponding to the obtained models has been done by ad-hoc software. For each type of terminological ontology translated to SKOS using the translation process described in this section (i.e., glossaries, taxonomies, and thesauri), a specific validation system has been created.

Many errors detected in different translation processes are usually caused by mistakes in the translation tool. Finding the problem and fixing the tool corrects all those errors. However, it has been found that it is also quite common to have errors in the terminological ontology source formats. Three types of errors have been detected: syntactic errors in the representation format (e.g., a file with a wrong name), semantic errors in the model (e.g., the format does not fulfill some part of the defined model), and structural problems related to the consistency (e.g., a model is supposed to be a thesaurus but some of the concepts have several preferred labels). Each of these types of errors is detected at a different stage of the translation process. Syntactic errors are directly found when the translation tool reads the sources. Semantic problems are detected by the matcher. Finally, errors in the general structure of the terminological ontology are detected by the validation process.

Management of the translation tool

Usually, the designed process for the creation of the translation tools is expected to produce simple tools that receive as input the source model and provide as output the translated SKOS file. However, this is not possible in all situations. Sometimes, the existence of errors in source models requires an additional preprocessing step to correct them. Other times, a simple manual processing of the source data reduces the complexity of the reader component. For instance, a transformation of the source files from ASCII to UTF-8 simplifies the work of managing the non Latin-1 characters. Another example is to save an Excel file as a text based tabular format to simplify the reader component (reading an excel file requires additional programming that is not needed to access a text file).

These additional steps are vital for a translation tool to perform its work properly. But since they must be done manually, the proposed methodology documents them in such a way that the next time a translation tool has to be used they can be easily identified and applied. The solution proposed is to define for each translation process a flow diagram that shows how the different transformation steps are concatenated. Figure 3.8 shows an example of a flow diagram for an XML based source where tree different steps are performed. First, a transformation of the source files to UTF-8. The second step is the correction of all the errors found in the source. The last step is the execution of the transformation tool that generates the SKOS file.

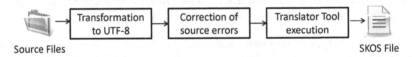

Source Files   SKOS File

Fig. 3.8: Example of transformation flow diagram

In addition to the flow diagram, the set of processes implied in a translation are described according to the model depicted in figure 3.9. In this model, a translation process is represented with the *Translator* class and identified with a name and a description of the source format. A translation consists of a set of translation tasks (*Task* class) that describe each process to perform. The *Task* class contains the following properties to describe a process: a name that identifies the task; the order of execution of the process (e.g., it has to be done in third place); the activity to perform (e.g., execution of the *EurovocTranslator* tool); a description of the task that describes how it has to be done; a description of the input and output of each task (e.g., a list of the files used as input, and the specific directory where they have to be located); and additional information that can be relevant for the process execution (e.g., the description of the different configuration files required to run the translation software).

The errors identified in the source model and the way used to correct them are documented with the *Problem* class described in figure 3.9. Table 3.2 describes the attributes in the *Problem* class: type, description, correction process, and comments.

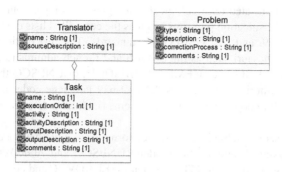

Fig. 3.9: Model used to describe the tasks involved in the translation step

ID	Description
Type	It indicates the type of error or issue detected. They can be syntactic, semantic or structural
Description	It describes the cause of the error. For example, there is an XML tag not closed (detailing the name and line where the tag is placed)
Correction process	It indicates what has been done to correct the error. In the previous case, it would be to add a close tag in the proper place
Comments	Additional information about the element that causes the error and how to correct it. For example, external sources used to determine how to correct an error

Table 3.2: Attributes in the *Problem* class used to describe the errors found in the source files

3.6.1.2 Testing the method

In order to test the feasibility of the methodology proposed, we have created a default implementation for the translation of different terminological ontologies. Table 3.3 shows a review of the translated ontologies indicating their name, the type of model they follow, the format in which they have been originally found, and an approximate number of concepts.

Name	Type of model	Original format	Concepts
GEMET	Thesaurus	Expanded SKOS	6500
AGROVOC	Thesaurus	Access Database	28000
EUROVOC	Thesaurus	XML based	6600
UNESCO	Thesaurus	Access Database	4400
URBISOC	Thesaurus	HTML based	3600
ISOC-GEOGRAFIA	Thesaurus	HTML based	5100
Spanish and French Administrative Units	Taxonomy-Authority File	Excel	45000
ISO-639 Language Code List	Authority File	Formatted text	7600
EPSG Reference systems	Authority File	Access Database	5200
40 ISO-19915 & ISO-19139 lists	Controlled vocabularies	Tables in a PDF file	300
12 CSDGM-FGDC lists	Controlled vocabularies	Tables in a PDF file	100
Inspire Spatial Themes	Controlled Vocabulary	Text document	35

Table 3.3: Review of translated models

Most of the translated terminological ontologies are simple controlled vocabularies used for classification purposes, such as the controlled lists contained in ISO-19115, ISO-19119, and CSDGM-FGDC standards. The rest of them are mainly taxonomies and thesauri such as the Spanish and French administrative unit models, AGROVOC, EUROVOC, GEMET, URBISOC[12], or UNESCO thesauri. There are also some authority files such as the ISO-639 language code list, and the set of EPSG codes for coordinate reference systems (including datums, ellipsoids, and projections).

As it can be seen in table 3.3, the source formats are quite heterogeneous. There are databases using different table models (UNESCO and AGROVOC thesauri), XML files following different DTD or Schemes (EUROVOC and GEMET thesauri), HTML representations (URBISOC and ISOC-GEOGRAFIA thesauri), Excel files with different degrees of organization (Spanish and French Administrative Units), and text directly extracted from text or even *pdf* files (ISO-19115 and ISO-639 code lists). This heterogeneity has increased the number of required translation tools because the created ones were not reusable in other translation processes. The only one that it has been possible to reuse has been the created for translating controlled vocabularies. Altogether, nine different translation tools have been required.

An additional factor that has complicated the creation of the translation tools has been the irregularities found in some of the terminological models. The existence of extensions to the basic model or the lack of some mandatory elements have hindered their processing. For example, GEMET and AGROVOC are thesauri but they do not completely follow the structure dictated by the thesaurus standards and include some ad-hoc elements and relationships.

Finally, the last problem tackled has been the existence of errors in the different translated source models. Many of them were not very important, but others were critical because it was not possible to perform a complete transformation if they were not corrected (e.g., syntactic errors). In the transformed models, all the critical errors have been manually corrected. However, it has not been possible to correct some of the non-vital consistency problems (e.g., the lack of a preferred label for a concept) due to the lack of information to fix them.

3.6.2 Terminological ontologies as a result of thesaurus merging

Reusing existent terminological ontologies is usually a good choice to reduce development efforts. However, it is not always possible to find a terminological model suitable for the required purpose. Existent terminological ontologies may not contain the required vocabulary, or may not provide enough semantics for the required purpose.

If no suitable model exists and a new ontology has to be created, instead of creating it from scratch (it takes a lot of effort), it is a good policy to take as base

---

[12] http://thes.cindoc.csic.es/index_URBA_esp.html

other existent ontologies and reuse as much as possible from them. Although existent models do not completely fit the needed requirements, part of their vocabulary and relations may be reused in the new model. These elements can provide the core of the new model saving a lot of time and effort in its construction.

To do this, it is important to take into account that each terminological ontology is a specific view of certain knowledge area. Each one provides a partial view of a knowledge area because its content is biased by the application context and purpose for which the ontology has been created. The meaning of a term in certain context can be completely different from the meaning in other contexts. It is said that one of the biggest challenges in information retrieval is the identification of concept meaning in a specific domain of interest. In terminological models this meaning is indicated by a natural language definition and by the context provided by the rest of the model structure (e.g., in a thesaurus the broader/narrower relations).

The use of several terminological ontologies (in this case thesauri) covering the same area of knowledge helps to obtain a more general interpretation of the domain. The different views provided by each terminological model complement each other. If a set of concepts and relations between them can be found in most of the source models, it indicates that the organization of these subsets of knowledge is generally recognized and it is quite stable. Therefore, due to its relevance in different contexts, it should be included in the model to generate.

The main issue to take into account when selecting these relevant knowledge elements is the identification of the set of them that is part of the desired knowledge area. The terminological models selected as source for the merging process contain terminology required by the model to construct. However, they also contain terms and relations relevant for other contexts that have to be removed.

This section describes a process to construct a terminological ontology using other terminological models as base. The objective of the process is to generate a terminological ontology following the thesaurus structure that is focused on a selected theme (that is, a domain model).

3.6.2.1 Proposed merging process

The objective of the developed process is to generate a thesaurus which contains the main concepts of the required area of knowledge and the relations between them. The process is based on two elements: a glossary of terms about the desired subject (set of required concepts) and a set of cross-domain terminological ontologies with a rich inter-concept structure such as thesauri or taxonomies (simpler models such as glossaries cannot be used due to the lack of term relationships) that contain subsets of terms about the desired theme. The glossary is used as the core of the new model (to focus the result in the desired theme) and it is enriched with the structure of concepts and relations between concepts in the desired area of knowledge through the analysis and comparison of cross-domain models. The structure resulting of such combination is a network of concepts that can be considered as a domain

terminological ontology of the area of interest. To obtain the desired thesaurus, this
network is processed adjust its structure to the specified by the thesaurus standards.

The obtained thesaurus provides a general view of the knowledge of the desired
area. It provides an initial structure of concepts and relations to work with that can be
updated and modified according to the desired requirements. Although the generated
model is not perfect and it has to be manually refined to adjust it to the application
requirements, the cost of doing it is much less than the cost of having to construct it
from scratch.

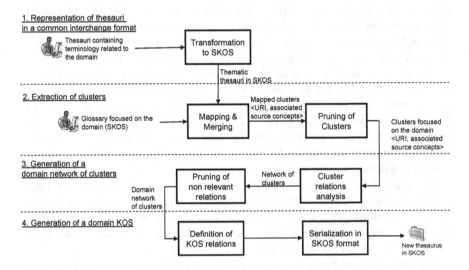

Fig. 3.10: Workflow for the generation of a new terminological ontology

Figure 3.10 remarks the different steps of the developed process showing the
inputs and the produced results. The creation process is divided into four different
tasks: the harmonization of the interchange format used for the thematic thesauri,
the mapping of concepts from the thematic thesauri, the generation of a network of
thematic concepts about the selected area of knowledge, and the transformation of
this network into a new thesaurus.

The harmonization of the interchange format is an external step required to provide a homogeneous input to the generation system. The other steps take this input
and transform it into a new thesaurus focused on the desired theme. Following sub-
sections describe in detail each one of these processes steps and the main components of software created to perform them (see figure 3.11).

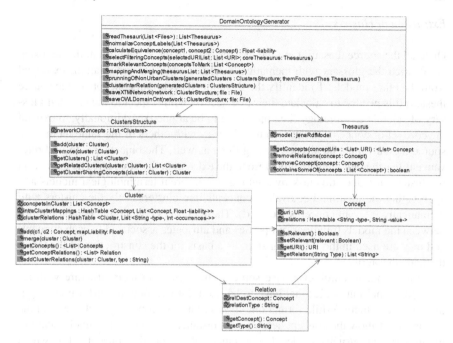

Fig. 3.11: UML model of the domain ontology generation tool

Harmonization of the interchange format

As it has been indicated in section 3.6.1, along the years, a lot of well-established terminological models have been created in different domains. However, the lack of standardization has produced a huge variety of incompatible formats.

Managing many different formats as input for the merging process is not viable because the process should be modified each time the set of used ontologies is changed. Therefore, to make the process reusable, the first step in the generation process is to homogenize all the source model representations to reduce the complexity of the whole process. The objective is to be able to increase or change the knowledge base used for the generation (using other thesauri) without having to modify the used generation software.

The format selected as input has been SKOS. If the glossary or any of the cross-domain thesauri are not in this format they have to be translated. To do so, a transformation tool has to be developed following the methodology described in section 3.6.1.

Extraction of clusters

Once all the source thesauri (and the glossary) are in the same format, the next step is to enrich the glossary with thematically related concepts and relations extracted from the other models. To identify the thematically relevant concepts in the source thesauri it is needed to calculate their intersection with respect to the selected glossary of suitable terminology (i.e., they have to be aligned). Additionally, to expand the core set of concepts in the selected glossary with others of the same theme, the source thesauri must be aligned among them as well. The objective is to find relevant entities that are thematically close to the existent in the glossary. The extraction of clusters step does this task by aligning the different terminological models and aggregating the identified equivalent concepts into clusters (only the clusters with thematically relevant concepts are used). These clusters contain the commonalities between the models (relations, properties and attributes associated to each concept) and they are used in the following steps as a basis for the construction of the target thematic thesaurus.

Terminological ontologies have some particularities in their structure with respect to formal ontologies that have to be taken into account to perform an alignment between them. While formal ontologies represent concepts as classes and the entities that follow the concept definition as instances of a class, terminological ontology terms are usually modeled as instances of a general "Concept" class which define the available types of properties and relations [141, 52].

This way of modeling terminological ontologies simplifies its use for classification, since the terms can be directly used as values of properties in the description of resources. As commented by Noy [157], representing each concept of a terminological ontology as a different class is problematic because it increases the complexity of the terminological model. For example, the classes have to be used as property values in the description of the resources, making the model to lose computational completeness (this can be avoided, but elaborated artifacts have to be defined).

The difference in structure of terminological ontologies with respect to formal ones reduces the number of alignment techniques that can be selected from the ones described in section 1.4. For example, the matching techniques based on the analysis of the classes, properties, and attributes are not applicable given that all the source models have the same types of properties and attributes (they are all represented using SKOS model). With respect to the techniques based on data analysis, the structure of the terminological ontology inhibits them to be used because the elements to relate in the used terminological ontologies are the instances.

The rest of techniques (e.g., techniques based on the analysis of entity names, techniques based on the use of external resources, or techniques based on semantic interpretation) can be applied but on instances and instance property values. For example, instead of using a linguistic technique to find equivalence between class names, the same technique can be used to find equivalences between term labels of different instances. For using these techniques, it is important to note that the multilingual characteristics of the glossary and terminological ontologies to align are of great use as additional resources in the generation of the matchings between the models.

The extraction of clusters process is divided into two different steps. First, the mapping & merging step that relates the thesauri and the glossary between them, merging equivalent concepts into a new one that acts as a cluster of source concepts (it groups concepts from the input thesauri). Second, the pruning of non-thematically related clusters step removes those clusters that do not contain terms of the glossary or that do not have a direct relation with other one that fulfills the previous condition.

Mapping & merging

In the mapping & merging step, every concept of every used terminological ontology (thesauri and glossary) is aligned to extract the commonalities and generate clusters of equivalent concepts. Each generated cluster represents a group of equivalent concepts and it is identified with one of the URIs of the original concepts. A code-oriented view of the process is shown in algorithm 1.

```
Procedure ClustersStructure mappingAndMerging(List thesaurusList);
begin
    normalizeConceptLabels(thesaurusList);
    ClustersStructure generatedClusters =new ClustersStructure();
    for int i=0;i<thesaurusList.size();i++ do
        List thesConcepts = thesaurusList.get(i).getConcepts();
        for int j=0; j<thesConcepts.size();j++ do
            Concept thesConcept = thesConcepts.get(j));
            Cluster clust= new Cluster(thesConcept);
            for k=i+1;k<thesaurusList.size() do
                List thesConceptsComp = thesaurusList.get(k).getConcepts();
                for int l=0; l<thesConceptsComp.size();l++ do
                    Concept thesConceptComp = thesConceptsComp.get(l));
                    int equivalenceValue = calculateEquivalence(thesConcept,thesConceptComp);
                    if equivalenceValue >0 then
                        | clust.add(thesConcept,thesConceptComp,equivalenceValue);
                    end
                end
            end
            Cluster existentCluster=generatedClusters.getClusterSharingConcepts(clust);
            if existentCluster != null then
                | existentCluster.merge(clust);
            else
                | generatedClusters.add(clust);
            end
        end
    end
    return generatedClusters
end
```

Algorithm 1: Matching process

In this context, two concepts from different thesauri are considered equivalent when at least one of the labels of a concept (preferred and alternatives) is equal to one of the labels from the other concept. To identify these equivalences, from the matching techniques described in section 1.4, the described process focuses on the comparison of preferred and alternative labels from concepts in the different available languages (string comparison), leaving the use of relations and other properties such as definition or scope notes as improvements of the basic technique.

To improve results of the matching procedure, the labels are normalized by removing the accents, capital letters and plurals (see character normalization and lemmatization techniques in section 1.4). Additionally, the matching could have been enriched with misspellings detection, stemming and word order analysis among others, but given the usual high quality of thesauri content no much improvement would be expected from the use of these techniques.

The use of multilingual thesauri provides additional labels for the matching process increasing the probability of finding an equivalence (two concepts may differ in a language but have a coincidence in another one). Additionally, the number of labels (in multiple languages) that coincide between two matched concepts can be used as measure of the similarity between the concepts and the quality of the matchings. The higher the number of labels two concepts share (from the total they have), the higher their equivalence is. Equation 3.1 shows the formula used to measure this similarity. It calculates the percentage of common labels between two concepts, being NMatLab the number of matched labels between two concepts, NLab_1 the total number of different labels of the first concept involved in the matching, and NLab_2 the equivalent for the second one. This formula is somewhat equivalent to the substring similarity formula used in matching systems to compute the distance between two strings (see [48, chap. 4]).

$$conceptSimilarity = \frac{2 * NMatLab}{NLab\_1 + NLab\_2}. \tag{3.1}$$

The concept similarity measure of equation 3.1 can be applied to each obtained mapping, but in this process it is only used to analyze the quality of the matching of each source thesaurus with respect to the glossary focused in the selected theme. This analysis has as objective to show the relevance that each different terminological model gives to the selected theme (see the experiments in section 3.6.2.2).

Figure 3.12 shows a simplified example of a generated cluster ("Inland Water" cluster). The example does not uses alternative labels for cluster construction and does not fix the plural differences but it is enough to show how the cluster generation works. In the figure, it can be seen that the AGROVOC "Inland Waters" concept is included in the cluster due to the presence of this label and its Spanish translation in the concepts of EUROVOC. The relevance of the matchings has been included to show that they can be seen as a measure of the similarity in the concepts definition.

Pruning of non-relevant clusters

From the clusters obtained in the mapping process, only those containing concepts about the desired theme are required in the following steps to generate the desired thesaurus. Therefore, the non-thematically relevant clusters have to be removed from the system. A schema of the pruning process is shown in the algorithm 2. The division between relevant and non relevant clusters is performed using the fol-

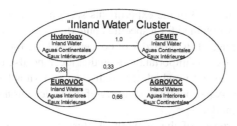

Fig. 3.12: Example of a possible cluster

lowing rule: A cluster is only considered relevant if it contains a concept from the glossary of selected terminology, or if it is directly related (*broader*, *narrower* and *related* relationships) to a cluster that fits in the first case. The rest of the clusters are considered as non-relevant and they are pruned from the system. The reason to include clusters that do not directly contain terminology from the selected glossary is to extend the set of core concepts with the relevant knowledge that different areas of knowledge (the provided by the different used thesauri) consider related to it.

```
Procedure pruningOfNonUrbanClusters(ClustersStructure generatedClusters, Thesaurus themFocusedThes);
begin
    List clusterList = generatedClusters.getClusters();
    for int i=0;i<clusterList.size();i++ do
        Cluster clust = clusterList.get(i);
        List relClustList = generatedClusters.getRelatedClusters(clust);
        relClustList.add(clust);
        boolean themFocusedCluster = false;
        for int k=0;k<relClustList.size();k++ do
            if themFocusedThes.containsSomeOf(relClustList.get(k).getConcepts()) then
                themFocusedCluster=true;
            end
        end
        if not themFocusedCluster then
            generatedClusters.remove(clust);
        end
    end
end
```

Algorithm 2: Cluster pruning process

Generation of a domain network of clusters

The clusters generated in the previous step contain the collected terminology about the desired theme (extracted from different knowledge models), but not how this knowledge is inter-related. The next step in the thesaurus generation process is to identify the relations and add them to the clusters. The result obtained is a network of clusters that can be seen as a domain ontology describing the knowledge of the area of interest. Figure 3.13 in the experiments section (section 3.6.2.2) shows an example of a network obtained for a specific context.

In addition to the use of the network of concepts as base for the generation of a new thematic thesaurus, it is important to note that it can be also used for tasks such as the analysis of the extent in which the studied area of knowledge is represented in the input thesauri. Additionally, it can serve for the detection of inconsistencies between the source models.

The generation process of the network of clusters is divided in two different subtasks: generation of inter-cluster relations and pruning of non-relevant relations.

Generation of inter-cluster relations

The creation of the relations between the clusters is done by converting the original relations of the concepts contained in the clusters into relations between the clusters that contain them. In addition to the basic relations (*broader*, *narrower* and *related*), *sibling* relations (*narrower* of its *broader*) have been also considered. They have been included to detect those concepts that are not directly related but they are close in meaning. Other more complex relations such as the *grandparent* (*broader* of its *broader*) or *grandchildren* (*narrower* of their *narrower*) could also have been considered to detect clusters relations, but they are left for future functionality expansions.

Algorithm 3 shows a schema of the cluster relation process. For each relation between concepts from two different clusters in their original thesauri, a relation of the same type is added between the clusters containing them. If several relations between two clusters are created, they are aggregated into a single one containing the number and types of the original relations. The number of original relations shows the relevance of the generated inter-cluster relation. The more relations are found in the source models, the stronger the generated relationship is (it has been found as relevant in more different contexts).

```
Procedure clusterInterRelation(ClustersStructure generatedClusters);
begin
    List clusterList = generatedClusters.getClusters();
    for int i=0;i<clusterList.size();i++ do
        Cluster clust = clusterList.get(i);
        List relatedC1 = clust.getConceptRelations();
        for int j=i+1;j<clusterList.size();j++ do
            Cluster clust2 = clusterList.get(j);
            for int k=0;k<relatedC1.size();k++ do
                Relation relR1 =relatedC1.get(k);
                if clust2.contains(relR1.getConcept()) then
                    | clust.addClusterRelation(clust2, relR1.getType());
                end
            end
        end
    end
end
```

Algorithm 3: Cluster interrelation

Pruning of non-relevant relations

The generated cluster relations can be classified by their relevance (depending on the number of source thesauri that contain them). This classification can be used to reduce the size of the generated network (it may be too complex and/or contain spurious clusters) by selecting only the most relevant relationships.

A specific process has been developed to perform this relationship punning. This process requires the selection by the user of a threshold that is used to determine if a relation is maintained. All the relations with a weight (number of occurrences) below the indicated threshold are pruned. Additionally, after the prune of relations, if some clusters have lost all their relations and do not contain terms from the source glossary they are removed (this is done to obtain a more compact network structure).

Generation of a new domain thematic thesaurus

The last step of the defined process is to take the network of clusters describing the content of the decided area of knowledge and transform it into a thesaurus. The structure of the network is reorganized into a hierarchical model. This is possible since the original models are also thesauri, i.e. the properties and relations of the clusters of the network are compatible.

The generation process is shown in algorithm 4. The process transforms the clusters in the network into concepts of the new thesauri. The cluster content (preferred and alternative labels, definitions and scope notes of the source thesauri) is transferred into the new concepts; and the cluster relations are modified to generate the hierarchical structure of a thesaurus.

The selection of the preferred label of each generated concept (one per language) is performed as follows. If the cluster contains a concept from the thematic glossary, its preferred label is selected. Otherwise, the selected label is the one in the concept whose source thesaurus has been loaded first in the system (it can be changed by configuration). The rest of the labels in the cluster are left as alternatives.

With respect to the relations structure, each relation between the clusters is marked with the type that has more occurrences (*broader/narrower* or *related* relationships). The *sibling* relationships are used as a concept closeness measure to determine the selection between a *broader/narrower* relationship and a *related* relationship in those situations in which there may be doubts. Algorithm 5 details the selection process of the most suitable relation. This algorithm is based on the application of the following set of rules:

- A relation in the new thesaurus is marked as *broader* if the number of *broader* relations found between the original clusters is greater than zero and the sum of the *broader* and *sibling* relations is greater than the number of *related* relationships. To maintain the consistency of the thesaurus, for each *broader* relationship that is defined an inverse *narrower* relation is also generated.
- In a thesaurus only a *broader* relation should be defined for each concept. Therefore, if more than one *broader* relation is generated using the previous rule, the

```
Procedure generationOfNewThesaurus(ClustersStructure generatedClusters, String schemaURI, File
fileToSave);
begin
        SKOSWritter writter = new SKOSWritter();
        SKOSModel newThesaurus = writter.createSKOSModel();
        SKOSConceptSchema schema = newThesaurus.createConceptShema(schemaURI);
        List clusterList = generatedClusters.getClusters();
        for int i=0;i<clusterList.size();i++ do
              Cluster clust = clusterList.get(i);
              SKOSConcept concept = SKOSModel.createConcept(clust.getURI(),schema);
              fillConceptProperties(concept, clust);
              List relationList = clust.getClusterRelation();
              List broaders, relateds; getSuitableRelations(relationList,broaders,relateds); if broaders.size()==0
              then
                  |  schema.addTopConcept(concept);
              end
              for int j=0;j<broaders.size();j++ do
                    ClusterRelation relation= relationList.get(j);
                    SKOSConcept destconcept =
                    SKOSModel.createConcept(relation.getDestinationUri(),schema);
                    concept.addRelation(SKOSRelation.broader,destconcept);
                    destconcept.addRelation(SKOSRelation.narrower,concept);
              end
              for int j=0;j<relateds.size();j++ do
                    ClusterRelation relation= relationList.get(j);
                    SKOSConcept destconcept =
                    SKOSModel.createConcept(relation.getDestinationUri(),schema);
                    concept.addRelation(SKOSRelation.related,destconcept);
                    destconcept.addRelation(SKOSRelation.related,concept);
              end
        end
        List topConceptList = SKOSModel.getTopConcepts();
        for int i=0;i<topConceptList.size();i++ do
            |  removeCycles(topConceptList.get(i), new ArrayList());
        end
        String skosFile = writter.generateSKOSFile(newThesaurus);
        fileToSave.write(skosFile);
end
```

Algorithm 4: Generation of the new thesaurus

broader relation that has the highest weight (biggest number of relations of this type in the original cluster) is preserved and the rest of them are tagged as *related* relationships. If two or more relations share the same weight, the one with more *sibling* is the selected. Finally, if they also have the same number of *sibling*s the user has to take the final decision.

- If a relation has not been tagged using the previous rules and the number of its inner *related* relationships is greater than zero, the relation is marked as *related* relationship.
- The relationships that are only marked as *sibling* type are discarded.

Having generated the concepts and relations of the thesaurus, it is needed to identify its top terms. This is quite easy, as a top term is a concept without a *broader* relationship. Therefore, it is only needed to review all generated concepts and mark those without a *broader* relationship as top terms of the thesaurus.

Finally, the last generation step is shown in Algorithm 6. It verifies that the *broader/narrower* structure in the obtained thesaurus does not cycles. Starting from the top concepts, all the *narrower* relationships are recursively analyzed until the

```
Procedure getSuitableRelations(List relationList, List broaders, List relateds);
begin
    ClusterRelation moreRelevantBroader = new ClusterRelation();
    for int i=0;i<relationList.size();i++ do
        ClusterRelation relation = relationList.get(i);
        int weightRelated=relation.getNumberof(SKOSRelation.related);
        int weightBroader=relation.getNumberof(SKOSRelation.broader);
        int weightSibling=relation.getNumberof(SKOSRelation.sibling);
        if (weightBroader>0) && hasBigestBroaderWeight(relation, moreRelevantBroader) then
            Forint i=0;i<broaders.size();i++ ClusterRelation relToTransfer = broaders.get(i);
            if relToTransfer.getNumberof(SKOSRelation.related)>0 then
            |   relateds.add(relToTransfer);
            end
            broaders.removeAll;
            broaders.add(relation);
            moreRelevantBroader=relation;
        else
            if (weightBroader>0) && hasSameBroaderWeight(relation, moreRelevantBroader) then
            |   broaders.add(relation);
            else
                if weightRelated>0 then
                |   relateds.add(relation);
                end
            end
        end
    end
end
```

Algorithm 5: Selection of the suitable relations between the available ones

end of the structure is reached or a cycle is found. When a cycle is found, the *broader/narrower* relationships that references to a processed concept are transformed into *related* relationships between the concepts (to remark that there is a relation between them).

```
Procedure removeCycles(SKOSConcept concept, List broaders);
begin
    List narrowList concept.getRelation(SKOSRelation.narrower);
    for int i=0;i<narrowList.size();i++ do
        SKOSConcept conceptRel = narrowList.get(i);
        if broaders.contains(conceptRel) then
            concept.removeRelation(conceptRel,SKOSRelation.narrower);
            conceptRel.removeRelation(concept,SKOSRelation.broader);
            concept.addRelation(conceptRel,SKOSRelation.related);
            conceptRel.addRelation(concept,SKOSRelation.related);
        else
            broaders.add(concept);
            removeCycles(conceptRel, new ArrayList(broaders));
        end
    end
end
```

Algorithm 6: Removal of cycles in the generated structure

The new thesaurus is stored in SKOS format to be able to integrate it, if needed, with other terminological ontologies. To do this, the SKOS writer component described in section 3.6.1 has been integrated as part of the generation software. The

SKOS writer receives the concepts and relations created by the generation software and it represents them in SKOS format.

3.6.2.2 Testing the method

This process has been applied in two different knowledge areas. In a first experiment, the method has been used to create a new thesaurus focused on the urbanism subject. In the second one, it has been applied in the hydrological domain.

Testing the method in the urban domain

Urbanism is usually defined as the study of cities including their economic, political, social and cultural environment. In this context, the ontologies have begun to be used to facilitate and improve the access to the urban resources (as it has happened in other knowledge areas). An example of the use of ontologies in the urban context is the COST C21 Action[13] project that has been created with the objective of increasing the knowledge and promoting the use of ontologies in the domain of Urban Civil Engineering projects.

Nowadays, there are terminologies containing urban vocabulary but not specifically focused on urbanism. In this context, the definition of stable terminological urban ontologies in the area is needed. However, the multidisciplinarity of urbanism makes the selection of the suitable terminology difficult. The collection of thematically related concepts requires an examination of all the cross-domain areas involved in the urbanism. As a step in this direction, a draft of an urban model has been created using the generation process described earlier.

The urban glossary required for the generation process as core of the urban ontology has been constructed using URBISOC[14] thesaurus as base. The URBISOC thesaurus was developed by the Spanish National Research Council to facilitate classification at bibliographic databases specialized in scientific and technical journals on Geography, Town Planning, Urbanism and Architecture. However, URBISOC is not suitable as a urban thesaurus since it also contains very general terms, not specifically related to urbanism.

In this context, the urban glossary has been constructed using an heuristic filtering process that extracts the urban concepts from URBISOC. Algorithm 7 shows the filtering process. This process requires the manual selection of a small set of initial concepts from URBISOC to work. Recursively, all the *narrower* and *related* concepts of this selected core are added to the set until no more elements are found. The rest of the concepts of URBISOC are considered as non-thematically relevant and are discarded.

---

[13] http://www.towntology.net/

[14] http://thes.cindoc.csic.es/index_URBA_esp.html

In this application example, the "Ordenación urbana" (Urban planning) concept has been selected as seed concept (it is used very frequently in urban contexts). The result obtained has been a glossary that has eliminated most of the general terminology and contains 3,091 concepts out of the 3,609 concepts of URBISOC.

```
Procedure selectFilteringConcepts(List selectedURIList, Thesaurus coreThesaurus);
begin
    List selectedConceptList = coreThesaurus.getConcepts(selectedURIList);
    markRelevantConcepts(selectedConceptList);
    List thesConcepts = coreThesaurus.getConcepts();
    for int i=0;i<thesConcepts.size();i++ do
        Concept thesConcept = selectedConceptList.get(i));
        if not thesConcept.isRelevant() then
            coreThesaurus.removeRelations(thesConcept);
            coreThesaurus.removeConcept(thesConcept);
        end
    end
end
Procedure markRelevantConcepts(List conceptsToMark);
begin
    for int i=0; i<conceptsToMark.size();i++ do
        Concept coreConcept = conceptsToMark.get(i));
        if not coreConcept.isRelevant() then
            coreConcept.setRelevant(true);
            markRelevantConcepts(coreConcept.getNarrowers(coreConcept));
            markRelevantConcepts(coreConcept.getRelateds(coreConcept));
        end
    end
end
```

Algorithm 7: Selection of filtering concepts

In addition to the urban glossary, the other input required by the generation system is a set of thesauri containing thematic related terminology. In this case the selected thesauri have been GEMET, AGROVOC, EUROVOC and UNESCO. They have been selected because they contain large sets of urban terminology and each one provides a different view of it. Additionally, all of them are multilingual and provide labels for the concepts in Spanish, English, and French (between others). The description of these thesauri and its content is shown in section 1.3.4.

Since the used cross-domain thesauri (including URBISOC) were published in completely different representation formats (see section 3.6.1.2), they had to be translated into SKOS format using the process described in section 3.6.1.

The clusters generated in the matching step have been used to analyze the degree of representation of the urban terminology in each of the used cross-domain thesauri. This has been done by counting the concepts of each thesaurus that have been matched to a concept in the glossary, and calculating the mean of the reliability of the mappings. Table 3.4 shows the obtained results. It contains the number of concepts of each thesaurus, the number of concepts mapped to the glossary extracted from URBISOC, and the average relevance of the mappings (see equation 3.1). These results show that all the thesauri selected to expand and relate the glossary contain a relevant subset of urban related concepts with a quire similar number of concepts (between 358 and 418 urban concepts). Independently, each matched subset only covers a reduced part of the core glossary (12% on average), but combining them the coverage is around a 35%.

Name	Concepts	Mapped Concepts	Reliability
GEMET	5244	388	0.765
EUROVOC	6649	418	0.588
AGROVOC	16896	369	0.684
UNESCO	4424	354	0.715

Table 3.4: Relevance of urbanism in cross-domain thesauri

In this use case, the generation of the relations between clusters has been performed a bit different from the described in the general process. The use of UR-BISOC to generate the core glossary provides a set of extra relations between the concepts of the glossary that have been taken into account for the construction of the network of concepts. These relations have been managed as the rest of relations between concepts from different clusters and used to determine the inter-cluster relationships.

The obtained network contains 4,698 clusters with 2,189 relations of weight 5 or greater, 2,181 of weight 4, 3,137 of weight 3, 12,000 of weight 2 and 44,518 of weight 1. In this context, the weight of the relations (number of occurrences) has been used to remove gradually the less relevant relations (and associated concepts) obtaining the set of results shown in table Table 3.5. Each row in the table shows the size of the network that includes all the relations of at least "Minimum Weight" weight. It includes the number of clusters, the average size of each cluster, the total number of relations between clusters, and the average number of relations of each cluster.

Minimum Weight	Clusters	Cluster Size	Relations	Cluster Relations
1	4698	1.83	64025	13.62
2	2568	2.39	42823	7.59
3	1514	2.90	17570	4.95
4	1082	3.10	11333	4.03
5	681	3.43	5622	3.21

Table 3.5: Size of the network of urban clusters

To facilitate the analysis of the structure and content of the network of clusters obtained for each pruning level, they have been represented using the XTM format [163]. XTM is an XML based format specifically designed to facilitate the visualization and browsing through network of concepts. Nowadays, there is a wide range of tools able to manage XTM, and from them the TMNAV tool created in the TM4J project[15] has been used to obtain the display of the network.

---

[15] http://tm4j.org/

The XTM files have been generated in such a way that the TMNAV tool shows the preferred English label (or the Spanish one if there is no any English label) of the clusters and the initials of the thesauri that have provided a concept to the cluster (i.e., AEGUR means that the concepts exist in A̲GROVOC, E̲UROVOC, G̲EMET, U̲NESCO and U̲RBISOC; and E̲_R means that the concept does only exist in E̲UROVOC and U̲RBISOC). With respect to the relations, they are labeled with the types and number of the original relations used to define it. BT indicates *broader* relation, NT is *narrower*, RT means *related*, and BR is used for *siblings*.

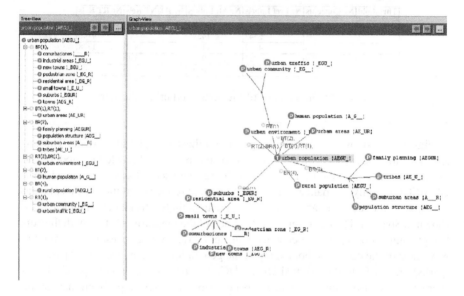

Fig. 3.13: Visualization of a part of the generated urban thesaurus

Figure 3.13 shows a screenshot of TMNAV tool containing all the obtained relations and clusters around the "urban population" cluster from the complete network of clusters (without prune). As it can be seen, the "Urban Population" cluster contains concepts from all the source thesauri except URBISOC and maintains relations with a lot of other clusters. For example, it is related to the "urban areas" cluster through a relation of type *broader* and *related* (both with weight 1).

Each of the generated network of clusters (each one with a different punning level) has been used to create a different version of the thematic thesaurus in SKOS format. Table 3.6 shows the dimensions of each thesaurus generated. It contains the total number of concepts of the generated thesaurus, the number of preferred and alternative labels, the number of *broader/narrower* relations and the number of related relationships. The output ontologies cannot be considered as a final work, but they are a helpful resource for ontologists and experts in the domain. On the one hand, the ontology with weight threshold 1 can be used to explain the relation between urban planning and other concepts that, at first sight, might seem far related. On the other hand, as the threshold increases, the derived ontologies help to discard spurious concepts, which are only considered in some of the original input thesauri. However, it must be taken into account that the increase of weight threshold implies as well a decrease of contributions from other domains. These different alternatives can be manually reviewed to select the most suitable one for the desired application. This selection can be done using any tool able to manage SKOS format. In the context of this book, it has been done using the ThManager tool described in section 5.4.

Threshold	Nr Concepts	Nr Pref Labels	Nr Alt Labels	Nr BT/NT Rels	Nr RT Rels
1	4698	9033	16225	4281	14022
2	2568	6347	14598	1482	4146
3	1508	4262	11556	852	1278
4	1069	3087	9135	550	570
5	672	1996	6653	317	302

Table 3.6: Dimensions of the generated urban thesauri

Figure 3.14 shows a subset of the generated thesaurus provided by the ThManager tool to give an idea of the structure of the resulting knowledge model. The obtained results are conditioned by the fact that the used glossary (extracted form URBISOC) is only in Spanish. This characteristic produces that those concepts that have not been matched to any other one do not contain English labels and have to be shown in Spanish. The figure shows the branch of the thesaurus starting with the "urban planning" concept. The generated concept hierarchy integrates, in a reasonable way, most of the concepts. For example, the generation system places the "parques" (parks) branch from the original URBISOC, as *narrower* of "green space". However, there are also some deficiencies. An example of a typical problem that can be found in the generated model is that the method has not detected that the concepts 'cinturones verdes" and "green corridor" are equivalent. The reason of this problem is that the Spanish translation of "green corridor" in the source thesauri is "pasillos verdes". This problem is not critical since both concepts have been classified as *narrower* terms of "green space" (this facilitates the identification of the problem). However, it is a nuisance because it must be manually corrected.

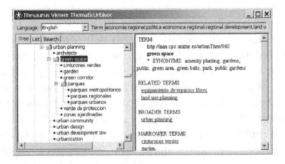

Fig. 3.14: Visualization of a part of the generated urban domain ontology

The translation of the glossary content to the languages provided by GEMET, EUROVOC, AGROVOC and UNESCO thesaurus (at least English, Spanish, and French) would improve the quality of the result thesaurus because it would reduce the non-identified equivalences. This translation could be done manually, or automatically with the help of a multilingual dictionary. Each approach has advantages and disadvantages. On the one hand, a manual translation provides high quality results but requires a lot of effort. On the other hand, an automatic approach is fast but it can introduce errors caused by synonymy problems that would affect to the generation process.

The translation of the glossary has not been included in the present version, but it is believed that an automatic translation process could be used since the specific character of the urban thesaurus would limit the polysemy problems. Additionally, polysemy problem could be partially detected and tackled by performing crossed translations. For example, each term translated to English could be translated from it to French and compared with the translation obtained through a direct translation. If the obtained translations match, the French translation is expected to be correct. In another case, there is a problem and the translation has to be manually reviewed (or directly discarded). The inclusion of a translation step would require the modification of the generated process. It should be performed after the step of normalization of the labels in the glossary with the objective of having more homogeneous labels to translate.

Testing the method in the hydrological domain

In recent years, there has been a general concern about environmental issues in the European context that has lead to the creation of national and international policies encouraging the development of information infrastructures about this issue. In the environmental field, the hydrology management is one of the most relevant and it has attracted a lot of attention and regulation. Hydrologists must monitor a great variety of features and phenomena that, although initially disconnected, may affect the status of water bodies. Due to this variety, information systems managing hydrological information require complete well-known domain models containing all the required terminology to classify and retrieve the hydrology related information. As an initial step in the creation of these models, the generation system described earlier has been used to create a draft of a thesaurus focused on hydrology that can be used to facilitate the management and integration of hydrological resources.

The first input required by the generation tool is a glossary of concepts focused on the desired domain (in this case hydrology). This glossary has been manually created using as base the existent terminology provided by the European Water Framework Directive[16] (WFD) for constructing hydrological models [196]. The resulting

---

[16] The European Water Framework Directive is considered to be the most important piece of legislation in the hydrology area. Its main objective is to achieve an accurate management of all water bodies and reach a "good status" for them by 2015.

glossary includes 108 concepts organized as a plain list of 56 concepts and two hierarchies containing the other 52 concepts.

With respect to the set of thesauri required to define the relation structure of the thesaurus to generate, the same ones that were used in the urban example have been selected (i.e., GEMET, AGROVOC, EUROVOC, and UNESCO). This has been done since they were already available in SKOS format and they contain a good deal of hydrology related terminology.

As in the previous example, the clusters generated in the matching step have been used to analyze the degree of representation of the hydrological terminology in each of the used cross-domain thesauri. Table 3.7 shows the obtained results. It contains the number of concepts of each thesaurus, the number of concepts mapped to the glossary, and the average relevance of the mappings according to equation 3.1 (section 3.6.2.1).

It can be seen from the results that the source thesauri contain a relevant subset of glossary concepts. Around a quarter of the glossary terms have been matched to AGROVOC, EUROVOC, and UNESCO thesaurus. GEMET performance is much better; it contains almost two thirds of the 108 concepts in the glossary. The combined coverage is around a 75% of the glossary concepts.

The difference of these results with respect to the obtained in the urban example is caused by two differences in the way that the generation process has been applied. Firstly, the glossary has been manually selected. Secondly, the glossary content is provided in English, Spanish and French. The manual selection of the glossary is an advantage in the sense that it increases its quality and the thematic closeness of the contained concepts. With respect to the use of a multilingual glossary, it increases the probability of mappings with the thematic thesauri that are provided in the same set of languages.

Name	Concepts	Mapped Concepts	Reliability
GEMET	5244	67	0.704
EUROVOC	6649	21	0.558
AGROVOC	16896	37	0.641
UNESCO	4424	27	0.726

Table 3.7: Relevance of hydrology in cross-domain thesauri

The obtained network of concepts contains 354 concepts with 250 relations of weight 5, 288 of weight 4, 395 of weight 3, 1387 of weight 2, and 2644 of weight 1. As in the previous example, the weight of the relations (number of occurrences) has been used to remove gradually the less relevant relations (and associated concepts) obtaining the set of results shown in table Table 3.8. Each row in the table shows the size of the network that includes all the relations of at least "Minimum Weight" weight. It includes the number of clusters, the average size of each cluster, the total number of relations between clusters, and the average number of inter-cluster relations.

Minimum Weight	Clusters	Cluster Size	Relations	Cluster Relations
1	354	2.77	4964	14.02
2	245	3.06	2320	9.46
3	174	3.16	933	5.36
4	116	3.34	538	4.63
5	75	4.11	250	3.33

Table 3.8: Size of the network of hydrology clusters

In the same way as in the urban example, each of the generated network of clusters (each one with a different punning level) has been used to create a different version of the thematic thesaurus in SKOS format. Table 3.9 shows the dimensions of each thesaurus generated. It contains the total number of concepts of the generated thesaurus, the number of preferred and alternative labels, the number of *broader/narrower* relations and the number of related relationships.

Threshold	Nr Concepts	Nr Pref Labels	Nr Alt Labels	Nr BT/NT Rels	Nr RT Rels
1	354	1062	2622	261	1014
2	245	735	2080	158	352
3	174	522	1585	93	134
4	116	348	1190	56	60
5	75	225	893	29	30

Table 3.9: Dimensions of the generated hydrology thesauri

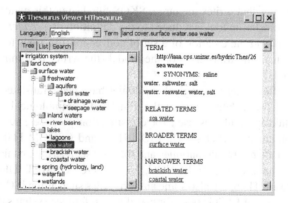

Fig. 3.15: Visualization of a part of the generated hydrology thesaurus

Figure 3.15 shows a subset of the generated thesaurus using the ThManager tool (described in section 5.4) to give an idea of the structure of the resulting knowledge model. The figure shows a branch of the thesaurus that starts with the "land cover" concept. It shows the generated hierarchy containing the different types of water bodies. Although it is true that the generated hierarchy is not the most appropriate (e.g., the "lakes" concept should be a narrower of "inland waters"). It only needs a minimal reorganization of the concepts to provide a much more suitable model.

3.7 Summary

This chapter has analyzed the problem of obtaining terminological ontologies suitable for the required purpose. It has reviewed the different approaches for the construction using as source corpora of data, dictionaries, schemata, or thesauri.

As cases of study of ontology learning methodologies for terminological ontologies two different approaches have been proposed. Firstly, methodology for the reuse of terminological models that gives as result updated models easier to integrate in any information infrastructure has been shown. Secondly, an ontology learning process of thesauri based on other terminological ontologies has been proposed.

Related to the reusability on existent models, the first problem identified has been their format heterogeneity. Ad-hoc formats are very common and extensions to the models are frequently created. Due to the need of a harmonized management of ontologies, this chapter has proposed a methodology to translate input models into a common format (the SKOS based format proposed in section 2.3.1). This process is based on the detailed description of the source and target terminological models. Once these models have been properly described, they are used to construct the translation tool. This construction is simplified thanks to the proposed architectural pattern that divides a translation tool into three separated components: a reader that access to the source format; a matcher that translates the source model to SKOS model; and a writer that writes the target SKOS file. Using this pattern, the task of creation a new translation tool is reduced to the definition of a *reader* component of the source model and the creation of a set of conversion functions to facilitate to a *matcher* component the translation of the model (the writer is common for all the translation tools).

Around 70 different terminological ontologies have been translated to SKOS using this process. From them, most of the translated terminological ontologies are simple controlled vocabularies used for classification purposes, such as the controlled lists contained in ISO-19115, ISO-19119, and CSDGM-FGDC standards. The rest of them are mainly taxonomies and thesauri such as the Spanish and French administrative unit models, AGROVOC, EUROVOC, GEMET, URBISOC[17], or UNESCO thesauri. There are also some authority files such as the ISO-639 language code list, and the set of EPSG codes for coordinate reference systems (including datums, ellipsoids, and projections).

With respect to the learning of a new thesaurus, the proposed method is based on the use of several terminological ontologies (in this case thesauri) covering the same area of knowledge helps to obtain a more general interpretation of the desired domain. The different views provided by each terminological model complement

---

[17] http://thes.cindoc.csic.es/index_URBA_esp.html

each other. If a set of concepts and relations between them can be found in most of the source models, it indicates that the organization of these subsets of knowledge is generally recognized and it is quite stable. The main steps of the generation process are: the harmonization of the input formats; the mapping between the concepts using linguistic similarity measures to generate clusters of equivalent concepts; the establishment of relations between the clusters on the basis of the original relations between the concepts contained in different clusters; the selection of the set of relations that conform a thesaurus structure; and the storage of the new generated model in SKOS format. This process facilitates the creation of different thesaurus versions through the selection of different prunning conditions for the cluster relationships.

The process has been tested to generate a thesaurus of urbanism and another one in the context of hydrology. The domain thesauri obtained as a result of the method proposed have several advantages in comparison with the models used as source:

- Consensus and focus: The concepts of the resulting network have been selected by consensus thanks to the mappings among the different sources, removing those concepts that are neither common nor focused on urbanism.
- Relations: With respect to the relation structure, the total number of available relations is bigger than the existent ones in each of the original sources. Besides, each relation has a weight that indicates its relevance. As future work, the semantics of these relations should be enriched. The information provided by definitions, examples, and naming patterns in the properties of the original concepts should help to refine the current relations (e.g., broader relations could be refined as *is-part-of*, *instance-of* or *generalization* relations).
- Multilingual support: Thanks to the combination of different sources of knowledge with multilingual support, the output network is enriched with alternative terminology in different languages.

Chapter 4
Formalization of terminological ontologies

4.1 Introduction

The applicability of thesauri in the classification and information retrieval context has promoted the creation and diffusion of well-established thesauri in many different domains. These simple models are useful for most of classification and retrieval systems where search requisites are not very elaborated; however, in contexts with an information model of great complexity, more elaborated ontologies with formal is-a hierarchies, frame definitions or even general logical constraints are needed to improve the retrieval quality.

Fisher [56] states that the advantage of replacing concept-oriented terminological ontologies with formal ontologies, is that it can cover a spectrum of functionality which, in principle, includes all the traditional services of a classical thesaurus, and it can offer additional ones. Soergel et al. [176] remark that thesauri should be transformed into other more formal models when at least one of the following requirements is needed:

- Improved user interaction with the ontology on the conceptual and the term level (query formulation, subject browsing, and user learning about the domain).
- Intelligent behind-the-scenes support for query expansion, both concept expansion and synonym expansion, within one language and across languages.
- Intelligent support for human indexers and automated indexing/categorization systems.
- Support for artificial intelligence and Semantic Web applications.

However, the creation of formal ontologies is much more complex than the creation of terminological ontologies because they include many more defined properties and relations. Nowadays, it is common to use (semi-)automatic processing of knowledge resources to alleviate the work of knowledge acquisition (see chapter 3). In this case, a terminological ontology can be used as a base for the construction of a formal model. As stated in [76], hierarchical classification standards, thesauri, and taxonomies are likely the most promising sources for the creation of domain ontologies at reasonable costs because they reflect some degree of community consensus

J. Lacasta et al., *Terminological Ontologies: Design, Management and Practical Applications*, Semantic Web and Beyond 9, DOI 10.1007/978-1-4419-6981-1_4, © Springer Science+Business Media, LLC 2010

and contain, readily available, a wealth of category definitions plus a hierarchy. The objective is to combine the terminological richness of good thesauri with the conceptual structure of full-fledged ontologies containing well-structured hierarchies of concepts connected through a rich network of detailed relations.

One of the most basic requirements to jump from terminological to formal ontologies is to be able to classify the *broader/narrower* relationships (that only indicate a general containment meaning) into specific categories such as *is-a*, *instance-of*, or *is-part-of*. Another important required transformation is the classification of the abstract *related* relationships into different specific subtypes. Once these basic elements have been correctly transformed, other elements such as value restrictions, cardinalities, or relations can be included to enrich the transformed ontology. Fisher [56] focuses on the problem of identifying these relations in a thesaurus model describing the issues inherent to the transformation.

This chapter analyzes the complexity and the viability of the formalization approaches for its use inside the global context of ontology management in Information Infrastructures. Additionally, this chapter describes a formalization prototype that implements some simple formalization rules. The results obtained are analyzed to see the viability of an approach of this kind.

4.2 Current approaches towards formalization

The objective of a formalization process is to increase the semantic level providing additional formal specifications for concepts properties and relations. Among the works related to the transformation of thesauri into formal ontologies, we must cite first a set of works that transform thesauri from its native format into Semantic Web languages such as RDF, OWL, or SKOS. The output of these methods cannot be categorized as a formal ontology because the relationships between concepts are still ambiguous, but at least it is a step forward. They move from the term-based approach recommended in ISO standards (ISO-2788, ISO-5964 and future ISO 25964), in which terms are related directly to one another, into a concept-based approach such as the proposed in the BS-8723 standard. In the concept-based approach concepts are interrelated, while a term is only related to the concept for which it stands; i.e. a lexicalization of a concept. Section 3.5 shows some format transformation works in which a thesaurus in translated into a formal language. An additional example in this area is the work of Wielinga et al. [207] which describes the transformation of the Art and Architecture Thesaurus (AAT) into an ontology expressed in RDFS. The full AAT hierarchy is converted into a hierarchy of concepts, where each concept has a unique identifier and a set of slots corresponding with the main term and its synonyms.

A second set of works are more ambitious and try to transform the ambiguous *broader / narrower* relationships of thesauri into more formal relationships such as *is-a* or *is-part-of* hierarchies. The ISO 2788 guidelines for monolingual thesauri contain a differentiation of the hierarchical relationship into *generic, partitive* and *instance* relationships. However, because the main purpose of thesauri is to facilitate document retrieval, the standards allow this differentiation to be neglected or blurred. In contrast to thesauri, formal ontologies are designed for a wider scope of knowledge representation and need all these logical differentiations in their relationships [56]. As stated in van Assem et al. [197], a major difference between them is that formal ontologies feature logical *is-a* hierarchies, while thesauri hierarchical relationship can represent anything from *is-a* to *is-part-of* relationships. Fisher [56] identifies several cases where the lack of semantics in the *broader / narrower* relationships may be a source of problems to transform a thesaurus into a formal ontology. In particular this work focuses on the problems of identifying subsumption and instance relationships behind the ambiguous *broader / narrower*.

Hepp and de Bruijn [76] describe an algorithm called GenTax to derive an RDF-S or OWL ontology from most hierarchical classifications available in the SKOS exchange format. This algorithm, implemented in the tool SKOS2Gentax[1], derives OWL classes from the instances of SKOS concepts and their *broader* and *narrower* relationships. The algorithm assumes that SKOS concepts can be used in different contexts with varying semantics of the concepts and their relationships. The algorithm has two main steps. Firstly, it creates two ontology classes per SKOS concept: one for the context of the original hierarchy, and a related second class (subclass of the first one) for the narrower meaning of the concept in a particular context. Secondly, GenTax inserts *subClassOf* relations between the classes in the original hierarchy context. However, since SKOS *broader* and *narrower* relationships are translated by default to an *is-a* taxonomy, the output of the algorithm requires many corrections. Another example is the work of Amann et al. [7]. This work uses a pre-existent ontology and combines it with a thesaurus to create a metadata schema for classification and querying.

Other works use natural language processing to refine the hierarchical relationship of thesauri. For example, Clark et al. [31] describe the experience of transforming a technical thesaurus (Boeing's technical thesaurus) into an initial ontology. In particular, this work introduces algorithms for enhancing the thesaurus connectivity by computing extra subsumption and association relationships. An important characteristic of technical thesauri is that many concept names are compound (multi-word) terms. They show a graph enhancement algorithm that automatically infers these missing links using word-spotting/natural language processing technology. Additionally, they also use natural language processing to refine the *RT* relationship into finer semantic categories.

Another remarkable work with the aim of automating the refinement of relationships is one the described by Soergel et al. [176] and Kawtrakul et al. [109]. It introduces a semi-automatic approach for detecting problematic relationships, especially *broader/narrower* and *use/use-for* relationships, and suggesting more appropriate ones. Upon the experience obtained with the transformation of AGROVOC into an ontology, their approach is mainly based on the identification of patterns and the establishment of rules that can automatically applied. The method is based

---

[1] http://www.heppnetz.de/projects/skos2gentax/

on three main ideas. Firstly, they try to find expert-defined rules. Assuming that concepts are associated with categories (e.g., geographic term, taxonomic term for animals ...), experts may define rules that can be generally applied to transform *broader/narrower* relationships of concepts under the same category into *is-a* or *is-part-of* hierarchies. Secondly, they propose noun phrase analysis to detect *is-a* hierarchies. If two terms in a *broader/narrower* relationship share the same headword, this relationship can be transformed into *is-a*. Alternatively, if two terms are in the same hierarchy of hypernyms in WordNet, their relationship is also transformed into *is-a*. Thirdly, in the case of *related* relationships, which are usually under-specified relationships, refinement rules, acquired from experts and machine learning, are applied. When a particular case of conversion for a *related* relationship is identified, a general rule for all the hypernyms of the involved terms that are related through another *related* relationship can be derived.

4.3 Increase of formalism in terminological models

With the objective of testing the complexity and the viability of the existent formalization approaches, a simple formalization process has been developed. Since the correct identification of *is-a* relationships is the minimum requirement to have a formal ontology, the process focuses on their automatic identification.

The purpose of the developed method is not to find all the existent *is-a* relationships in the source terminological model (a thesaurus). The objective is to determine a lower limit (as closest as possible to the real one) of the percentage of the source model structure that can be directly translated into a formal model without additional restructuring. That is, the objective is to obtain a measure of the inherent formalism of the analyzed thesaurus. Additionally, as consequence of this analysis, it can be deducted which areas of the thesaurus require little formalization effort and which ones require a complete transformation.

In this context, the identification of a *broader/narrower* relationship between two concepts as an *is-a* relationship has been done using the heuristic described in algorithm 8. According to this algorithm, a *broader/narrower* relationship is transformed into an *is-a* relationship if the narrower concept has the same headword (substantive) in at least one of their labels (preferred or alternatives) in any of the available languages (in this case only Spanish and English have been considered). Here, the language difference is critical because the position of the headword is completely language dependent. Additionally, in order to simplify the identification of equivalences between the headwords, they are processed to remove the plurals. The relations that are not identified as *is-a* relationships are left as *narrower/broader* relationships. Their formalization is left for future work.

Figure 4.1 shows the steps performed to formalize the source thesaurus. The result of the formalization is stored into an OWL file. The formalization process transforms each source concept into an OWL class (it is modified to facilitate its

```
Function boolean detectIsARelations(Resource res1, Resource res2);
begin
    List res1Labels = getPrefAndAltLabels(res1);
    List res2Labels = getPrefAndAltLabels(res2);
    for int i=1;i<res1Labels.size(); i++ do
        LabelStructure lR1 = res1Labels.get(i);
        String langR1=lR1.getLanguage();
        for int k=1;k<res2Labels.size(); k++ do
            LabelStructure lR2 = res2Labels.get(k);
            String langR2=lR2.getLanguage();
            String[] campos1 = l1.getLabelString().split(" ");
            String[] campos2 = l2.getLabelString().split(" ");
            if lang1.equalsIgnoreCase("en") && lang1.equalsIgnoreCase(lang2) then
                if removeEnglishPlural(campos1[campos1.length-1]).
                equalsIgnoreCase(removeEnglishPlural(campos2[campos2.length-1])) then
                    return true
                end
            else
                if lang1.equalsIgnoreCase("es") && lang1.equalsIgnoreCase(lang2) then
                    if removeSpanishPlural(campos1[0]).
                    equalsIgnoreCase(removeSpanishPlural(campos2[0])) then
                        return true
                    end
                end
            end
        end
    end
    return false
end
```

Algorithm 8: Identification of *is-a* relationships

visualization by formal ontology management tools such as Protégé[2]). The preferred and alternative labels of each source concept are stored as *rdfs:label* properties. With respect to the relationships, the identified *is-a* relationships are represented as inheritances between OWL classes. The rest of them (non-formalized relations) are generated as named *owl:ObjectProperty* (generating a different identifier for each one).

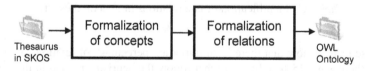

Thesaurus in SKOS → Formalization of concepts → Formalization of relations → OWL Ontology

Fig. 4.1: Workflow for the formalization of a terminological ontology

---

[2] http://protege.stanford.edu/

4.4 Application of the formalization process

To test the suitability of the described thesaurus formalization process, two different analysis have been performed. On the one hand, it has been applied to a set of
thesaurus (GEMET, AGROVOC, EUROVOC, UNESCO) also used for other experiments in this book, in order to detect if the pattern used to identify the *is-a* relationships is effective in general thesauri covering different areas of knowledge. On the
other hand, it has been applied to the urban and to the hydrological thesaurus generated in the section 3.6.2.2 to analyze the structural quality of the output models. The
process described in section 3.6.2 allows creating different versions of each generated thesauri by selecting the relations with higher weight (by modifying different
parameters of their respective generation processes). This characteristic facilitates
the analysis of the formalization suitability in the sense that it allows determining if
there is some kind of correlation between the strength of the relationships (number
of times they are contained in the generated thesaurus) and the percentage of *is-a*
relationships detected in the formalization process (i.e., it allows determining if the
most common relations are usually *is-a* relations).

Table 4.1 shows the results of applying the formalization to GEMET, AGROVOC,
EUROVOC, and UNESCO. For each thesaurus, it shows: the number of original
broader/narrower relationships of each thesaurus; the number of these relations that
have been identified as *is-a* relationships (separating those relations found through
the analysis of Spanish labels from the ones found through the analysis of English
labels); and the percentage of the total number of relations that have been transformed into *is-a* relationships.

Thesaurus Name	Nr BT/NT	Nr is-a	% is-a rels	English is-a	Spanish is-a
GEMET	5332	1563	29%	1042	1042
AGROVOC	16579	2498	15%	1379	1722
EUROVOC	7149	2748	38%	1888	1775
UNESCO	14827	699	3%	378	397

Table 4.1: Identification of is-a relations in general thesaurus

These results show that there is an important percentage of relations in the thesaurus (between a 15% and a 38%) that follow the heuristic applied in the formalization process. In this context, the cases of GEMET and EUROVOC are specially
relevant because around a third of the concepts in these thesauri can be formalized
by applying a simple heuristic. That is, it can be said that they have a better organization and their formalization would be easier.

Table 4.2 shows the results of the formalization of the different urban thesaurus
versions described in section 3.6.2.2. Each version is identified with the weight
threshold used to generate it. The rest of the table has the same structure as table 4.1.
That is, the number of original *broader/narrower* relationships of each thesaurus;
the number of these relations that have been identified as *is-a* relationships (separating those found though the analysis of Spanish labels from those found through the

analysis of English ones); and the percentage of the total number of relations that have been transformed into *is-a* relationships.

Weight threshold	Nr BT/NT	Nr is-a	% is-a rels	English is-a	Spanish is-a
1	4281	883	20%	685	625
2	1482	686	46%	535	508
3	852	453	53%	375	325
4	550	307	56%	248	241
5	317	191	60%	157	146

Table 4.2: Identification of is-a relations in the urbanism thesaurus

From the results obtained it can be seen that the percentage of identified *is-a* relationships increases with the weight of the considered relationships. That is, stronger relationships have a much higher chance to be *is-a* relationships than weaker ones.

The comparison of the formalization results of the different versions of the generated thesauri allows determining which one of the generated models provides a better balance between the number of generated concepts and the underlying formal structure. This information can be used to improve the selection of the most suitable thesaurus version performed in section 3.6.2.2. Previously, the only available criteria for the selection of the most suitable thesaurus version were the number of concepts, and a measure of quality obtained through a manual examination of the model. In this context, the measure of the underlying formalism can be used as a third selection criterion. It can be considered that a thesaurus model with a higher percentage of underlying *is-a* relationships is better organized than another one more heterogeneous, and therefore it is more suitable for classification purposes. Additionally, if it is expected to generate in a near future a formal model based on the thesaurus, having a model with a better structure simplifies the formalization process.

If this additional criterion is applied to urban thesauri, it can be seen that the most suitable model is the one considering the relations of weight 2. The obtained data shows that using this weight (the relations that are only contained once in the source models are removed) the percentage of *is-a* relations jumps from a 20% to almost a half of the obtained relationships. A lower weight provides a very heterogeneous structure and a higher one reduces in a great extent the number of concepts included in the model.

Finally, table 4.3 shows the formalization results of the different hydrology thesaurus versions described in section 3.6.2.2. The structure of table 4.3 is the same as the one in table 4.2. That is, each version is identified with the weight threshold used to generate it and the information provided is the following: the number of these relations that have been identified as *is-a* relationships (separating those found though the analysis of Spanish labels from those found through the analysis of English ones); and the percentage of the total number of relations that have been transformed into *is-a* relationships.

A similar analysis to the one performed for the urban thesaurus has been done for the hydrology thesaurus. In this case, the results obtained are much better. In the complete thesaurus (without pruning) half of the relations have been identified as *is-*

Weight threshold	Nr BT/NT	Nr is-a	% is-a rels	English is-a	Spanish is-a
1	261	135	51%	110	90
2	158	102	64%	85	63
3	93	64	68%	51	54
4	56	42	75%	35	33
5	29	25	86%	23	22

Table 4.3: Identification of is-a relations in the hydrology thesaurus

a. And if the less relevant relations are pruned, this percentage can be increased up to a 86%. In this case, due to the reduced size of the thesaurus and the high number of *is-a* relations identified, the hydrological thesaurus obtained without performing any pruning should be the selected.

4.5 Summary

This chapter has analyzed the problem of generating formal ontologies using as input terminological models. We have studied the need of using formal ontologies with formal *is-a* hierarchies, frame definitions, or even general logical constraints. There are systems that require improved user interaction with the ontology on the conceptual, intelligent behind-the-scenes support for query expansion, improved indexing/categorization systems, or support for artificial intelligence. And for these purposes, the use of terminological ontologies is not enough. However, since the creation of formal ontologies is even more complex than the use of terminological ones, the use of simpler models for its construction is expected to save a lot of effort.

This chapter has proposed a method to determine the feasibility of constructing formal models through the automatic formalization of terminological ontologies. The method focuses on the deriving of *is-a* relationships from the *broader/narrower* relationships of thesauri. The objective is to find how much the original model structure directly fit into a formal model. This prototype has been tested with the set of thematic thesauri used along the book (see section 1.3.4), and the different versions of urban and hydrology thesauri generated in the previous merging. The results obtained for the thematic thesauri are quite heterogeneous. The number of identified *is-a* relationships out of *broader/narrower* relationships range from a minimum 13% in the UNESCO thesaurus to a maximum 38% in EUROVOC. These results show that the complexity of the formalization depends greatly on the structure of each processed model (it is easier to formalize the EUROVOC than the UNESCO thesaurus). With respect to the urbanism and hydrology thesauri, the comparison of the results obtained with each one of the generated versions (according to different prune levels) clearly show that the most common relations have a much higher chance to be an *is-a* relationship. Additionally, it has been shown that the obtained results can be used as a measure of the structural quality of each thesaurus. That is to say, they can be used as an additional factor in the decision of the thesaurus to select for each purpose.

Chapter 5
Access to terminological ontologies

5.1 Introduction

Typical information infrastructures manage different terminological ontologies with a very different levels of specificity, language coverage integrated in their systems (e.g., from monolingual lists of terms to multilingual thesauri covering more than 20 languages), formalization, (e.g., from simple glossaries to well-structured thesauri), or size, (e.g., AGROVOC thesaurus [126] contains more than 16,000 concepts).

Each of these different ontology models have been traditionally stored, managed, used and updated independently from the rest of them. This lack of coordinated management makes very difficult to determine which models are used in which service and with which purpose. Additionally, this lack of coordination leads to the replication of the terminological ontologies along the infrastructure. Ensuring that all the copies of each ontology are identical requires high maintenance effort. Moreover, the lack of coordination makes the upgrade process very prone to errors. For example, it is very easy to forget updating one of the copies; and if this happen, the service using the obsolete terminology would produce deficient results. Additionally, the lack of knowledge of the used ontologies leads to a dispersion in their use. For instance, different but similar terminological ontologies are used for situations where a single one would be a better selection.

When ontologies are provided to the public by their creators, they are distributed through ad-hoc services developed by the institution providing each ontology. However, in systems which use a great amount of them, it is not viable to access a large amount of different incompatible services to retrieve the needed vocabularies. It is needed to collect all the required models obtained from external and internal sources and provide them homogeneously, using a single inner model, storage system, and access procedures.

Section 5.2 reviews the existent works in this area to determine if the proposed solutions cover all the required management needs. This study has shown that existent solutions tackle specific management problems independently of the rest. In this context, with the objective of managing terminological ontologies in a homoge-

J. Lacasta et al., *Terminological Ontologies: Design, Management and Practical Applications*, Semantic Web and Beyond 9, DOI 10.1007/978-1-4419-6981-1_5, © Springer Science+Business Media, LLC 2010

neous way, section 5.3 describes the general architecture that has been proposed for the management of terminological ontologies. Each one of the following sections describes in detail a specific component of this architecture. Firstly, section 5.3.2 focuses on the need of a common repository to store all the required terminological ontologies and it makes a proposal for such a repository. Secondly, at management level, section 5.4 describes the management needs for terminological models and it proposes a solution for an efficient management. Finally, section 5.5 focuses on access issues and it describes the requirements and structure of a Web service to facilitate the distribution of the most suitable terminological models to the components of an information infrastructure.

The components described in this management architecture have been implemented and tested to verify their suitability for working with terminological ontologies. Section 5.6 shows the experiments performed and the results obtained.

5.2 Terminological ontology management

Because of the variety and large number of terminological models used in an information infrastructure, the harmonization of their management is a priority. The interest in creating terminological ontologies in the digital libraries field and other related disciplines has led to an increasing number of software packages for the construction of different types of terminological models. The web site of Willpower Information[1] offers a detailed analysis of more than 40 tools, most of them designed for thesauri edition. Some tools are only available as a module of a complete information storage and retrieval system, but others also allow the possibility of working independently of any other software. Among these creation tools, one may highlight the following products:

- BiblioTech[2]. This is a multi-platform tool that forms part of BiblioTech PRO Integrated Library System and can be used to build an ANSI/NISO standard thesaurus [9].
- Lexico[3]. This is a Java-based tool that can be accessed and/or manipulated over the Internet. Thesauri are saved in a text-based format. It has been used by the U.S. Library of Congress to manage vocabularies and thesauri such as the "Thesaurus for Graphic Materials", the "Global Legal Information Network Thesaurus", the "Legislative Indexing Vocabulary", and the "Symbols of American Libraries Listing".
- MultiTes[4]. This is a windows based tool that provides support for ANSI/NISO relationships plus user defined relationships and comment fields for an unlimited number of thesauri (both monolingual and multilingual).

---

[1] http://www.willpowerinfo.co.uk/thessoft.htm

[2] http://www.inmagic.com/

[3] http://www.pmei.com/lexico.html

[4] http://www.multites.com/

- TermTree 2000[5]. TermTree is a windows based tool that uses Access, SQL Server or Oracle for data storage. It can import/export TRIM thesauri (format used by the Towers Records Information Management system[6]) as well as a defined TermTree 2000 tag format.
- WebChoir[7]. WebChoir is a family of client-server web applications that provide different utilities for thesaurus management in multiple DBMS platforms. Term-Choir is a hierarchical information organizing and searching tool that enables to create and search varieties of hierarchical subject categories, controlled vocabularies, and taxonomies based on either pre-defined standards or a user-defined structure and exported to an XML based format. LinkChoir is another tool that allows indexers to describe information sources using terminology organized in TermChoir. And SeekChoir is a retrieval system that enables users to browse thesaurus descriptors and their references (broader terms, related terms, synonyms ...).
- Synaptica[8]. Synaptica is a client-server web application that can be installed locally on a client's intranet or extranet server. Thesaurus data is stored in a SQL Server or Oracle database. The application supports the creation of electronic thesauri in compliance with ANSI/NISO standard. The application allows the exchange of thesauri in CSV (Comma-Separated Values) text format.
- SuperThes [15]. SuperThes is a windows based tool that allows the creation of thesauri. It extends the ANSI/NISO relationships allowing many possible data types to enrich the properties of a concept. It can import/export thesauri in XML and in tabular format.
- TemaTRES[9]. TemaTres is a web application specially oriented to the creation of thesauri, but it also can be used to develop web browsing structures or to manage the documentary languages in use. The thesauri are stored in a MySQL database. It provides the created thesauri in Zthes format [10] or in SKOS format.

In addition to the tools specifically designed for editing terminological ontologies, general ontology editors can also be used. In this context, Denny [39] describes a detailed survey of general ontology editors. Other edition alternatives are the family of RDF edition tools such as SWOOP [105], Protégé [158], or Triple20 [206]. However, these general editing ontology tools do not provide specific adapted interfaces to create ontologies following a specific model. Additionally, they are too complex as they provide too many options and capabilities not needed in terminological ontology models.

Having all the required terminological models available, the harmonization in their management becomes a priority. The Canadian Geospatial Data Infrastruc-

---

[5] http://www.termtree.com.au/

[6] http://www.towersoft.com/

[7] http://www.webchoir.com

[8] http://www.synaptica.com/

[9] http://www.r020.com.ar/tematres/

[10] http://zthes.z3950.org/schema/index.html

ture project [11] advanced in 1999 that such a infrastructure would need a centralized ontology management service when the number of ontologies to manage would increase. In 2004 they published a prototype of a web service, the Multilingual Geospatial Ontology (M3GO)[12] to try to fulfil this need. However, the main standardization organizations have not provided any specification to develop this kind of service. The most advanced approach for providing an standard specification for ontology services is found in the geospatial community. In this context, a specification draft describing how RDF and OWL ontologies may be included within an Web Catalogue Service has been proposed [180]. However this work is still quite preliminary and it has not been still adopted.

The uniform management of terminological models is not a simple task. It is needed to be able to share them with other components of the infrastructure, and identify them adequately to be able to locate the required one. Additionally, the size of this kind of models creates the need to provide additional communication protocols to access to the required area instead to the whole ontology.

Traditionally, in the information community, the classical approach to share terminological ontologies has been to create different ad-hoc web services that provide access to a particular ontology. Some examples of this kind of service are:

• ADL project: The Alexandria Digital Library project is focused on the creation of a distributed catalog of resources around the world. In this project there is a HTTP-XML service[13] whose objective is to provide the thesaurus used to classify the repository content.
• GEMET Service: HTTP-XML service[14] created to provide access to GEMET thesaurus.
• The service detailed in Binding and Tudhope [19] and Tudhope and Binding [191] that provide access to a thesaurus (concepts and relations).
• Agrovoc Concept Server Workbench: HTTP-XML service[15] that provide access to AGROVOC thesaurus.

These services provide access to a single terminological model through their own ad-hoc communication protocol making nonviable its direct integration in systems using multiple terminological ontologies. Integration problems are partially solved thanks to the use of standardized approaches for providing access to the models. An example of a standardized access protocol is Zthes[16], a Z39.50 [8] profile for thesaurus representation, access, and browsing.

The use of a standardized access protocol for terminological models can be a solution for systems using only a few ontologies, but systems using lots of models cannot afford creating different services for each one. A homogeneous solution that

---

[11] http://www.geoconnections.org/CGDI.cfm

[12] http://www.geoconnections.org/en/aboutGeo/projects/id=256

[13] http://www.alexandria.ucsb.edu/ gjanee/thesaurus/

[14] http://www.eionet.europa.eu/gemet

[15] http://www.fao.org/aims/ag_intro.htm

[16] http://zthes.z3950.org/z3950/zthes-z3950-1.0.html

integrates the access into a single service is required. The most recent works in this area go in this direction, for example:

- TemaTres[17]: It is a web application to manage documental languages. It provides access to thesauri and other similar knowledge models.
- OCLC terminological service: The Online Computer Library Center is dedicated to provide global access information. It provides an HTTP-XML terminological service[18] to give access to the used knowledge models.
- SWAD-E project: This project has as objective to support the semantic web initiatives provided by the W3C in Europe. Between its works it is the definition of a web service with a SOAP interface[19] to provide access to a repository of terminological ontologies.
- Star project: This project focus on the use of semantic technologies in the archeology area. One of the components provided is a SOAP service[20] containing the knowledge models used in the system.

In the area of formal ontologies there is also a similar concern with respect to the need of reusing existent ontologies. Swoogle [41] is a crawler-based indexing and retrieval system for the Semantic Web that allows searching for Web documents in RDF or OWL (that is, ontologies). It extracts metadata for each discovered document, and computes relations between documents. Watson [36] goes in the same direction by collecting and giving access to ontologies and semantic data available online. Oyster [162] is a bit different in the sense that it focuses on the description of the ontologies as the way to provide a better access. The access is not provided through a traditionally web service but through a Peer-to-Peer network. Other different approaches for accessing formal ontologies are KAON [202] or Ontolingua [50]. They are complex infrastructures which have been designed to share ontologies in general contexts. They include different components such as editors or reasoners that access to the repository containing the stored the ontologies through a predefined API.

The problem with all these solutions is the lack of search capabilities to find the desired terminological ontology. SKOS server does not provide any facility to locate the desired ontology, and the same happens in the KAON tool (it identifies the desired ontology by means of a URI). A better approach is the one followed by Ontolingua and STAR projects where a list of ontologies with the name plus a short description is provided.

All these projects have identified that the use of a centralized service is a step forward to facilitate access and management of ontologies in complex information infrastructures. However, the lack of discovery services for the contained models (e.g., search for the ontology name, creation date or description) limits its integration possibilities in systems requiring a dozens of terminological models. In these

---

[17] http://www.r020.com.ar/tematres

[18] http://www.oclc.org/research/activities/termservices/default.htm

[19] http://www.w3.org/2001/sw/Europe/reports/thes/skosapi.html

[20] http://hypermedia.research.glam.ac.uk/kos/terminology_services/

systems, it is required to provide the most suitable model for each context. Therefore, they must be described to be able to locate the required ones. In addition, the
use of these ontologies adds new requirements not needed in more general services,
such as searches of ontologies focused on a specific geographic area, application
domain, or even data creator.

5.3 Terminological ontology storage and access

5.3.1 Architecture

In order to advance in the improvement of the management of terminological ontologies in infrastructures with an important need of access to these types of models,
the architecture of components shown in figure 5.1 is proposed.

The system consists of a core component called *ontology manager* that provides
the storage for the terminological models and a software components that provide
access to the *ontology repository*, allowing the addition, removal, and update of the
desired ontologies. The manager provides a metadata oriented access to the terminologies. Each model has to be described and identified using metadata. The
metadata are then used to provide a search system in the repository simplifying
the location of the required ontology. Additionally, the manager provides access to
equivalences between ontology concepts. These equivalences can be used, for example, to expand the user queries with similar concepts in a search system with access
to the repository of terminological ontologies. To provide access to the repository,
the *ontology manager* provides an API with all the required access functionality.
The *ontology repository* stores the terminological ontologies, their metadata and
additional components used for interrelation of models.

With the objective of controlling the contents of the repository and making the
required changes when needed, on top of the *ontology manager* a desktop editor
(ThManager) that allows visualizing, adding, updating, deleting and modifying the
terminological ontologies and their metadata descriptions has been designed. This
desktop editor follows an architectural pattern that simplifies the creation and composition of different graphical components for the visualization and modification of
terminological models.

Finally, to provide access to terminological ontologies to components requiring
it, a Web Ontology Service (WOS) that provides the access to the ontologies stored
in the repository through the *Ontology Manager API* has been designed. It offers
different interfaces to cover a broad range of applications with different functionality
requirements. Some possible client applications (e.g., query expansion, browsing)
are described in chapter 6.

The first step to provide a harmonized access to terminological models has been
to create a repository for the ontologies and a management component able to provide access to the stored models. The repository layer not only stores the termino-

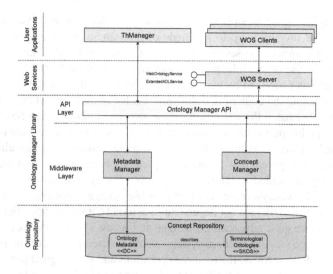

Fig. 5.1: Architecture of the management and access proposal

logical ontologies (concepts and relations) but also the metadata describing them and a concept core used for the interconnection of ontologies. With respect to the *Ontology Manager*, its main function is to provide access to a repository. It is used by the *ThManager* and the *Web Ontology Service* to harmonize the access to the ontologies. As it is shown in figure 5.1, the *Ontology Manager* consists of two main layers: the middleware layer that is in charge of accessing the repository, and the API layer that provides the external interface for tools requiring access to its functionality.

5.3.2 Terminological ontology repository

As proposed in the representation framework presented in section 2.3, the format selected for representation of terminological ontologies is SKOS based. The access to the RDF SKOS documents is provided in the application layer through *Jena*[21]. *Jena* is a popular library that simplifies the manipulation of RDF documents, storing them in text files or in a relational database. One important advantage of using *Jena* is that it has an open model that can be extended with specialized modules to provide other ways of storage such as the *Jena-Sesame adapter*[22], which provides access to *Sesame*[23] databases.

---

[21] http://jena.sourceforge.net/

[22] http://sjadapter.sourceforge.net/

[23] http://www.openrdf.org/

Since terminological models vary enormously in size, ranging from hundreds of concepts and properties up to hundreds of thousands, the time spent on load, browsing, and search processes is a functional restrictions to take into account. In this context, the use of the default Jena component to load the SKOS files with the terminologies has proven to be very inefficient. SKOS is RDF based, and reading RDF and extracting the content is a slow process for terminological models of big size. On the other hand, the use of a database storage system such as Sesame provides an acceptable performance. However, for those situations where the use of an external database access is not suitable (e.g., simple desktop tools) an alternative storage model is required. The solution adopted has been to transform the SKOS files when they are added to the repository into a binary format, whose access is more efficient. Nowadays, there are other possible storage alternatives that provide file based storage and that are not dependent of external databases. Specifically, Jena TDB [24] provides a quite advanced file storage and access system that uses SPARQL as query language [25]. Any of these systems could be used instead of the proposed storage model if they provide the required operations and show a good performance.

The data structure used in the developed storage model is shown in figure 5.2. The model is an optimized representation of the RDF triplet structure. The *Concepts* map contains the concepts and their associated relations in the form of key-value pairs: the key is a URI identifying a concept; and the value is a *Relations* object containing the properties of the concept. A *Relations* object is a map that stores the properties of one concept in the form of <*property type, property values*> pairs. The keys used for this map are the names of the property types in the SKOS model (e.g., narrower, or broader). The only special cases for encoding these property types occur when the property has a language attribute (e.g., *prefLabel*, *definition*, or *scopeNote*). In those cases we propose the use of a [lang] suffix to distinguish the property type for a particular language. For instance, *prefLabel_en* indicates a *prefLabel* property whose content is in English. Additionally, it must be noted that the data type of the property values assigned to each key in the *Relations* map varies upon the semantics given to each property type. The data types used fall into the following categories: a string for a *prefLabel* property type; a list of strings for *altLabel*, *hiddenLabel*, *definition*, *scope note*, and *example* property types; a list of URIs for *narrower*, *broader* and *related* property types; and a list of *Notation* objects for a *notation* property type. The data type used for *notation* values is a complex object because there may be different *notation* types. A *Notation* object consists of type and value attributes. The type attribute is a URI which identifies a particular notation type and qualifies the associated *notation* value. Some other elements of the SKOS model such as *collections* and different types of *notes* have been omitted given its lack of use in the managed ontology models, but they could be easily added to the model and supported in the repository if required.

With the objective of increasing the speed of some operations (e.g., browsing or search), some additional optimizations have been used. Firstly, for terminological

---

[24] http://jena.sourceforge.net/TDB/

[25] http://www.w3.org/TR/rdf-sparql-query/

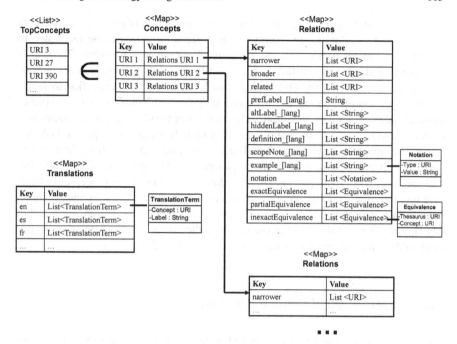

Fig. 5.2: Persistence model

models with a hierarchical structure such as taxonomies or thesauri, the URIs of the top concepts are stored in the *TopConcepts* list. This list contains redundant information, because those concepts are also stored in the Concepts map, but it makes immediate the location of the top concepts. Secondly, to simplify and speed up the process of search of concepts, and to reduce the time required to provide the concepts in an alphabetical order, the *Translations* map has been created. This map contains, for each language in which the terminological ontology is available, a list of pairs <URI, *prefLabel*> in that language ordered by the *prefLabel*. *Translations* map also contains redundant information, but the improvements obtained compensate the small overhead in load time (as it is shown later). If the alphabetic viewer and the search component are not needed, this structure can be removed without any collateral effect.

The storage model includes some elements used to represent the interrelations between terminological ontologies. As it can be observed in Figure 5.2, the solution allows defining direct mappings for *exact*, *inexact* and *partial* equivalences.

This storage solution has proven to be useful to manage the kind of terminological models used in the infrastructures considered in this book (the ontology models used do not surpass the size of 50,000 concepts and about 330,000 properties). They can be loaded in a reasonable time allowing an immediate browsing and search. See section 5.6 for a detailed performance analysis.

A fundamental aspect in the repository is the description of ontologies. Metadata for describing ontologies are considered as basic information to be facilitated to clients. These metadata are depicted in figure 5.1 as *Ontology Metadata*. The reason for this metadata-driven interface is that centralized ontology storage is not enough to manage them efficiently. Ontologies must be described and classified to facilitate the selection of the most adequate ontology for each situation. The purpose of these metadata is not only to simplify the location of terminological ontologies to a user, but also to facilitate the identification of models useful for a specific task in a machine-to-machine communication. The lack of metadata describing them makes very difficult the identification of ontologies provided by other services, producing a low reuse of them in other contexts. Metadata are used in search processes to facilitate ontology retrieval, allowing users to search them not only by an agreed *name*, but also by the *application domain* or the associated *geographical area* among other descriptors. The metadata profile used is the indicated in the representation framework to describe the terminological ontologies (section 2.3.1).

5.3.3 Terminological ontology manager

The purpose of the components contained in the ontology manager shown in figure 5.1 is to simplify the access to the information stored in the repository to the applications constructed on top of it. The ontology manager component (in the middleware layer) has as main objective to separate the upper layers from the complexity of the repositories. This simplifies to a great extent the interchange of repositories, allowing the selection of the most suitable one for each situation.

In addition to the repository of terminological models, it is needed to provide access to the repository storing the metadata that describe the ontologies. This functionality is provided by the *metadata manager* component in the middleware layer. The methods provided are shown in figure 5.3. A query method to search the ontologies for the metadata content is provided; additionally, methods to retrieve, update, and delete metadata elements have been included. The metadata contain a reference to the ontology URI in the field *identifier*; therefore, accessing to the metadata allows a user to locate the desired terminological ontology in the ontology repository.

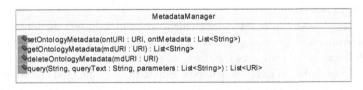

Fig. 5.3: Metadata manager

The upper layer in the *ontology manager* is the *API layer* containing the *ontology manager API*. The objective of this API is to unify the functionality provided by the *metadata manager* that gives access to the metadata describing the terminologies, and the *concept manager* that aggregates the *ontology manager* providing access to the ontology. The resulting set of procedures includes all the required methods to allow other components to access and manage the stored terminological ontologies. These methods, displayed in figure 5.4, can be classified in two categories: query and administration.

- With respect to query methods, *query* and *getRelatedConcepts* methods allow users to browse through the relations between concepts and to search concepts by their label in different languages. The *query* method uses the disambiguation mechanism described before to expand the results returned, providing equivalent terms from the same or different ontologies.
- As regards to administration methods, they allow users to create a new ontology given its metadata, modify its metadata, delete it, and import or export it in SKOS format. Additionally, the API includes methods to update concept properties and relations between concepts from different ontologies.

OntologyManagerAPI

getCapabilities(request : OWSGetCapabilities) : ServiceMetadata
setOntologyMetadata(ontURI : String, ontMetadata : Array)
getOntologyMetadata(mdURI : String) : Array
getRelatedConcepts(ontURI : String, conceptURI : String, relation : String) : List<Concepts>
query(ontURI : String, queryType : String, queryText : String, parameters : List<String>) : List<Concepts>
importOntology(ontContent : String, ontMetadata : Array)
exportOntology(mdURI : String) : String
createOntology(ontMetadata : Array)
deleteOntology(mdURI : String)
createConcept(ontURI : String, conceptURI : String)
deleteConcept(ontURI : String, conceptURI : String)
createRelation(ontURI : String, conceptSourceURI : String, conceptDestURI : String, relationURI : String)
deleteRelation(ontURI : String, conceptSourceURI : String, conceptDestURI : String, relationURI : String)
createProperty(ontURI : String, conceptURI : String, propertyName : String, Value : String)
deleteProperty(ontURI : String, conceptURI : String, propertyName : String)

Fig. 5.4: Web Ontology Service implementation

5.4 Edition of terminological ontologies

Having defined the structure, functionality and access methods to the repository of terminological ontologies, the next step has been to design a editor able to create the required ontologies, to fill the repository, to load the existent ones, and to export them in a suitable interchange format.

The required terminological ontologies have to be created in a suitable format, updated with the latest changes, and described appropriately with their metadata to allow the clients to find them. As commented in the representation framework described in section 2.3, the most accepted format to define simple knowledge models such as terminological ontologies is SKOS. SKOS provides a rich machine-readable language, but nobody would expect to have to create an ontology following this format just using a general-purpose RDF editor (SKOS is RDF based).

Section 5.2 has reviewed different tools for the edition of terminological models. However, none of them is suitable here. Some of them are unable to manage properly structures with tens of thousands of concepts. Others are deeply integrated in bigger systems and cannot be easily reused in other environments because they need specific software components to work (as DBMS to store terminologies). Those systems that are independent terminological editors have an architecture difficult to integrate within other information management tools. Moreover, they use incompatible interchange formats and do not provide support for SKOS. Finally, they are not focused on providing an integrated management of collection of ontologies and their metadata descriptions as is required in this context.

To fill this gap, an editor called ThManager that facilitates the construction of SKOS based terminological ontologies has been designed. It has been thought to manage thesauri but it is also appropriate to create and manage any other terminological models that can be represented using SKOS format. It provides a dual functionality. Firstly, it has the ability to visualize the terminological models in the repository to validate that their content are correct. And secondly, it facilitates the creation/update of the required ones. To facilitate its use in different computer platforms, ThManager has been developed using the Java object oriented language. Additionally, the tool is distributed as Open Source software and it is accessible through the SourceForge platform[26].

This section shows the architecture of ThManager editor. The main features that have guided ThManager design have been the following: a metadata-driven design, an efficient management of terminological ontologies, and the reusability of ThManager components.

ThManager has been constructed on top of the *Ontology Manager* described in section 5.3.3 (it provides access to a repository of terminological ontologies). The complete architecture structure is shown in figure 5.5.

ThManager has a layered architecture to facilitate its integration in desktop tools requiring the access to terminological models. On top of the repository layer (constituted by the *Ontology Manager*), a GUI layer that offers different graphical components has been placed in order to visualize terminological models (specifically thesauri), search by their properties, and edit them in different ways. Among the graphical components, there is a hierarchical viewer, an alphabetic viewer, a list viewer, a searcher, and an editor; but more components can be built if needed. The GUI layer is designed as a factory of reusable graphical components that makes possible to create tools able to manage terminological models with a minimum effort. Additionally, it also allows the integration of this technology in other applications that need controlled vocabularies to improve their functionality. For example, in a metadata creation tool, it can be used to provide the graphical component to select values from controlled vocabularies and automatically insert them in the metadata.

---

[26] http://thmanager.sourceforge.net/

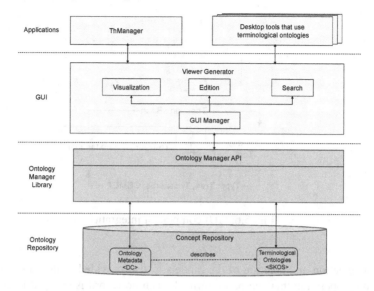

Fig. 5.5: ThManager layer architecture

Figure 5.6 shows the integration process of a thesaurus visualization component in an external tool. The provided thesaurus components have been constructed following the Java Beans philosophy (reusable software components that can be manipulated visually in a builder tool), where a component is a black box with methods to read and change its status that can be reused when needed. Here, each thesaurus component is a *ThesaurusBean* that can be directly inserted in a graphical application to use its functionality (visualize or edit thesauri) in a very simple way. The *ThesaurusBeans* are provided by the *ThesaurusBeanManager* that, given the parameters of the thesaurus to visualize and the type of visualization, returns the most adequate component to use.

The ThManager editor is an application component that uses the GUI layer elements to provide the user with the management and edition of terminological ontologies. The tool groups a subset of the provided components, relating them to obtain a final user application that allows the management of the stored thesauri, their visualization (browsing by the concept relations), their edition, and their importation/exportation using SKOS format. In the same way as ThManager has been constructed, other tools requiring access to terminological models can use the visualization components or the methods provided by the persistence layer to provide access to stored models.

The management of the models stored by the ThManager tool is metadata oriented. The first window visualized by the graphical interface of the editor shows a table including the metadata records describing all the terminological models stored in the system (figure 5.7). The selection of a record is used by the rest of the components of the application to know the model they have to work with.

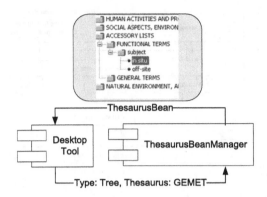

Fig. 5.6: GUI component integration

The creation and deletion of the models is also provided in the same window. The only operation that can be performed when no record is selected is to import a new thesaurus stored in SKOS. To import it, the name of the SKOS file has to be provided. If available, the metadata of the ontology are extracted directly from the input SKOS file. Otherwise, it can be provided as well as an associated XML metadata file. If no metadata record is provided, the application generates a new one with minimum information, using the name of the SKOS file as basic descriptor. Once the user has selected a model, it can visualize and modify its metadata, content, export it to SKOS or, as commented before, delete it.

Unique Id	Title	Subject	Responsible Party	On-Line Linkage
AGROVOC	Thesaurus of agriculture AGROVOC	POLITICS, LAW A...	Food and Agriculture Organizati...	http://www.sdiger.org/dc-spatial/AGROVOC
EuropeanTerrit...	Thesaurus of territorial units of Spain ...	COUNTRIES AND ...	University of Zaragoza. Advanc...	http://www.unizar.es/iaaa/thesaurus/Europe
GEMET	Multilingual environmental thesaurus	SCIENCE.NATUR...	European Network of Informati...	http://www.cen.org/dc-spatial/GEMET
ISO639	List of languages of the world	CULTURE.LINGUI...	University of Zaragoza. Advanc...	http://purl.org/dc/terms/ISO639-2
UNESCO	Thesaurus of UNESCO	EDUCATION	University of Zaragoza. Advanc...	http://www.cen.org/dc-spatial/UNESCO

Records count 5

Search

Fig. 5.7: General metadata based selector

The metadata describing a terminological ontology is visualized by a metadata viewer in an HTML based view. Different HTML views can be provided by adding different CSS presentation files to the application. The edition is performed by a customizable metadata editor. To add or delete metadata elements to the metadata edition window, the user needs to modify the description of the IEMSR profile followed by the metadata (see the profile described in section 2.3.1).

One of the basic functionalities of the tool is to visualize the terminological ontology structure, showing all properties of concepts and allowing the browsing by

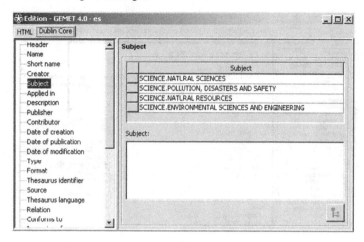

Fig. 5.8: Metadata editor

relations (Figure 5.9). To do this, different read-only viewers are provided. There is an alphabetic viewer, which shows all the concepts ordered by the preferred label in one language. There is also a hierarchical viewer that provides navigation by broader and narrower relations (used for taxonomies and thesauri). And finally, a hypertext viewer shows all properties of a concept and provides navigation by all its relations (e.g., broader, narrower and related) by means of hyperlinks.

To simplify the location of concepts, there is a search system that allows the typical searches needed for terminological modes such as thesauri (equals / starts with / contains). Currently, search is limited to preferred labels in the selected language, but it could be extended to allow searches by other properties such as synonyms, definitions, or scope notes. All these viewers are synchronized, so the selection of a concept in one of them produces the selection of the same concept in the others.

The third available operation is to edit the model structure. Here, to create terminological ontologies following the SKOS model, an edition component for the ontology concepts is provided (figure 5.10). The graphical interface shows a list with all the concepts created in the selected model, allowing the creation of new ones (providing their URIs) or the deletion of selected ones. Once a concept has been selected, its properties and relations to other concepts are shown, allowing their edition. To facilitate the creation of relations between concepts, a selector of concepts (one of the previously described terminological ontology viewer) is provided, allowing the user to add related concepts without the need of manually typing the URI of the associated concept. Also, to see if the created thesaurus is correct, a preview of the terminological model can be shown, allowing the user to easily detect problems in the defined relations.

As mentioned in section 5.3, for efficiency, the format used to store the thesauri in the repository may change, but the interchange format used is SKOS. Therefore, a module to import and export terminological ontologies is provided. This module

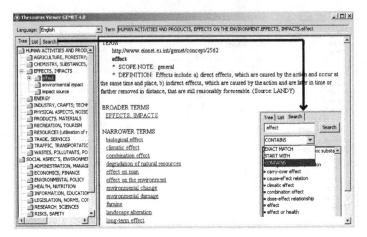

Fig. 5.9: Concept selector

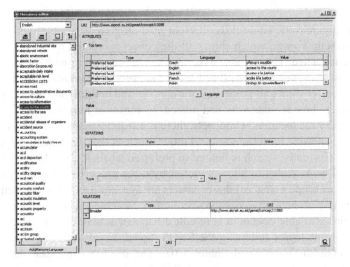

Fig. 5.10: Concept editor

is able to import from SKOS and export to SKOS, but also the interrelation with
respect to other terminological ontologies (if it has been created) using the format
described in section 2.4.1.

The layered architecture described before allows all the different described components to be reused in other contexts. ThManager tool itself reuses some of the
components in different areas. For example, the terminological ontology viewer is
used in the editor of terminological ontology metadata to facilitate the selection of
values for the subject section of metadata. Additionally, the viewer is used in the
concept editor to simplify the selection of concepts, providing the list of all the cre-

ated ones, and a preview of the created terminological model (to help to detect errors in the creation process).

5.5 Accessing terminological ontologies through a web service

Once the repository of terminological ontologies described in section 5.3.2 has been filled with the required models, and once they have been properly described and updated to fit with the required functionality, the last step is to provide these ontologies to the services requiring them. The access needs can be multiple: they can range from the need of a list of possible values for specifying criteria in a web search system, to a thesaurus based browsing of a collection of resources in an exploratory search system.

This section describes a web service specification called *Web Ontology Service* (WOS) that provides the access functionality focusing on the communication protocol and the underlying architecture. Figure 5.1 depicts the server providing *Web Ontology Service* on the web services layer. It provides access to the ontology repository through the *Ontology Manager API* contained in the *Ontology Manager* described in section 5.3. It provides access to the external components requiring access to terminological ontologies through two different HTTP based interfaces. Each of the interfaces is focused on providing access to a different family of clients.

For applications in general environments having to access terminological models such as thesauri, an interface following the service architecture proposed in the Alexandria Digital Library (ADL) project [96] and following the ADL Thesaurus protocol [97] (a protocol designed for the distribution of thesauri through the Web) has been created. The *ADLService* interface at the bottom of figure 5.11 contains the methods provided by this protocol. Given the limitations of ADL Thesaurus protocol to provide access to a single monolingual thesaurus, an extension of the *ADLService* interface called *ExtendedADLService* has been developed to provide access to multiple multilingual thesauri. As depicted in figure 5.12, the *ExtendedADLService* is implemented by the *MultilingualServiceImpl*, which provides the bridge to the *OntologyManagerAPI* to access the repository.

Additionally, a second alternative interface has been proposed for this web service in order to fulfil the needs of the geospatial community. Nowadays, geographic information has acquired a great importance as an instrument to facilitate decision-making and resource management in diverse areas. This potential has promoted the creation of Spatial Data Infrastructures (SDI), a specific kind of information infrastructure, to encompass the relevant base collection of technologies, policies and institutional arrangements that facilitate the availability of and access to geographic information [147]. With the aim of adopting open and spatially enabled reference architectures, the Open Geospatial Consortium (OGC) is a widely known organization in the geospatial community that promotes the definition of specifications to facilitate interoperability. In particular, OGC has defined an architecture of components called OGC Web Services Architecture (WSA) [205, 130]. The objective is to

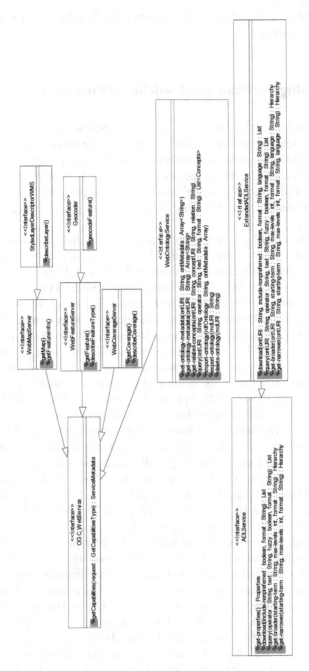

Fig. 5.11: External interfaces of the WOS

promote interoperability among OGC service specifications by increasing commonality and discouraging non-essential differences. According to this API, every OGC
service inherits from a general service whose unique operation is *getCapabilities*
[205]. The *getCapabilities* operation provides a description of the service, its operations, parameters and data types. It is used for clients to identify whether a service
provides the needed functionality and how to access it.

The top elements of figure 5.11 show the integration of *WebOntologyService*
with the rest of OGC services. The *WebOntologyService* extends the standard
OGC_WebService interface (as the rest of services in the OGC WSA) with methods that provide the functionality to access terminological ontologies. As shown in
figure 5.12, the interface is implemented by the *WebOntologyServiceImp* that uses
the *OntologyManagerAPI* to provide the required functionality.

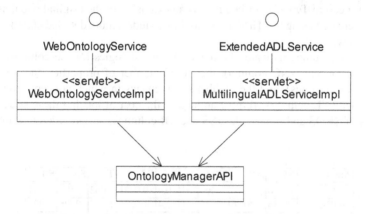

Fig. 5.12: Implementation of WOS interfaces

It must be noted that none of the service interfaces include update methods for
concepts and relations. With respect to the clients accessing the models, each ontology is considered as a whole, managing their changes as different versions of the
whole ontology.

5.6 Performance analysis

Around 70 terminological ontologies among thesauri and other types of controlled
vocabulary have been managed and distributed using the components and tools described in this chapter.

Some of the managed terminological models have a considerable size. Therefore, to test that the developed components are able to work with them without
problems, a performance test has been done. For the test, a set of terminological
ontologies including thesauri, authority files and classification schemes commonly

used by the geographic information community have been selected. Table 5.1 shows the selected models: the ADL Feature Types Thesaurus (ADL FTT)[27], the ISOC thesaurus of Geography (ISOC-G)[28], the ISO-639 codes for the representation of names of languages [82], the UNESCO Thesaurus[29], the OGP Surveying and Positioning Committee Code Lists (EPSG)[30], the Multilingual Agricultural Thesaurus (AGROVOC)[31], the European Vocabulary Thesaurus (EUROVOC)[32], the European Territorial Units (Spain and France) (ETU), and the GEneral Multilingual Environmental Thesaurus (GEMET)[33]. They have been selected because they are very different in sizes and they can be used to show how the load time evolves with the terminological ontology size. The size of these models varies greatly from a few hundred of concepts to thousands of concepts and/or relations. All of them, except the ADL Feature Types vocabulary have been transformed to SKOS using the processes described in section 3.6.1 and then imported into the ontology repository. The ADL Feature Types described here is an extension of the original one that was manually created using the ThManager tool to include a more detailed classification of features types.

Table 5.1 columns indicate: the name of the ontologies (Name column), their number of concepts (NC column), their total number of properties and relations (NP and NR columns), and the number of languages in which concept properties are provided (NL column). To give an idea of the cost of loading these structures, the sizes of SKOS and binary files (SS and SB columns) are provided in kilobytes (KB).

Name	NC	NP	NR	NL	LT	BT	JT	SS	SB
ADL FTT	210	210	408	1	0.4	0.047	0.062	103	41
ISOC-G	5136	5136	1026	1	2.4	1.063	1.797	2796	1332
ISO-639	7599	16247	0	6	5.1	1.969	2.89	3870	3017
UNESCO	8600	13281	21681	3	2.1	1.406	2.984	4034	2135
EPSG	4772	9544	0	1	1.8	0.969	1.796	2935	1682
AGROVOC	16896	103484	30361	3	7.5	4.953	14.75	15859	5089
EUROVOC	6649	196391	20861	15	11.1	9.266	15.828	18442	11483
ETU	44991	89980	89976	2	13.3	10.625	17.844	23828	10412
GEMET	5244	326602	12750	21	13.7	11.828	25.61	28010	15048

Table 5.1: Sizes of some thesauri and other types of vocabularies

Table 5.1 includes the performance in load time of the analyzed terminological models. The times have been measured using a 3 Ghz Pentium IV processor. The

[27] http://www.alexandria.ucsb.edu/gazetteer/FeatureTypes/ver070302/

[28] http://thes.cindoc.csic.es/index_esp.html

[29] http://www.ulcc.ac.uk/unesco/

[30] http://www.epsg.org/

[31] http://www.fao.org/aims/ag_intro.htm

[32] http://europa.eu/eurovoc/

[33] http://www.eionet.europa.eu/gemet

measures obtained allow comparing the time difference between loading a terminological ontology stored in SKOS using the Jena library and loading the same model
when it is stored using the binary model described in section 5.3. Three different
load times (in seconds) have been computed. The BT column contains the load
time in seconds of binary files without the cost of creating the GUI for the thesauri
viewers (load time for the WOS). The LT column contains the total load time in seconds of binary files (including the GUI creation and drawing time). The JT column
contains the time in seconds spent by Jena library to load the SKOS into memory
(it does not include GUI creation). The difference between the BT and LT column
shows the time used to draw the GUI once the thesauri have been loaded in memory.
The difference between BT and JT columns shows the gain in terms of time of using
a binary storage instead of a RDF based one.

These measures can be used to determine the size of the models that each type
of storage model can manage. Figure 5.13 depicts the comparison of the different
load times shown in table 5.1 with respect to the size of the RDF SKOS files. The
order of the terminological models in the figure is the same as in the table 5.1. It can
be seen that the time to construct the model using a binary format is almost half the
time spent to create the model using a RDF file.

It can be seen that once the binary model is loaded, the time to generate the GUI
for the ThManager is not very dependent on the thesaurus size. This is possible
thanks to the redundant information added to accelerate the load of the top terms
and the alphabetic list of the concepts in all the available languages (which is very
costly). This redundant information produces an overhead in the import and load
processes but it is compensated by a reduction in the graphical drawing time.

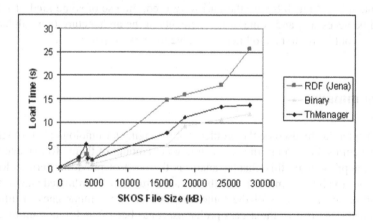

Fig. 5.13: ThManager load times

Despite using the binary representation model described in section 5.3, the load
time of the biggest terminological models shown in figure 5.13 is still high. However, once it is loaded, future accesses are immediate; negligible for WOS and less

than 0.5 seconds for ThManager. The ThManager time accesses include: opening it again, navigating by thesaurus relations, changing the visualization language, and searching concepts by their preferred labels. To minimize the load time, the terminological models can be loaded in background when the application is launched, reducing in that way the user perception of the load time.

Another interesting aspect shown in figure 5.13 is the peak of the third element. It corresponds with the ISO-639 classification scheme. It has the special characteristic of not having hierarchy and having many notations. These two characteristics produce a little increase in the load time of the model, given that the top concepts list contains all the concepts and the notations are more complex than other relations. However, most of the time is used to generate the GUI of the tree viewer. The tree viewer gets all the top terms and their preferred labels in the selected language and sorts them alphabetically to show the first level of the tree. This process is fast for a few hundred of concepts but not for the 7599 of the ISO-639.

This problem can be solved using the *type* field in the metadata describing the terminological ontology (see section 2.3.1) to distinguish between terminological models and perform the different optimized tasks for each type of model. If the tool knew that the terminological ontology does not have broader/narrower relations, it could use the structures used to visualize the alphabetic list, which are optimized to show all the concepts of the ontology very fast, instead of trying to load it as a tree.

The use of the persistence approach based on binary files has the advantage of not having to use external persistence systems such as a DBMS, and it provides a very fast access after the load, but it has the drawback (in time and space) of having to load all the terminological ontologies in memory (up to 512 MBs for the analyzed terminological models). For the context considered in this book it has been found to be enough but if much bigger thesauri were used, the use of some kind of DBMS would be necessary, and some of the elements in the architecture (e.g., alphabetic viewer) would have to be modified to be able to work properly.

5.7 Summary

This chapter has focused on the problems of managing terminological ontologies in infrastructures that require the access to a great amount of them. To manage these models appropriately, this chapter analyzes the need of providing terminological ontologies to all the components of the infrastructure in a coordinated way to avoid the use of several copies of the same ontology or very similar ones in different components. As part of the access problems, it has been found important to tackle the storage problem, the status management, and the relations with other models.

In order to provide a single access to the terminological ontologies an architecture for an *ontology manager* has been proposed. It facilitates the access to different types of storage repositories for the ontologies, allowing the selection of the most appropriate for each situation. The stored terminologies are described through metadata to facilitate their thematic location and access through search services. The *on-*

tology manager acts as an independent layer and on top of it different management applications can be built.

To fill the repository and manage the stored terminological ontologies, an open source editor called *ThManager* has been designed. It provides the functionality to create, describe, update, and delete terminological ontologies stored in a repository (accessed through the *ontology manager*). Additionally, *ThManager* architecture facilitates the design and implementation of different edition and selection components to provide access to terminological models.

In order to provide access to the ontologies contained in the repository, a centralized web service called *Web Ontology Service* (WOS) has been designed. In the same way as the *ThManager*, the service access to the ontologies using the *ontology manager*. Designed as a centralized service, its architecture aims at reducing the need of creation of new terminological ontologies, using existent ones, improving reusability, and avoiding duplicities and inconsistencies. To facilitate access two different interfaces are provided, one for general access and the other one compliant with the OGC Web Services Architecture specification for its integration in the geospatial community as a component of spatial data infrastructure..

Nowadays, tools and systems managing terminological model are not very effective in loading terminological models with hundreds of thousands concepts and relations without the use of a DBMS, so the storage model developed for situations when the use of a DBMS is discouraged has been tested calculating the load times of a set of terminological models. The performance of the tool is proved through a series of experiments on the management of a selected set of thesauri. This work analyzes the features of this selected set of thesauri and compares the efficiency of this tool with respect to their load directly from a RDF file. The results obtained show that the designed storage is good enough for the required terminological ontologies, providing an acceptable load time and an immediate access. The fast access to typical operations such as browsing, sorting or changing the visualization language increases the usability of *WOS* and *ThManager*.

As future work, it is planned to extend the *WOS* functionality to give support for non-terminological ontologies expressed in formal ontology languages such as OWL. This would not imply a complete redesign of the described architecture because SKOS is based on both RDF and OWL. Nevertheless, it requires a further analysis of the implications derived from the inclusion of non-terminological models and how this would affect the present API.

Future work could be oriented as well towards the enhancement of *ThManager* functionalities. On the one hand, the ergonomics to show the connections among different thesauri could be improved. Currently, these connections can be computed and annotated but the created GUI does not allow the user to navigate them. The base technology has been already developed, only a graphical interface is needed. On the other hand, *ThManager* could be extended to support data types different from texts (e.g., images, documents, or other multimedia sources) for the encoding of property values of concepts. This and the possibility to add user defined relations would increase the flexibility to support more complex models. Finally, improvements in usability could be added thanks to the component-based design of *ThManager* widgets. New viewers or editors can be created with little effort to meet the needs of specific users.

Chapter 6
Applicability of terminological ontologies to information retrieval

6.1 Introduction

The previous chapters have focused on describing different strategies, processes, components and systems to improve the management of terminological ontologies. This chapter takes all those elements and applies them to improve information discovery and retrieval in an information infrastructure.

In order to help in the classification of resources, section 6.2 proposes the integration of the terminological ontology management component described in section 5.4 with a tool for the creation of metadata. The objective of the integration is to simplify the semantic annotation of resources.

Another basic element in the discovery process is the development of search components. In order to improve the recall in search systems, section 6.3 shows a retrieval model that uses terminological ontologies for query expansion. These terminological ontologies are accessed through a web service following the architecture described in section 5.5.

In addition to search interfaces, browsing systems are also usually used to locate information in many different contexts. Instead of performing blind searches the user task in a discovery scenario might be one of browsing [13, p. 20]. These systems are based on providing an ontology more or less complex that is used as a core structure for the browsing process. However, the direct use of ontologies is not appropriate because usually neither a unique ontology nor their complete structure have been used in the collection. Somewhat related to the information browsing problem is the need to identify the content of different data catalogs that contribute from the different nodes of an information system. Having an overview of the content of a catalog helps to identify if the content may be suitable for the required purpose. This is important when there are multiple catalogs instead of a unique one and an indiscriminate search may consume a lot of processing time only to obtain that many of them contain nothing about the desired subject. This problem can be attended by using suitable content summary descriptions for the collection contents that help to reduce the scope of the searches. However, given that manual gener-

J. Lacasta et al., *Terminological Ontologies: Design, Management and Practical Applications*, Semantic Web and Beyond 9, DOI 10.1007/978-1-4419-6981-1_6,
© Springer Science+Business Media, LLC 2010

ation is costly (the summary gets obsolete if the collection changes), an automatic approach is more effective. Section 6.4 describes two approaches to provide adapted categorizations of a collection. On the one hand, it proposes a method to generate a topic map adapted to the collection content that can be used for browsing. On the other hand, it describes a set of methods to generate a collection classification that can improve the efficiency of distributed discovery systems.

6.2 Resource classification

Information systems can integrate information from many different sources, which may range from individuals (e.g., concerned citizens or graduate students in geography) and non-profit institutions (e.g., universities or non-governmental organizations) to large companies or governmental institutions. This great variety of sources implies a consequent heterogeneity in the classification process, both in the wide choice of metadata models and in the different expertise of metadata creators.

According to the different resources and organizational procedures of the institutions contributing to the information system, metadata may be created by scientific data producers, by library cataloguers, or by administrative staff. Therefore, it is important to provide users with metadata edition tools that facilitate the content creation, i.e. generating those metadata elements that can be automated, and guiding them in the edition of descriptive elements that must be typed manually. Moreover, since typing errors in metadata creation can imply not finding a resource, control of content quality is very important. Being homogeneous in the selection of the terms used to describe a resource is another important issue. If two resources have similar characteristics, they should be described with the same terms. Otherwise, a query system will only return a subset of the records it should return.

The use of different metadata standards can be solved by matching the metadata models and establishing crosswalks between them. Works such as Lacasta et al. [120], Zarazaga-Soria et al. [209], and Nogueras-Iso et al. [154] show the problems that affect to the relation of metadata models and propose approaches for the creation of crosswalks between them. However, even if all the metadata describing the resources have been transformed to a single model, the differences in their content still persist.

Tolosana-Calasanz et al. [186] describes a process to identify those metadata elements that affect to a greater extent to the overall quality of the metadata. The use of a controlled vocabulary for the most relevant of these fields can help to increase the homogeneity, to minimize the number and impact of human errors, and to reduce the time of creation. In order to reuse these vocabularies in different services, it becomes essential to manage them uniformly by means of services such as the Web Ontology Service proposed in section 5.5 or the ThManager tool shown in section 5.4.

Metadata standards such as Dublin Core [85], ISO-19119 [87] and ISO-19115 [84] define a large number of metadata elements for their application field, and many of them must (or may) contain terms from terminological ontologies such as controlled vocabularies or thesauri. Some examples in ISO-19115 are the *descriptive keywords*, the *topic category*, the *distribution format*, or the *spatial representation type*.

These controlled elements are usually facilitated by the used metadata edition tool. However, in most of these tools it is difficult to update them (and to add new ones) due to each one is managed independently of the rest. To facilitate the use of the terminologies in the metadata creation process and with the objective of managing them uniformly, a metadata edition tools with the capability to access to a repository of terminological models is needed.

The solution adopted has been to integrate the management components provided by ThManager (see section 5.4) into a metadata edition tool for the documentation of resources called *CatMDEdit*, which makes a special emphasis on the annotation of geographic information. *CatMDEdit* [210] is an Open Source cross-platform desktop tool[1], whose main aim is to promote metadata creation as a mechanism that facilitates the processing of data in a more effective way. *CatMDEdit* facilitates semi-automatic mechanisms for the generation of metadata in order to hide the complexity of metadata standards and minimize the interaction with users. Additionally, it provides mechanisms for integrating Geographic Information System (GIS) tools that enable the access to datasets through their associated metadata.

Figure 6.1 shows the three-layered architecture of CatMDEdit. The upper-layer contains the main functional components of the application: a *Resource Browser* (to manage the metadata records), a *Metadata Editor* (to modify the metadata), and a *Resource Viewer* (to visualize the resources associated to the metadata). The second layer contains the middleware software libraries that support the development of the functional components. Finally, the data layer includes the repositories needed for configuration and storage of data and metadata. In this architecture, the thesaurus tool component uses the ThManager visualization components to access to a local repository of terminological ontologies. The *ThesaurusBeans* provided by the ThManager library have been used to facilitate the selection of values for some metadata elements. Moreover, it must be noted that, thanks to this integration, *CatMDEdit* not only facilitates the selection of terms in different languages, but it also gives access to their definitions, synonyms, and narrower / broader / related concepts to help the user to select the most suitable one.

Some more complex ontology models such as those used to describe *spatial reference systems* (datum, ellipsoid, and projection) or *citations* (name, organization, address ...) could be also managed in the same way. However, special interfaces would be required to create / visualize each one of them.

If a stronger coordination of terminological models were required, the use of a local repository for the ontologies would not be adequate. For these situations, the Web Ontology Service - WOS (section 5.5) can provide the remote access to a central repository. Then, the ThManager components integrated in CatMDEdit would act as WOS clients.

---

[1] http://catmdedit.sourceforge.net/

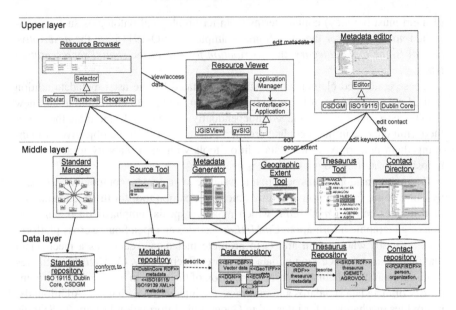

Fig. 6.1: Integration of ontology management with CatMDEdit

6.3 Improvement of information discovery through query expansion

In many situations, users (including computer applications) do not have a clear understanding about which keywords they should introduce in their queries to an information system, and they use query terms that differ from the keywords used by metadata creators. Sometimes the users are professionals with a high level of expertise, but it is also usual to find citizens and novice users just exploring for the first time the possibilities offered by a service.

This problem is partially solved by offering search interfaces that guide the user through a single thesaurus or other type of linguistic/terminological ontology that contains the more appropriate terms (the used by metadata creators). However, a project that implies the cooperation of different institutions usually derives in a collection of metadata records using a wide range of thesauri and other classification schemes. Content creators from different organizations and application domains apply their own criteria for the classification of resources, using very diverse terminology even for the description of similar resources. This situation is even more problematic when the catalog system stores metadata records written in different languages. In that case, the terminological differences between users and metadata creators become a really complex barrier for information retrieval.

The heterogeneity of metadata content and the great variety of users has been shown as a factor that may reduce the retrieval performance, despite guiding the user in the construction of queries by means of a terminological ontology. In this context, the initial query formulation can be improved with techniques such as query expansion where query terms are enriched with additional elements that are expected to improve the query specification [13, Chap.5]. The integration of query expansion techniques into a retrieval model helps to understand the sense of user vocabularies and to link this meaning to the underlying concepts expressed in metadata records. The objective behind its incorporation is to enhance its capabilities, moving from data retrieval strategies to information retrieval ones.

This section describes an information retrieval model that uses query expansion techniques on thesaurus indexed records to improve the results. The required terminological ontologies are provided to the retrieval model through the integration of the Web Ontology Service (section 5.5). The information provided by the terminological models (e.g., translations, synonyms, and related concepts from other terminological ontologies) is used to create an automatic approach for the expansion of user queries. Subsection 6.3.1 reviews the query expansion issues analyzed along all the section. Next, subsection 6.3.2 describes the proposed information retrieval model. Finally, section 6.3.3 shows the results of applying the proposed method for the retrieval of a metadata collection.

6.3.1 State of the art in query expansion

A classical way to expand queries is to use the semantic relations of the natural language. Relations such as *synonymy*, *hypernymy-hyponymy*, or even *holonymy-meronymy* and *gender* relations can be used to improve the query. However, adding new elements comes to a cost, if *polysemic* or *homonymic* terms (they have several meanings) are included in the queries the precision of the results obtained is reduced (not desired resources are returned).

The most basic semantic relationship between terms is the *synonymy*. Two terms are synonyms if they have the same meaning. However, prefect synonymy is scarce, most of synonymy relations are partial-synonyms that only share part of their meanings. In a retrieval system, the use of synonyms should produce the same results (with records classified according to one of them). This task can be done by a query expansion system that includes all the possible exact synonyms in the query. Additionally, partial synonyms can also be added if in the application context the meaning cannot be misinterpreted. In this context, the identification of the intended meaning of each query term is very important because it can help to add additional close synonyms that improve the results.

An special case of *synonymy* is the relation between terms from different languages with equivalent meaning. Multilingual terminological models have an important applicability in multilingual systems where it is needed to retrieve results independently of the language of the user query and the language used to classify the resources. The expansion of query terms to those equivalents to other languages greatly simplifies this task.

In addition to *synonymy*, *hypernymy-hyponymy* relationships between terms are also interesting to expand the queries. In most situations, the *hyponyms* of a query term are relevant to improve the query formulation since their meaning is completely included in the meaning of the original one. On the other hand, *hypernyms* are discouraged for query expansion. They have a more general meaning and their use can include non-desired items to the result set. However, in some specific contexts were it is known that the hypernym has been only used for classification with the same intended meaning than the corresponding hyponym (i.e., no records classified with other of the hypernym meanings exist in the collection), they can be used for expansion.

More specific than general *hypernymy-hyponymy* relation, there is the *holonymy-meronymy* relationship. A term is meronym of another one if it denotes a constituent part of, or a member of something. For example, a tributary *is part of* a river, a specific mountain *is part of* a mountain chain, and a specific administrative division of the territory *is part of* another bigger one. *Meronymy* relationship is especially useful to expand queries in the GIS context since the nature of the information is mainly based on spatial earth surface divisions. For example, in a query about the "flora in Aragón" (a sub-division of Spain), to increase the number of suitable records returned, the term "Aragón" could be expanded to include additional subdivisions such as "Jaca".

Gender relation is another semantic relation to deal with. From the different terminological models, usually only the dictionaries contain this type of relationship. When it is available, a search term can be expanded with the term used for the other gender (a search for "horses" should include results about "mares"). Most of the times, the gender difference is reduced to a small change in the ending of the word that can be removed through a lemmatization process (it depends on the language). However, in other situations the words used for each gender are completely different (e.g., uncle-aunt).

There are many expansion related works in the field of geographical information. For example, Jones et al. [100] combines a hierarchical distance measure (using a toponym thesaurus) with the Euclidean distance between place centroids to create a hybrid spatial distance measure. This measure is integrated with a thematic distance, based on classification semantics, to create the semantic closeness measure used for relevance ranking in the retrieval system. Other works are the proposals of Alani et al. [3] and Tudhope et al. [190], which illustrate how hierarchical spatial relationships can be used in applications employing online gazetteers and geographical thesauri to provide more flexible retrieval for queries incorporating place names. Additionally, they explore how to combine spatial and associative relationships by filtering the context of the associative link and their subtypes. Taking into account multilingual issues, query expansion can be used to provide language independent query systems by using multilingual terminological ontologies to translate the query terms to other languages [68, 155].

6.3.2 A proposal for terminological based query expansion

As it has been described previously, user queries can be expanded by using the concepts contained in terminological ontologies and the relations that hold among them. To be able to perform this expansion, an information retrieval model must have a suitable access to the required terminological models. This subsection describes an information retrieval model for metadata catalogs and an expansion model for the user queries that integrate the Web Ontology Service (WOS) proposed in section 5.5 to provide access to the terminological models.

6.3.2.1 General context

An information retrieval process implies a series of typical operations such as text processing, indexing of documents, query processing, searching, and ranking of retrieved documents. Figure 6.2 shows a schema of these operation interactions based on the model proposed by Baeza-Yates and Ribeiro-Neto [13], but customized to the special characteristics of metadata management. Additionally, the figure remarks where the interaction for query processing with the WOS component is placed.

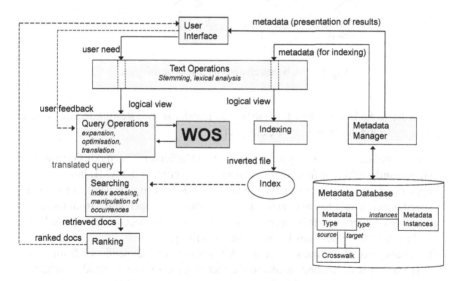

Fig. 6.2: Structure of an information retrieval system (IRS) [13]

As regards the specific decisions taken in the operations involved in this information retrieval process, CatServer is proposed for the storage of the resource descriptions. This catalog system, described in Tolosana-Calasanz et al. [188], provides a functional kernel for catalog services handling XML-encoded metadata. With respect to the information retrieval model applied, CatServer is based on the Extended

Boolean Model [13], i.e. it combines the simplicity of the Simple Boolean Model with the slightly more sophisticated ranking of results supplied by the Extended Model. Additionally, it is worth noting that this catalog system fulfils two main requirements. On the one hand, the system is independent from the metadata standards or schemas followed by the metadata inserted in the catalog. The idea behind this requirement is to use CatServer as a basis for the implementation of different metadata-driven services such as geographical data catalogs, service catalogs, or even Web Feature Servers (including its gazetteer variant). On the other hand, CatServer is able to manage large amounts of metadata records and be efficient enough in response time.

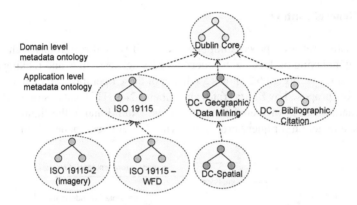

Fig. 6.3: A hierarchy of metadata ontologies

In order to be independent from metadata standards, two design decisions have been taken in the development of CatServer:

- Firstly, metadata are directly stored in XML at CatServer. This modus operandi is significantly different from other catalogs which convert the XML into a persistent object model. The great advantages of the adopted approach are its retrieving speed (since it only has to retrieve the XML) and its independence from metadata standards. Otherwise, as it happens with the persistent object model approach, the inclusion of new standards involves code rewriting.
- Secondly, apart from the storage in XML format, the independence from metadata standards is fulfilled thanks to the fact that the different metadata schemas share a common core [187]. This common core is needed if the system wants to provide the user with the functionality of querying all the metadata instances stored, independently of the metadata schema used (e.g., we need a common set of queryable properties). As depicted in figure 6.3, the only prerequisite of the standards supported by our system is to provide their XML Schema and their mapping to the common core of Dublin Core. That is to say, as it is shown in figure 6.2, the metadata database maintains a knowledge base of the supported

metadata types (schemas) and the *crosswalks* between them (at least a crosswalk towards the Dublin Core common core).

With respect to the need related to the efficiency and the management of huge amounts of metadata records, it must be noted that the Inverted Index structure [13] was chosen and adapted to speed up queries. This structure could be defined as a sequence of *(key, pointer)* pairs where each pointer refers to a record in a database which contains the key value in some particular field. The index is sorted by the key values to provide fast searching for a particular key value (e.g., using binary search). The index is "inverted" in the sense that the key value is used to find the record rather than the other way around. For catalog systems enabling searches with filters on more than one database field, multiple indexes (sorted by those keys) may be created.

The index structure of CatServer is slightly different. It consists of a pair *(key, array)* where the key has the same meaning, but there is an array instead of a pointer to a register. The array represents those metadata records that contain the word in a specific XML metadata element tag. The index structure has been implemented by means of a relational database table. The usual way of working is to build an Inverted Index for every XML metadata element tag for which the clients need to search. Figure 6.4 (left) shows two Inverted Indexes built over the Dublin Core elements *title* and *subject* (the examples uses an excerpt of metadata describing the *Natura 2000 sites* dataset, a set of areas of special interest for biodiversity protection across Europe).

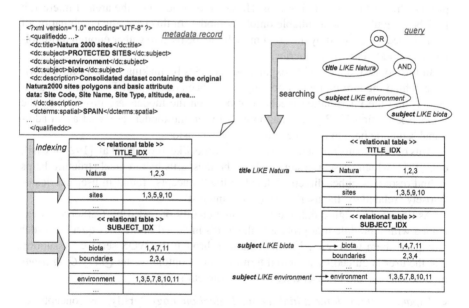

Fig. 6.4: Retrieval example: XML tags and Inverted Index implementation correspondence (left); querying process (right)

Once the indexes are built, the system can retrieve the information with only the tag name, which determines the index to examine, and the key. For instance, let us consider the query represented in figure 6.4 (right). This query aims at retrieving those metadata records whose *title* contains *Natura* or whose *subject* contains *biota* and *environment* (*title LIKE '%Natura%' OR (subject LIKE '%biota%' AND subject LIKE '%environment%'*)). Thus, CatServer would obtain three arrays of metadata identifiers: one for *Natura*, one for *biota*, and another for *environment*. The next step in the process is to combine these arrays as sets of metadata records. The *AND* implies an intersection operation between the *biota* array and the *environment* array. The *OR* implies a union operation between the *Natura* array and the subset obtained in the previous step.

Evidently, not all the results are equally important. As mentioned at the beginning of this subsection, the ranking process is based on the Extended Boolean Model. Therefore, the subset of metadata is in fact a list of metadata records ordered by relevance. Following with the example, metadata records satisfying both operands of the *OR* logic expressions are more relevant than those which only satisfy one of them, i.e. they appear before in the ranked list.

6.3.2.2 Proposed expansion model

The query expansion requires the identification in the specific application area of a subset of the relationships described in section 6.3.1. Terminological ontology can provide these semantic relationships. However, depending on the area of interest, it may be difficult to find a suitable ontology model. In this case, the combination of the knowledge provided by different models can be used to gather enough terminology to properly enrich the queries.

In this context, a method to expand user queries by making profit of the knowledge behind the terminological ontologies has been developed. The terminological models and the interrelation mechanism between the models are provided by the WOS (see section 5.3.3). The mappings between the models are used as an additional semantic base to produce better query expansions.

This query expansion model is similar to works like Tudhope et al. [192] or Clark et al. [31], which present systems where the thesaurus hierarchical structure helps to find resources either directly related to the "concepts" found in user queries or "closely" related to "the user's concepts of interest".

As depicted in figure 6.2, the basic functionality provided by CatServer is extended with a module that processes the terms included in the user query in order to expand them with related terms obtained through the WOS service. Assuming that the user is guided by an initial terminological ontology, the *Query Operations* module will expand the user queries in two directions:

- *Expansion through the initial terminological ontology.* Firstly, the concepts selected by the user through an initial terminological ontology (and displayed in a particular language) are expanded with all the labels (preferred and alternatives) in the different languages supported by this initial terminological ontology.

- *Expansion through related terminological ontologies.* Secondly, the *Query Operations* module tries to expand the query with the labels corresponding to related concepts in other terminological ontologies managed by the WOS. This strategy helps to find synonyms or translations in related ontologies that have a richer vocabulary or support more languages than the initial one.

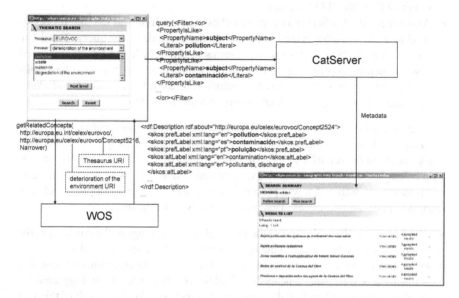

Fig. 6.5: Example of query expansion for a thematic catalog

Figure 6.5 shows an example of the first type of query expansion (*expansion through the initial terminological ontology*). This example can be described in a sequence of three main steps:

- Firstly, a thematic search interface[2] allows the user to browse the concepts contained in a terminological ontology (left side of figure 6.5). Although the search interface only shows the preferred labels in the language the user has selected, it can be assumed that the terminological ontology is multilingual, i.e. it gives support for several languages. Whenever the user browses the narrower concepts of a selected concept (e.g., the concept *deterioration of the environment* identified by the URI *http://europa.eu/eurovoc/Concept5216* in the EUROVOC terminological ontology), the thematic search interface interacts with the WOS service to retrieve all the preferred and alternative labels of the narrower concepts in all the available languages (e.g., *pollution* in English but also *contaminación* in Spanish). Figure 6.5 shows an excerpt of the *getRelatedConcepts* request sent to the WOS service and the response returned in SKOS format.

---

[2] This search interface belongs to the set of search services offered by the SDIGER project - http://sdiger.unizar.es- (see section 6.3.3 for more details)

- Secondly, a click on the *search* button represents that the user has stopped browsing the terminological ontology and has decided the final concepts to be included in the query. Then, the search interface constructs the query that will be sent to the catalog system (CatServer). This query is compliant with the OGC Filter encoding specification [204] and it contains an expression that includes all the possible alternatives of preferred and alternative labels in different languages obtained from the WOS service.
- And thirdly, the CatServer system launches the searching and ranking processes to obtain the metadata records that satisfy the expanded user query. Thanks to the fact that WOS provides preferred terms in different languages, the returned result contains records written in multiple languages. For instance, the results shown on the right side of figure 6.5 include records in French (*Rejets pollutants des systèmes* ...) and Spanish (*Presiones e impactos sobre* ...).

With respect to the second strategy for query expansion (*expansion through related terminological ontologies*), the *Query Operations* module applies a basic routine to estimate the reliability of expanding an original set of keywords with a new term belonging to a different ontology. In this particular case, we have used the disambiguation algorithm that was presented in section 2.5 as an example of defining mappings between ontologies. This process consists of four steps:

- The first step is the collection of the more reliable mappings of the concepts in the original query with respect to the upper-level ontology used by the WOS service. From now on we will use the name *synset* for these major mappings because this is the name given to the concepts in WordNet (the upper-level ontology used for the disambiguation functionality described in section 2.5). As a result of this first step, for each concept in the query we obtain an initial collection of *synsets*.
- Secondly, we collect the *synsets* corresponding to a candidate concept for query expansion from a different ontology. Initially, all the concepts of the ontologies stored in the WOS are considered as candidates.
- Thirdly, we compute the reliability of a candidate concept as the number of *synset* coincidences with the *synsets* of the original query concepts divided by the number of *synsets* of the new concept and multiplied by 99:

$$reliability = \frac{|synset\ matches\ of\ new\ concept|}{|synsets\ of\ new\ concept|} \times 99 \qquad (6.1)$$

The reason to use a final factor of 99 and not 100 in equation 6.1 is to obtain a maximum reliability percentage of 99 for automatically expanded concepts, reserving a 100-reliability percentage uniquely for the concepts which were originally in the query.

- Finally, the reliability of a new candidate concept is compared with a *threshold* reliability. If the reliability percentage is greater than a selected *threshold*, the query is expanded with this new concept. This means that the query expression will include as alternatives the preferred and alternative labels of this new concept in the different available languages. A *threshold* of 50% is considered as an appropriate value to detect suitable concepts related to the initial set.

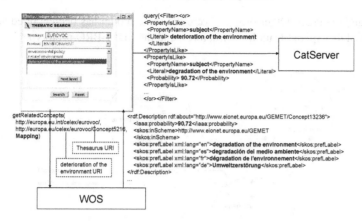

Fig. 6.6: Expansion through disambiguation

The core of this expansion technique is integrated in the WOS service. The disambiguation functionality is provided through the *getRelatedConcepts* operation, using *Mapping* as relation type. Figure 6.6 shows an example of this type of query expansion. The concept *deterioration of the environment* belonging to the EUROVOC vocabulary is expanded with the concept *degradation of the environment* of GEMET. This concept of GEMET has been mapped to the original concept of EUROVOC with a reliability of 90.72%.

6.3.3 Testing the retrieval model

In order to quantify the retrieval effectiveness of an information retrieval system, performance measures such as precision (number of relevant hits divided by the number of hits) and recall (number of relevant hits divided by the number of relevant documents) must be computed upon the results obtained from evaluation experiments. This requires a testbed comprising a fixed number of documents, a standard set of queries, and relevant and irrelevant documents in the testbed for each query.

For the testing the retrieval model and verifying the influence of WOS in the improvement of information retrieval performance, this model has been applied within the context of the SDIGER project. This project includes a thematic catalog searcher (see left side of figure 6.5) that makes use of a WOS instance to access multilingual terminological models to help in the construction of user queries, which are automatically expanded with cross-language terminology by means of the strategies explained in section 6.3.1. The multilingual models managed by the WOS instance integrated within the SDIGER project are the Multilingual Agricultural Thesaurus (AGROVOC), the European Vocabulary Thesaurus (EUROVOC), the GEneral Multilingual Environmental Thesaurus (GEMET), and the UNESCO Thesaurus. All of them have been defined by well-known organizations and give support to several

European languages. Other projects were the same model has been applied are the Spanish SDI[3] (Spatial Data Infrastructure), and the SDI-EBRO prototype[4].

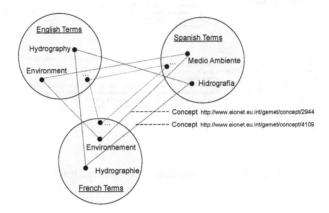

Fig. 6.7: Mapping between terms in different languages

The SDIGER metadata corpus consists of around 26,000 metadata records in Spanish, English, and French (each one in a single language) that contain about 350 different keywords to describe their associated data. Many of these keywords have been extracted from different thesauri but others have been randomly typed by metadata creators. All these characteristics make the corpus appropriate to analyze the impact of multilingual dispersion in the information retrieval performance.

Previous to the performance analysis, it was necessary to obtain a series of topics and their relevance with respect to metadata records. This way, it would be possible to compare different retrieval (and query expansion) strategies. The topics were selected upon an analysis of the concepts behind the 350 different keywords found in the metadata records. After mapping terms in different languages, identifying synonyms, and eliminating redundancies introduced by plurals and other derived lexical forms, 204 different concepts were obtained.

To extract the topics, the following semi-automatic process was developed. Firstly, the language of each of the 350 keywords was identified by means of the *language* descriptor found in the metadata records containing these keywords. Additionally, the language assigned to each element was verified with a multilingual dictionary. Secondly, as shown in figure 6.7, a manual mapping between terms in different languages was applied to identify the concepts that would be used later as topics for the experiments. Thirdly, the identification of synonyms and elimination of related lexical forms was applied as well with the aid of a multilingual dictionary. Finally, spatial data experts from the institutions contributing to the SDIGER project assigned manually the relevance of metadata records with respect to each topic.

---

[3] http://www.idee.es/

[4] http://ide-ebro.chebro.es/

For the sake of facilitating topic relevance assignment, experts were provided with the *Inverted Indexes* automatically created by CatServer and an initial pre-assignment of relevance according to the following rule: *"a metadata record is relevant to a topic if it contains one of the possible terms (labels) that represent the concept in that topic"*. The experts only had to revise this initial pre-assignment for possible mistakes due to word-sense ambiguity. However, in most cases the initial pre-assignment was accurate. In contrast to text information retrieval (where full documents are indexed), we are indexing metadata records, which are short summary texts created by experts. This has two important advantages in comparison with classical text information retrieval. On the one hand, the texts are short and there are few noise words, reducing the possibilities of mistaking a noise word for a label representing a real topic of the resource described. And on the other hand, most terms found in metadata are quite specific, reducing the possibilities of polysemy. In fact, a search system just based on word-matching of topic terms would yield a high precision. The main problem that affects the performance of search systems over this metadata corpus is the problem of detecting the correspondence among translation of terms and some synonymy issues. That is to say, a simple word-matching strategy for retrieval yields a low recall.

Once the corpus was fully established, a series of experiments were conducted using CatServer in order to compare different alternatives for query expansion. These experiments can be classified into three categories according to the query expansion strategy applied:

- *No query expansion*. The first three experiments consisted in selecting a particular language (e.g., English, French, or Spanish) and sending queries to CatServer using topic terms in that particular language without applying any strategy for query expansion. In other words, these three experiments were oriented to study the three original languages separately (used in metadata records) and the problems derived from the multilingual dispersion.
- *Expansion through the initial ontology*. A second series of three experiments was oriented to analyze the effect of expanding queries thanks to the knowledge stored in the terminological ontologies. This strategy matches with the first heuristic described in section 6.3.1 for query expansion. In these experiments, it is assumed that the user is browsing a terminological ontology (GEMET, AGROVOC, or UNESCO) for the definition of user queries. When the user decides the final concepts to include in the query, each query term is automatically expanded with all the equivalent terms in the other languages of the ontology.
- *Complete query expansion*. The final experiment is devoted to analyze the effect of applying the two heuristics for query expansion described in section 6.3.1. This experiment assumes that the user is using the GEMET terminological ontology for the definition of the query. As regards to the query expansion, apart from extending the topic concepts to all possible terms, the expansion also considers related concepts in the terminological ontologies of AGROVOC and UNESCO. Using the strategy called *expansion through related terminological ontologies*, based on the disambiguation mechanism (see section 2.5) and the reliability for-

mula (explained in section 6.3.1), the concepts of GEMET were connected to related concepts in UNESCO and AGROVOC.

With respect to the performance measures obtained upon these experiments, it is worth mentioning that they have been focused on the analysis of recall. Given the characteristics of the metadata corpus, the comparison of precisions for each experiment is not relevant. As stated before, the results obtained in the experiments that not use query expansion always get a high precision because the metadata collection contains very specific concepts, which are rarely affected by polysemy conflicts. Additionally, the topics used for the queries correspond to concepts extracted from the own keywords contained in metadata records. This can be also extrapolated to the other two series of experiments using query expansion. Again, thanks to the lack of polysemy and the specificity of the topics used in the experiments, the automatic expansion is supposed to be precise. On the one hand, the translations of terms derived from the use of a terminological ontology are inherently accurate (the terminological ontology has been constructed by experts with knowledge in different languages). On the other hand, the expansions with concepts from different ontologies are also accurate because of the specificity of the topics.

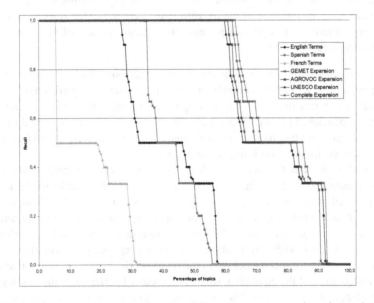

Fig. 6.8: Comparison of recall using different query expansion alternatives

Figure 6.8 shows the recall curves obtained in each of the aforementioned experiments. The topics in the *x-axis* of each recall curve are ordered by the recall obtained in the experiment strategy. This fact does not allow the comparison of recall for a particular topic in two experiments. However, the main purpose of the figure is to provide a general idea of the average recall in each experiment. The area covered in the polygons bounded by the recall curves and the positive sides of both *x-axis* and *y-axis* denotes the recall improvements in each experiment.

As a result of the experiments, it can be observed that query expansion strategies based on terminological ontologies (i.e., use of translations and synonyms) imply an important recall improvement. Without query expansion, only 6% of topics using French terms have a full recall. This is slightly improved in the case of experiments using English and Spanish terminology: 26% and 32% of topics with full recall respectively. But anyway, it can be verified that this strategy produces low recall measures in a multilingual corpus. Quite the opposite, the experiments guided by the use of a terminological ontology such as GEMET, AGROVOC and UNESCO obtain a high recall for most of the topics: 60% of topics have a full recall, and 80% of topics have a recall higher than 50%. Finally, the experiment using complete query expansion provides a small increase in recall with respect to the use of a single ontology.

Theoretically, the experiment with complete query expansion should have been obtained a perfect recall. However, there are still a small number of concepts that are not contained in the terminological ontologies used for the experiments. It must be taken into account that topics are derived from the keywords found in metadata records, but these keywords may not have been selected from a terminological ontology. Additionally, the labels (terms in multiple languages) used for a concept in a terminological ontology may not necessarily match with the terms manually mapped for the extraction of topic concepts.

Finally, it must be noted that independently of the query expansion method and the terminological ontology used, the results obtained are similar. This is caused by the fact that the ontologies selected for the experiment are thematically related to the metadata collection and all of them contain a similar subset of the required keywords.

This information retrieval model based on the WOS component has been applied to different Spatial Data Infrastructure (SDI) projects (Spanish SDI, SDIGER Geoportal, and SDI-EBRO prototype). The search clients constructed for these systems have been based on the client prototype described in section 5.5 but adjusting them to the specific requirements of each system (in general, through the change of the configuration parameters).

From the different projects where the WOS has been integrated, the Spanish SDI project is the most relevant. The search services of the infrastructure use a collection of search components (e.g., graphical display to restrict results by coordinates, or a free text area to introduce query elements) to construct the final user queries that include some components constructed according to the architecture described in section 5.5 to access the WOS. For instance, Figure 6.9 shows two of these search services. On the one hand, figure 6.9a depicts the catalog search service of the Spanish SDI. In this search interface, the controlled lists that are shown (category, scale) are specialized WOS clients that provide access to the required terminology. On the other hand, figure 6.9b shows a subset of the Spanish SDI Gazetteer service interface that contains two different WOS clients. The first one (on the right side of the figure), shows all the types of features contained in the gazetteer (it is a controlled vocabulary without hierarchy). The second one (on the left side of the figure), shows the content of the Spanish administrative division thesaurus.

(a) Spanish SDI catalog search interface

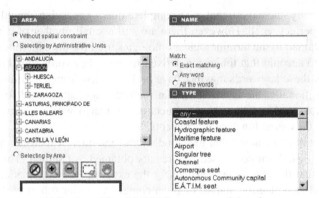

(b) Section of Spanish SDI Gazetteer search interface

Fig. 6.9: Spanish SDI search services

6.4 Information browsing

The use of terminological models in search interfaces is a simple way to guide the user in the selection of query terms. However, if some of the concepts of the ontology model have not been used in the collection, a search using them would return zero results. This problem is especially important in browsing interface since it is not suitable to provide a term for selection if it is not going to return any results. Additionally, even if all the concepts of the terminological model have been used for classification, when the used model is too big it becomes difficult to know what the collection is about. It is needed to provide a small classification of the collection that acts as an overview of the main themes in the collection.

The provided terminological models have to be adjusted to the user needs. In this context, the analysis of the metadata describing data collections is required to generate a suitable terminological model. Depending on the user needs, the desired model can range from a whole terminological model, such as the one used previously but adapted to the collection, to a much reduced list containing the general themes of the collection.

This section describes a set of processes to generate terminological models of different specificity from a data collection that can be later be used to facilitate the browsing and the identification of the collection content. It describes two different approaches to generate a collection classification, one based on the construction of a topic map, and the other one based on the use of different clustering techniques.

6.4.1 State of the art in information browsing approaches

If the terminological model used for the classification (or annotation) of data is available, the content of data collections may be browsed using this terminology. However, a common situation when integrating data from different collections is not to know the origin of the keywords used in the metadata. In this context, the keywords can be used to try to reconstruct the original terminological ontology. Although a process of this type can only generate a model which is poor in relations, it reflects the current contents of the collection.

From the different terminological ontology models that can be generated from the keywords, the most suitable for information browsing is the topic map. The structure of topic maps has been specifically designed to associate terminological concepts to resources that are about the theme (simpler models does not allow storing the relation of a keyword with the resources containing it). This structure makes the browsing process immediate (the associated resources are related to the topic) but it requires a reconstruction of the topic map if the associated collection changes. Depending on the detail required, the resulting model can vary from a detailed topic map of the collection to a reduced classification containing only the main topics of the collection.

Several works have advanced in how to construct automatically topic maps in a way that represents the source collection in a trustworthy way [2, 38, 173]. Boulos et al. [22] presents a system that creates a graphic topic map to enhance the access to a medical database using a graphical representation to locate the different topics over a graph of the human body. Schlieder et al. [174] and Schlieder and Vögele [173] insist on the idea of accessing to metadata collections through a network of intelligent thumbnails, being those thumbnails either concepts or locations. For instance, in the case of locations, the network of thumbnails corresponds to the hierarchical structure of administrative toponyms. Schlieder and Vögele [173] proposes the use of XTM [163] as the topic map exchange format, which can be easily visualized by a wide range of tools compliant with this format. Demšar [38] and Podolak and Demšar [164] provide a visual data mining approach to explore in an easier way the complex structure/syntax of geographical metadata records. Podolak and Demšar [164] also describe a system to convert a collection of metadata elements into clusters of similar metadata elements using the cluster algorithm of Fisher [55]. Albertoni et al. [4] describes a system to visually show traditional representations of statistical information about a collection to facilitate the identification of patterns.

Many of these works base their generation algorithms on pattern analysis techniques, known as clustering, that are focused on dividing resource collections (i.e., metadata) into clusters of resources with similar characteristics. These techniques are useful to find groups of metadata records (clusters) that share similar values in one (or more) metadata elements according to a mathematical correlation measure (e.g., the Euclidean distance, Bernoulli, Gaussian or polynomial functions among others). It can be said that elements in a cluster share common features according to a similarity criteria [38].

Clustering techniques have proved to produce good results in the classification of big collections of resources for different purposes (data mining, signal analysis, image processing...) [179]. Kaufman and Rousseeuw [108] and Jain and Dubes [95] show a great variety of clustering and classification techniques and their applications. The MetaCombine project [114] is a good example of classification of heterogeneous metadata. It focuses on providing a browsing service, i.e. the exploration or retrieval of resources (OAI and Web resources) through a navigable ontology. It shows the effectiveness of different clustering techniques for heterogeneous collections of metadata records according to different factors, such as the time used to locate a resource, the number of clicks needed to reach it, or the number of failures in locating the resource. Other related works are the proposed by Kang [106], which proposes a clustering method based on the document keywords; or Krowne and Halbert [114] and Cutting et al. [35] that use the clustering to improve browsing interfaces of digital libraries. They classify the resources in such a way that these classifications can be used later for information browsing.

Clustering techniques can be grouped according to the way each element is associated to each cluster in two different families of techniques:

Hard clustering: It associates each element of the collection to a unique cluster. An example of this category is *K-means* and its variants [44, 108].

Fuzzy clustering: It associates each element to each cluster with a different probability. It includes fuzzy and probabilistic techniques between others. Some examples are fuzzy *C-means* [189] and finite mixture models (as Bernoulli or polynomial) [6].

In this section, techniques from each of the families have been used to identify the main topics of a resource collection.

6.4.2 Topic map based browsing

As it has been described in section 1.3.5, topic maps are a representation of knowledge with an emphasis on the find-ability of information. The international standard ISO 13250 [86] that defines the topic map concept (the standard proposes a model for representation and an interchange format) indicates that topic maps allow easy and selective browsing to the requested information. It shows a thematic view of the collection of metadata and facilitates in that way the access to the information.

This subsection describes a method to generate a topic map for information browsing that provides a thematic global vision of the collection and gives information about what metadata records in the collection use each term of the topic map and about the weight of each keyword in the collection. Another objective is to use the generated topic map to obtain a reduced classification of the collection and circumscribe the collection to a concrete theme.

The designed generation process extracts a topic map from a metadata collection using the keywords section of the metadata records. The problem has been circumscribed to a collection of metadata records that, in their keywords section, use terms from a single terminological ontology following the thesaurus model. The process to automatically generate the topic map from the metadata collection is shown in detail in Figure 6.10.

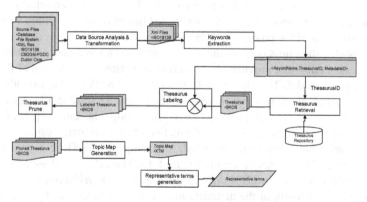

Fig. 6.10: Topic map generation Process

The first step is to obtain the metadata collection in a format readable for our system. The metadata records can be stored in different repository sources such as a metadata catalog, a relational database, or even in a directory of XML files. Their structure can follow different standards such as ISO 19115 [84], Dublin Core [85], or CSDGM-FGDC [51]. The input required in the designed generation process is the XML format described by ISO-19139 [88]; therefore, metadata in other formats have to be transformed to it. For the most typical situations where the source format is an XML file following other metadata standard, transformation process such as the crosswalks described by [156, chap. 3] can be used. For more complex situations, dedicated transformation software may have to be constructed.

The second step is the analysis of the metadata collection and the generation of the list of triplets <KeywordName, ThesaurusID, MetadataID> with the values of the keywords of the metadata, the identifier of their source thesaurus, and the identifier of the metadata record where the keyword has been found. Such triplets are the base elements used to construct the topic map classification.

The third step consists in the retrieval of the thesaurus used to create the keywords of the metadata collection. It is obtained by accessing to the ontology repository described in section 5.3. Once the thesaurus used in the metadata records has been identified and retrieved, it is labeled with the information of the triplets obtained in the second step. This labeling process considers not only the direct uses but also those inherited through the thesaurus hierarchy (it stores separately the direct relations from the inherited ones) to allow identifying in future steps if a term is used directly by some metadata records or if the used is one of its descendants.

The next step consists in pruning the branches and leaves of the labeled thesaurus whose terms are not referenced directly or by inheritance in any metadata record of the collection. Only terms with no direct or inherited references are deleted. Inner nodes with inherited relations are not deleted to maintain a more detailed hierarchy useful for browsing. This is useful when the user is not an expert in the themes of the metadata collection: if he does not understand the meaning of some of the more specific terms used in the lower levels of the hierarchy, he can select one of its more general ancestors to retrieve the associated information. Algorithm 9 shows a general overview of the process for generating topic maps.

The labeled thesaurus is to all intents and purposes a topic map adjusted to the metadata collection that provides the resources associated to each term of the used terminological model. The topic map is generated in SKOS format, extending this format to include the direct and indirect relationships. The SKOS file can then be used in a search service as topic map to navigate through the data, as part of a keyword selection system, or to provide information about how many results are going to be returned when a keyword is selected. An example of the SKOS representation of a topic map element can be seen in Figure 6.11. The extension done to the basic SKOS format has been to add the *directReference* and *inheritedReference* properties that store the identifiers of the metadata records using (directly of by inheritance) the keyword.

The generated file can be directly used as topic map if the system to use it is able to read it, or it can be transformed into a topic map standard format to allow other applications to directly use it. Among the available formats for topic maps representation, the XTM format [163] seems to be the most adequate for its use as topic map interchange format for the topic map generated. This format is quite simple and a great number of applications are able to use it.

The last step analyzes the generated topic map generated to extract the main themes of the collection. This can be manually done using visualization tools that allow the load of SKOS or RDF (such as Protégé) and detecting manually the most used themes. However, since the metadata collection updates usually change the

```
Procedure keywordExtractionandLabeling(List XMLMetadataList, ThesaurusCatalog thesCatalog);
begin
    List triplets = new ArrayList();
    for int i=0;i<XMLMetadataList.size();i++ do
        Metadata metadat = XMLMetadataList.get(i));
        tripletList.addCollection(metadat.getControlledTags());
    end
    Thesaurus thes=thesCatalog.get(tripletList.get(0).getThesaurusID());
    for int i=0;i<tripletList.size();i++ do
        Triplet triplet = tripletList.get(i);
        Concept concept = thes.getConcept(tripl.getKewWordName());
        concept.addRelation("directReference",triplet.getMetadataID());
        addIndirectReferences(concept, triplet.getMetadataID();
    end
    pruneNonUsedConcepts(thes.getTopConcepts(),thes);
    saveToSKOSFormat(thes,"topicMap.xml");
end

Procedure addIndirectReferences(Concept concept, String metadataID);
begin
    concept.addRelation("indirectReference",triplet.metadataID());
    List conceptList = concept.getBroaders();
    addIndirectReferences(conceptList.get(i)),metadataID);
end

Procedure pruneNonUsedConcepts(List conceptList, Thesaurus thes);
begin
    for int i=0;i<conceptList.size();i++ do
        Concept concept = conceptList.get(i);
        List narrowerList = concept.getNarrowers();
        pruneNonUsedConcepts(narrowerList,thes);
        if (!concept.hasRelation("directReference")) && (!concept.hasRelation("indirectReference")) then
            thes.remove(concept);
        end
    end
end
```

Algorithm 9: Generation of the topic map

main themes of the collection, to reduce the human work, an automatic process to extract this information has been designed. The process described here is based on the idea of concept density used for the disambiguation of free text in Agirre and Rigau [1]. The objective is to obtain the representative nodes of the tree that aggregate a relevant percentage of records in the metadata collection. Clustering techniques analyze different properties of data to statistically group together the most similar. Elements in a cluster share common features according to a similarity criteria [38]. Inherently, the topic maps described above can be considered as hierarchical clusters. However, our intention in this last step is to obtain a 1-dimensional cluster that summarizes the collection at a first glance. Here, the hierarchical structure of the thesaurus provides a thematic context of similarity that enables terms of the same branch to be summarized by the root node of the branch. In order to identify this 1-dimensional cluster the Formula 6.2 has been proposed.

$$\frac{\sum_{\forall node \in Branch} numberOfRecords}{\sum_{\forall recods \in Collection} numKeywords} > threshold \qquad (6.2)$$

```
<skos:Concept
rdf:about="http://www.eionet.eu.int/gemet/concept/2405">
    <skos:prefLabel xml:lang="es">ciencias de la tierra</skos:prefLabel>
    <skos:prefLabel xml:lang="fr">sciences de la terre</skos:prefLabel>
    <skos:definition xml:lang="en">
    The science that deals with the earth or any part thereof;
    includes the disciplines of geology, geography, oceanography and
    meteorology, among others.(Source: MGH)</skos:definition>
    <topicMap:directReference>
        digital-data-30-boundary<topicMap:directReference>
    <topicMap:directReference>
        digital-data-30-P-13-cells<topicMap:directReference>

    <topicMap:inheritedReference>
        digital-data-30-P-4-conventional<topicMap: inheritedReference>

    <skos:narrower rdf:resource=
        "http://www.eionet.eu.int/gemet/concept/5270"/>

</skos:Concept>
```

Fig. 6.11: Labeled SKOS concept

The criterion used to identify a representative node divides the number of records containing this node (or any of its descendants) by the number of keywords in the collection. If this value is greater than a threshold, then this node is considered as a relevant node. This threshold has been selected experimentally, using a range of values between 0.05 and 0.2 (see section 6.4.4.2).

6.4.3 Cluster based browsing

Section 6.4.2 has described a method to generate a topic map from a metadata collection based on the keywords section of metadata. It makes profit of the terminological ontologies (e.g., classification schemes, taxonomies, or thesaurus) that have been selected to pick up those terms in the keywords section to create a hierarchical topic maps. However, in distributed systems where the different catalogs store thousands of metadata records, the topic map summarizing the thematic contents of a collection may still be fairly complex. In this sense, section 6.4.2 already identifies the necessity of obtaining a reduced set of representative terms from the generated topic map.

It has been analyzed the thematic classification and structuring of resources by means of clustering techniques. The clusters obtained as output of these techniques may help in two important issues of information retrieval systems operating on a network of distributed catalogs. On the one hand, the information of the clusters (e.g., names) may serve as metadata for describing the whole collection of metadata records. On the other hand, the output clusters provide the means for structured guided browsing.

The technique proposed here improve classic clustering techniques with the hierarchical relations that may be derived from keywords found in metadata records, whenever these keywords have been selected from well-established terminological ontologies following thesaurus model. Clustering techniques group the resources by the similarity of some properties but do not have into account the relations that can exist between the analyzed properties. This section describes how to adapt some clustering techniques to make profit of the hierarchical structure of the thesaurus concepts used to fill the keyword section of metadata records. Specifically, this idea has been applied to improve the results obtained by classic hard and fuzzy clustering approaches:

Clustering keywords selected from thesauri: The keywords of the metadata records are transformed into numerical codes that maintain the hierarchical relations between thesaurus terms. These numerical codes are then grouped by means of clustering techniques.

Clustering keywords as free text: Hard and fuzzy clustering techniques are directly applied over the text found in the keywords section. Previously to the clustering, some keyword expansion techniques are used to improve the results.

6.4.3.1 Selection of algorithms for hard and fuzzy clustering

As mentioned in Steinbach et al. [179], there are several techniques of hard clustering. From them, the *K-means* family of algorithms [44, 108] has been selected for the test with hard clustering algorithms. It has been selected by its simplicity, its general use in other areas of knowledge to find patterns in collections of data, the availability of numerous tools to perform it. The *K-means* algorithm is based on the partitions of N records into K disjoint subsets S_j (being $j \in 1..K$) that minimize the sum of the distances of each record to the center of its cluster. The mathematical function used to measure this distance varies depending on the *K-means* implementation (e.g., correlation functions, Spearman rank, Kendall's Tau...). The function that has been used here for the experiments is the Euclidean distance, which is one of the most frequently applied.

The implementation of *K-means* used in the testing (section 6.4.4) is the proposed in equation 6.3. The objective of this equation is to minimize the value of J, where x_n is a vector representing the n-th data record and v_j is the S_j centroid. v_j is calculated with formula 6.4, where N_j is the number of elements contained in S_j. The algorithm starts assigning randomly the records to the K clusters. Then, two steps are alternated until a stop criterion is met (number of iterations or stability of J). Firstly, the centroid is computed for each record. Secondly, every record is assigned to the cluster with the closest centroid according to the Euclidean distance.

$$J = \sum_{j=1}^{K} \sum_{n \in S_j} \left| x_n - v_j \right|^2 \qquad (6.3)$$

$$v_j = \frac{\sum\limits_{n \in S_j} x_n}{N_j} . \tag{6.4}$$

The main problem of this implementation is the need to select the number of clusters to create, because it is not able to automatically adjust the number of cluster returned. Other more advanced implementations use adaptive techniques. For instance, ISODATA algorithm [14] creates or joins clusters when needed, returning a number of clusters adjusted to the collection distribution. Another improvement of the proposed techniques would be to use clustering algorithms requiring no previous knowledge on the number of clusters (e.g., Extended Star [63]) to estimate the initial number of clusters before applying the approaches presented here.

With respect to the fuzzy clustering family, it includes techniques as fuzzy *C-means* (a fuzzy variant of *K-means*) or finite mixture models (Bernoulli, Gaussian or Polynomial). They assign a metadata record to each cluster with a probability value. Usually, the cluster that has the higher probability is considered as the cluster to which the record belongs, but in doubtful situations more than a cluster can be selected. That is, fuzzy clustering allows measuring to what extent a metadata record belongs to a cluster, distinguishing between the records that are clearly contained in a subgroup from those that may belong to several clusters. This distinction makes possible to sort the records of each subgroup by their degree of membership and to include a record in more than a cluster with different levels of relevance.

The fuzzy algorithm selected for the experiments has been the *C-means* algorithm proposed in Torra et al. [189]. It minimizes the distance of each record to every cluster centroid, adding the probability of the record to belong to each cluster. It minimizes the function in equation 6.5, where $A_j(x_n)$ stands for the probability of record n to be in the cluster j. Additionally, this algorithm takes into account the constraints in equation 6.6. The exponent m is a weighting parameter used to adjust the fuzziness of the clustering algorithm. As it can be seen, the function to minimize is similar to the one used in the *K-means* algorithm. The difference in this case is that the Euclidean distance of each record to a cluster center is multiplied by the probability of being in that cluster.

$$J = \sum_{j=1}^{K} \sum_{n \in S_j} (A_j(x_n))^m \left| x_n - v_j \right|^2 . \tag{6.5}$$

$$(A_j(x_i)) \in [0,1] , \; \sum_{j=1}^{K} A_j(x_i) = 1 \; for \; all \; j . \tag{6.6}$$

6.4.3.2 Thematic clustering using the thesaurus structure

To detect the main themes of the collection, this first approach encodes the keywords of the metadata records into numerical values that preserve the hierarchical relations among the thesaurus concepts. Then, these encodings are clustered. This process let us group metadata records that share similar thematic characteristics without losing the benefits provided by the hierarchical structure of the thesaurus used to fill the metadata records.

The goal here is to generate a numerical identifier for each concept of the thesaurus that describes the hierarchical relations of the concepts, i.e. its position in the thesaurus. This identifier is similar to the Dewey Decimal Classification System [161]. It consists of a set of numbers where each number indicates the position of the term in the thesaurus branch to which it belongs (a branch is a tree whose root is a top concept and contains all the descendants of this concept in the *broader/narrower* hierarchy). For example, as shown in figure 6.12, the identifier *"02 03 00"* indicates that the term *Geotechnology* is the third child of the second top term (*Earth Science*) of the thesaurus.

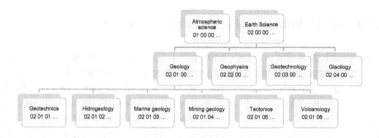

Fig. 6.12: Numerical encoding of concepts

The result of clustering using these identifiers is the detection of groups of records containing concepts that are close in the thesaurus structure. These clusters are then processed to obtain a reduced set of branches that concentrate most of the keywords used in the metadata records, i.e. its main themes. The approach consists of four sequential steps:

- As an initial step of this approach, the metadata collection is processed to extract a list of pairs $< keywordInRecord\_URI, keyword\_id >$. In these pairs, *keywordInRecord _URI* represents a string that consists of a record identifier and a keyword term found in a record with this identifier. The second element in the pair (*keyword_id*) is the numerical identifier of the term found in the record. This list of pairs has been used as input for the hard and fuzzy clustering algorithms.
- The second step is the application of the hard and fuzzy clustering algorithms. The result of hard clustering is a list of clusters indicating the set of *keyword InRecord_URIs* contained in each cluster. Fuzzy clustering returns a matrix where the rows represent the different *keywordInRecord_URIs* and the columns represent the identified clusters. Each row in the matrix contains the membership degree of *keywordInRecord_URI* to each cluster. A *keywordInRecord_URI* is assigned to the cluster with the highest probability.
- Obviously, the results obtained in the second step are not the final output, because each record may have been assigned to several clusters (as many clusters as the number of times it appears in a *keywordInRecord_URI*). Therefore, in order to

detect the most proper cluster for each record, the records are associated to the clusters where they appear more times.

- Finally, the fourth step determines the names of the clusters. The numerical codes representing the keywords in each cluster are processed back to obtain the terms behind them. Then, the common ancestors of the keywords are analyzed to select the cluster names. The name given to each cluster is the most specific common ancestor of the keywords in the records grouped in the same cluster. To make the name more representative, there is an exception in this rule when all the records in a cluster can be grouped under a maximum number of three sub-branches. In this case, the name of the cluster is the concatenation of the sub-branches names (e.g., "Product, Materials, Resource" cluster in section 6.4.4.3).

6.4.3.3 Thematic clustering using keywords as free text

The main problem in the previous approach is that it can only be used on metadata collections that contain terms from a single selected vocabulary. However, one can find metadata containing terms from a wide range of thesauri, or even keywords typed randomly by the users. In this context, it seems relevant to explore other alternatives with not so restrictive prerequisites that facilitate the thematic characterization of collections described with heterogeneous metadata. Therefore, a different approach that considers the keywords section as a free set of terms that do not belong necessarily to a selected vocabulary or thesaurus structure has been analyzed.

In this approach, the keywords of the metadata records are clustered using the vector space model. In this model, documents are encoded as N-dimensional vectors where N is the number of terms in the dictionary, and each vector component reflects the relevance of the corresponding term with respect to the semantics of each document in the collection [18]. This relevance is directly proportional to the number of occurrences of a keyword in a metadata record. Additionally, not only the terms that exist in the keywords section of the metadata records are included but also all the ancestors (*broader* terms) of those terms extracted from a thesaurus. That is to say, making profit of thesaurus structure, we expand the text found in keywords sections when the terms belong to selected thesauri.

Since metadata collections can be very heterogeneous, the output clusters can be seen as a set of different homogeneous sub-collections centered on very different themes. Thus, the naming of clusters may be quite problematic (the names of clusters should represent the theme of each cluster). The generation of the main theme of each sub-collection is done differently for hard and for fuzzy clustering approaches. When hard clustering is used, the name is composed of the most frequent keywords in the output cluster. With fuzzy clustering, the selected name contains the terms with the highest degree of cluster membership.

6.4.4 Browsing methods comparison

This section describes the set of experiments performed to test the viability of the process for the creation of a hierarchical topic map and a thematic classification of a metadata collection.

6.4.4.1 Description of the metadata corpus

As metadata corpus for experiments, the contents of the Geoscience Data Catalog at the U.S. Geological Survey[5] (USGS) were used. The USGS is the science agency for the U.S. Department of the Interior that provides information about Earth, its natural and living resources, natural hazards, and the environment. Despite being a national agency, it is also sought out by thousands of partners and customers around the world for its natural science expertise and its vast earth and biological data holdings. This metadata collection was processed as indicated in Nogueras-Iso et al. [156] until a collection of 753 metadata records compliant with CSDGM-FGDC [51] standard was obtained. The 626 keywords from GEMET thesaurus in the metadata collection have been the selected to be used in the experiment. The GEMET version used contains 5542 terms from which the metadata collection uses 104 different ones (about 1.9% of the thesaurus size).

6.4.4.2 Topic map extraction

The topic map creation process has been applied to the described corpus using GEMET as base for the creation of the topic map. The topic map generated contains 216 nodes (the 104 used in the collection plus 112 inner nodes), i.e. a 4% of GEMET size. This huge reduction of size provides a much more adjusted selection tool to locate a resource. To visualize the correctness of the generated topic map and to provide to the users a tool able to navigate by the topic map and to locate the associated information, we have selected the TMNAV tool created in the TM4J project[6]. This tool allows the visualization of topic maps stored in XTM format [163] providing a graphical visualization of the properties of the records and facilitating the browsing by the relations. The *Atmosphere (air, climate)* branch of the generated topic map is shown in Figure 6.13. The figure shows its relations with other terms of the topic map and the two metadata records of the collection that indirectly contain this term of the topic map (one of its children is contained in the metadata records of the collection). The example shown does not contain direct relations (metadata records that directly contain the term of the topic map), but they would have been also shown in the visual representation if they existed.

---

[5] http://geo-nsdi.er.usgs.gov/

[6] http://tm4j.org/

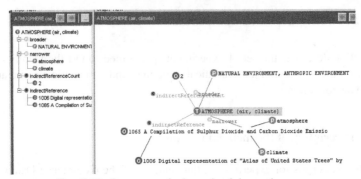

Fig. 6.13: Structure of a branch of the topic map

When the topic map is presented to the user in a graphical view, at first sight he can see how many results is going to obtain if he selects a term from the hierarchy (records that contain the selected keyword or one of its descendent). Then, the user can refine the selection navigating for the tree until he finds the most adequate term to query. This avoids him the execution of several queries that produce too many results or the selection of terms not used in the metadata records (queries produce zero results). Using the topic map as base, the main themes of the collection have been extracted. The algorithm for the selection of relevant nodes (shown in section 6.4.2) was applied to the topic map using as threshold the values of 0.05, 0.1 and 0.2. With these parameters, the thematic classifications of table 6.1 has been obtained.

Table 6.1 shows the keywords selected as main themes of the metadata collection given a threshold. From the terms selected during the generation process, only those that have no descendants in the extracted terms are marked as main keywords (in bold face); the rest of the terms in the figure are their hierarchical ancestors in the topic map. These results shows that the main themes of the metadata collection are *earth science* and *human activities and products, effects on the environment* terms, because they have been obtained with the highest threshold. It is also shown that the secondary themes are *geology* (child of *earth science*) and *natural gas*, both obtained if the clustering threshold is reduced to 0.1. The terms *coal*, *marine geology* and *natural environment, anthropic environment* are less relevant, because they have been obtained with the lowest threshold.

6.4.4.3 Application of clustering techniques

The different clustering techniques described in section 6.4.3 have been applied with the following results.

Threshold = 0.05	Threshold = 0.1	Threshold = 0.2
human activities and products, effects on the environment	human activities and products, effects on the environment chemistry	**human activities and products, effects on the environment**
chemistry, substances, processes	chemistry, substances, processes	——
products, materials	——	——
product	——	——
fuel	——	——
fossil fuel	——	——
coal	——	——
material	material	——
raw material	raw material	——
natural gas	**natural gas**	——
social aspects, environmental policy measures	social aspects, environmental policy measures	social aspects, environmental policy measures
research, sciences	research, sciences	research, sciences
science	science	science
natural science	natural science	natural science
earth science	earth science	**earth science**
geology	**geology**	——
marine geology	——	——
natural environment, anthropic environment	——	——

Table 6.1: Threshold effect for the extraction of representative nodes

Thematic clustering using the thesaurus structure

The process has been performed with both hard *K-means* and fuzzy *C-means* clustering techniques to discover the difference between using them.

The collection selected for the experiment contains keywords with terms picked up from the GEMET thesaurus. This thesaurus was processed to generate identifiers in the form described in section 6.4.3.2. Since none of the branches of this thesaurus has more than 99 terms as *narrower* of a concept, two digits were enough to encode each level of the thesaurus.

In the case of hard *K-means* algorithm, five clusters (K=5) were asked to obtaining the five branches of GEMET most used in the collection. However, the results obtained were disappointing because the algorithm did not converge (it produced clusters with heterogeneous keywords). The results obtained with fuzzy *C-means* algorithm were quite better since the clusters contained groups of records with similar keywords. The following clusters were obtained:

Hydrosphere, Land: 19 records about the following topics (including hierarchical path):

- Natural Environment, Anthropic Environment. Hydrosphere
- Natural Environment, Anthropic Environment. Land

Biosphere: 10 records about the following topic (including hierarchical path):

- Natural Environment, Atrophic Environment. Biosphere

Product, Materials, Resource: 211 records about the following topics (including hierarchical path):

- Human activities and products, effects on the environment. Products, Materials. Materials
- Human activities and products, effects on the environment. Products, Materials. Product
- Human activities and products, effects on the environment. Resource

Chemistry, Substances and processes: 39 records about the following topics (including hierarchical path):

- Human activities and products, effects on the environment. Chemistry, Substances and processes

Research Science: 291 records about the following topic (including hierarchical path):

- Social Aspects, Environmental, politics measures. Research Science

These results exhibit how the metadata records of the collection are related. The existence of upper level branches (the most generic) indicates disperse keywords in the metadata records, the existence of lower level branches (more specific) expose a high relation with a specific theme, and the lack of a branch of the thesaurus indicates that the metadata in the collection are not related to that theme.

Thematic clustering using keywords as free text

In the second approach of section 6.4.3, the keywords of the metadata are considered as free text keywords and expanded with the relations deduced from terminological ontologies. With this approach, similar results have been obtained from the use of hard and fuzzy clustering algorithms.

Keywords as free text and hard clustering

The keywords of the USGS metadata records were transformed into a $C(NxM)$ matrix where N is the number of metadata records to cluster, and M the set of keywords contained in the collection plus the terms added from the GEMET thesaurus. An element $C(i, j)$ of the matrix takes value 1 when the term j is contained in the metadata record i or j is an ancestor in GEMET hierarchy of a term in record i. Otherwise, $C(i, j)$ takes value 0. The *K-means* algorithm were applied to the matrix asking for five clusters ($K = 5$). Then, the clusters obtained were processed to generate a representative name (combination of the most frequent keywords, or the name of the thesaurus branch that contains them). The following results were obtained:

Natural gas, Geology, Earth Science: This cluster consists of 151 metadata records all of them containing the keywords *Natural gas*, *Geology* and *Earth Science*.

Coal: 116 of its 117 metadata records contain the *Coal* keyword, and the other has *Lignite*, a keyword related hierarchically with *Coal* (its father).

Geology: This third cluster contains 128 metadata records from which 92 contain *Geology* and 34 *Marine geology* (narrower term of *Geology*). The remaining two records contain keywords with terms related to *Geology*. One of them contains *Earth Science* (broader term of *Geology*) and the other one contains *Mineralogy* (sibling term of *Geology*, i.e. they share *Earth Science* as broader term).

Chemistry, substances and processes: This cluster contains 53 metadata records with keywords from the *Chemistry, substances, and processes* branch of GEMET.

Parameter & Others: This cluster of 32 metadata records is heterogeneous. It contains 14 metadata records from the *Parameter* branch of GEMET. However, the other 18 metadata records have no relation with them or among them.

Using the result obtained, the generated classification from the whole collection of metadata would be *Geology* (contained in 151+92 records), *Natural gas*, *Earth Science*, *Coal* and *Chemistry, substances and processes*. Each one being less relevant than the previous one (it appears fewer times). The obtained results also show that inside the set of metadata records about *Geology* an important part of them is more specialized (they are also about *Natural gas* and *Earth Science*)

The expansion through the GEMET hierarchy in conjunction with clustering techniques allows detecting semantic aggregations not directly visible. For example, the cluster *Chemistry, substances, processes* is not detected when no hierarchy relations are considered. In addition, this technique also separates in different clusters records not sharing enough keywords. An example of this occurs in the *Geology* cluster. There are records that contain the terms *Geology* or *Earth Science*, also present in the *Natural gas* cluster, but do not contain the *Natural gas* term. This has produce that the clustering algorithm assigned to a different cluster to each of these groups. This can cause confusion when accessing the information, since two subsets are said to be about the same matter (*Geology*). When this happens, the solution adopted is to include all the elements of the more specific cluster inside the most general one. That is, considering the *Natural gas, Geology, Earth Science* as a subset of the *Geology* cluster.

Another problem found in the obtained results is that the *K-means* algorithm assigns very heterogeneous records to the smallest cluster (in the example, the *Parameter* cluster), because they cannot be classified in the rest of clusters. The result is that the smallest cluster is quite useless. Therefore, the name obtained for the *Parameter* cluster is not adequate as it contains many heterogeneous elements. In order to remark this heterogeneity, the generic term *Others* has been added to the cluster name.

Keywords as free text and fuzzy clustering

The same $C(NxM)$ matrix generated for the previous example was used with the fuzzy *C-means* algorithm. Initially, asking for five clusters ($K=5$) with $m=2$. However, due to the low degree of cluster membership of the records in two of the clusters, the experiment was redone with $K = 4$. In the results obtained, these two clusters were joined producing a new cluster whose main keyword was *parameter* with a probability of 0.5. There were no changes in the other clusters. The following results were obtained; they include the cluster name and the number of records that have been assigned to each cluster:

Natural gas, Earth Science (151 records)   : The occurrences of *Natural gas* and *Earth science* keywords are contained in metadata records near the cluster center, with a mean probability of being in the cluster of 0.99, *Geology* is the following with a probability of 0.64.

Coal (117 records)   : The occurrences of *coal* keyword are contained in metadata records near the cluster center, with a mean probability of being in the cluster of 0.8.

Marine geology (128 records)   : The occurrences of *marine geology* are contained in metadata records near the cluster center, with a mean probability of being in the cluster of 0.75.

Others (85 records)   : It contains the set of records that it has not been possible to assign to the other clusters because of their low probability of belonging to them.

In order to generate the name of each cluster (its main themes), the concept names contained in the records with the highest cluster membership were selected. Depending on the requirements of the systems, concepts in records with a lower degree could be also included (e.g., *Geology* in the first cluster). In this situation, the membership degree could be displayed to indicate that not all the categories represent the collection in the same way.

6.4.4.4 Comparison of results

The results obtained in each experiment are quite different. Figure 6.14 displays an skeleton of the GEMET hierarchy and how the collection classifications obtained by each approach are distributed.

The results obtained with the topic map approach using the process described in section 6.4.2 are quite similar to the obtained using the different clustering techniques. The difference lies on the way the keywords are aggregated. The topic map approach shows the keywords that are frequently used in the collection. Clustering techniques also show how the keywords are distributed and aggregated in the metadata collection (see figure 6.14). That is, clustering techniques provide a more detailed description of the thematic structure of the collection.

Regarding the first clustering approach (using the thesaurus structure), it has been shown that hard clustering does not work, and that fuzzy clustering produces very general results. Additionally, it only works correctly if the keyword section has been created with terms of a single thesaurus. But, since metadata usually contain terms from a wide range of thesauri, or even keywords randomly typed by the users, the second clustering approach is more flexible.

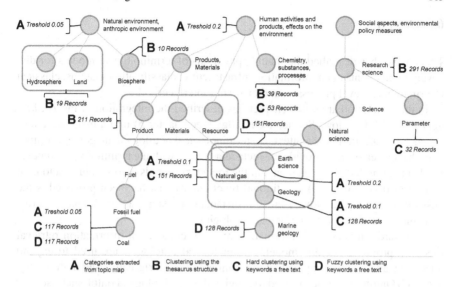

Fig. 6.14: Clusters generated with the different approaches proposed

In the second clustering approach (using keywords as free text), fuzzy clustering produces more specific results than hard clustering. This second approach expands the keywords contained in the metadata (to improve the results) using the thesauri used as source. Nevertheless, it also works properly with several thesauri or even with keywords not contained in a controlled vocabulary.

In general, hard clustering has the advantage of being more simple, but fuzzy clustering enables the identification of records with doubtful allocation (they have similar probability for two or more clusters). This is a clear advantage of fuzzy with respect to hard clustering. Fuzzy clustering detects a cluster not only on the basis of the number of times a keyword appears in a metadata record, but also taking into account that a keyword can be found in other clusters. An example of this is the treatment of the *Geology* concept in the second approach. When hard clustering is applied, *Geology* was as important for the cluster theme as the rest of the main keywords. However, with fuzzy clustering it is shown that the records containing *Geology* are less centered in the cluster than the other ones.

As summary, it can be said that each approach provides a vision of the collection from a different perspective: ranging from the more general vision of the first approach to the more specific vision of the last experiment. Therefore, the selection of the technique to use to obtain a classification is quite dependent of the needs of the application the context where it is going to be used.

6.5 Summary

This chapter has described the main applications of terminological models for discovery components of an information infrastructure: classification systems, classical information retrieval processes, and browsing interfaces.

In the annotation area, this chapter has described the integration of the *ThManager* and Web Ontology Service technology (see chapter 5) into a metadata editor called *CatMDEdit*. In this context, the terminological ontology management components have been used to provide the metadata creator with the terminological models needed to complete those elements in the metadata records whose values belong to a controlled vocabulary. An additional functionality that has been proposed is the possibility to validate already created metadata and suggest for alternative terms contained in different terminological ontologies.

As regards the classical information retrieval context, an information retrieval model is proposed. In this model, terminological ontologies are used to expand queries by adding terms equivalent in meaning to those originally used in the query. The Web Ontology Service is used to provide the terminological ontologies used for term selection in the query construction interface, and for expansion of the query terms. Two different methods are proposed: first, a system where the expansion is based on the use of alternative concepts and translation to different languages; and second, a system more elaborated in which the queries are expanded with equivalent terms from other terminological ontologies. To relate the different terminological models, mappings are defined in the way indicated in section 2.4.1. Here, it is important to remark that the terms obtained by the use of mapping between ontologies should not have the same relevance that the original ones typed by the user in the query context. They are derived information extracted from mappings that usually are not perfect. Here, the concepts obtained are weighted according to the mapping reliability to provide results sorted by relevance. The results obtained show that the provided term expansion systems increase the recall of the user queries.

The last use of terminological ontologies described is related to browsing information. This chapter has described a process to generate a topic map from a collection of geographic metadata records and a set of methods to obtain a thematic classification of the metadata collection.

With respect to the method to obtain a topic map, the method proposed assumes that the terms used in the keywords section have been selected from a well established thesaurus, and the aim of the method is to extract a hierarchical topic map that reduces significantly the size of the original thesaurus. Additionally, the method proposed also suggests a formula to obtain from the topic map a more reduced set of representative nodes (a 1-dimensional cluster), which summarizes the main themes of the collection at a first glance. Overall, it can be highlighted that the proposed topic maps facilitate enormously selection of the terms in a query system and that the generated themes (the reduced set of representative nodes) give a synthesized and accurate summary of the contents of the metadata collection. A preliminary version of the process described here is shown in Lacasta et al. [119].

Following the line of obtaining a reduced set of representative categories for a collection in situations where a reduced set of categories is required and the topic map size is excessive, some techniques to automatically generate a classification of a collection of metadata records using the elements of their keywords section have been proposed. These techniques are based on hard (*K-means*) and fuzzy (*C-means*) clustering techniques and they have into account the hierarchical structure of the concepts contained in the terminological ontologies used to select these keywords. Lacasta et al. [118] shows a resume of this process.

Two different approaches have been analyzed. In the first approach, the keywords in the metadata records picked up from a single thesaurus have been encoded as a numerical value that maintains the inner structure of the thesaurus. Then, this encoding has been used as the property for the definition of the thematic clusters. In the second approach, all the keywords in the metadata collection have been considered as free text. Additionally, in order to improve the results, when it has been recognized that a term belongs to a terminological ontology, the terms in the hierarchy of ancestors have been added to the set of keywords. Then, these sets of expanded keywords have been clustered using hard and fuzzy clustering techniques.

The generation of a model adjusted to a metadata collection provides several benefits. These benefits can be grouped in the following categories:

- Facilitate the browsing. Ontologies provide a different way to navigate for the data in the collection. The concepts can directly have the list of metadata records that use a term, avoiding free text or even controlled queries that can easily produce empty result sets.

- Contribute to the improvement of distributed catalog strategies. The metadata keywords section of most metadata standards indicates the theme of the data provided by the service. Those keywords can be used by a distributed catalog to reduce the response time of the query and the network overhead by redirecting user queries only to the local catalogs with the appropriate themes. These metadata can be created manually by analyzing the metadata collection with visual data mining tools but they have to be updated each time there is change in the collection. In this situation, it is better to use an automatic approach (such as the described in this chapter) to generate the collection classification.

- Facilitate the construction of queries. In a metadata creation process it is usual to provide terminological ontologies in the form of controlled lists or thesauri to facilitate the creation of metadata records and to use the same structures in search systems to facilitate the location of resources. Providing directly to the user the thesauri used to create the keywords section of the metadata records sometimes is not useful because of the number and size of the used thesauri. Here, the use of a topic map from the metadata collection facilitates the user the location of the desired information (it avoids the construction of queries that produce zero results).

- Metadata quality evaluation. The identification of the main themes of a collection can be used to analyze if the thesaurus used in the metadata collection is the most adequate. For example, if almost all the keywords of the collection are in the hydrology path of UNESCO thesaurus, a thesaurus specialized in hydrology should have been used to allow the selection of more specialized keywords in the metadata records, and to provide to the user a more detailed description of the data.

It is important to note that the work described along this chapter does not stay in a simple declaration of intentions. To test their applicability, the systems, tools, and techniques have been integrated in the following real information projects:

- The Spanish SDI project[7]. It has as objective the integration of the geographical data, metadata, and services that are produced in Spain.
- SDIGER project[8]. SDIGER is a pilot project on the implementation of the Infrastructure for Spatial Information in Europe (INSPIRE) to support access to geographic information resources concerned with the European Water Framework Directive [208, chap. 6], [125].
- SDI-EBRO prototype[9]. This project aims to publish the geographical data produced by the Ebro River Basin District. In this project, catalog and gazetteer search interfaces provide terminological ontology selectors according to different criteria such as thematic or organizational.

---

[7] http://www.idee.es/

[8] http://sdiger.unizar.es/

[9] http://ide-ebro.chebro.es/

Chapter 7
Concluding remarks and outlook

In any information infrastructure, the information retrieval components have a special relevance because they are the components that provide the first point of access to the contents. Improving these components involves an improvement in the entire infrastructure environment, making the resource holdings easier to find and access.

Ontologies are knowledge organization systems often used within the information retrieval context to improve the performance of systems. Terminological ontologies are the models most frequently used for classification and information retrieval. Thanks to their extensive use in digital and traditional libraries, these resources cover almost every area of interest.

However, existent terminological models are scarcely reused across different communities. Each organization has its own systems to interpret, use, and represent them, generating an heterogeneity that hinders their reuse. Ontologies are used to solve specific problems for different components without providing an integrated framework of ontology management.

Within this book, we have faced the problem of defining a common representation framework for terminological ontologies, together with a set of methods, architectural patterns, and guidelines for the development of accompanying artifacts that facilitate their creation, management, and access. In particular it has addressed the following issues:

- Homogeneous representation of terminological ontologies: The ontologies used by different components of an information infrastructure have to be managed in a harmonized way, using the same model and format. Due to the applicability to a wide range of application domains, there is a great variety of terminological ontologies with very different levels of specificity, language coverage, formalization, or size. Additionally, the need to relate different terminological models to improve semantic interoperability has created the additional need to analyze how to represent the defined mappings properly.
- Creation and reuse of terminological ontologies: Information retrieval systems need different terminological models depending on their purpose and required functionality. If the required terminological models exist but they are not rep-

resented in the desired format, they must be transformed and customized to the user requirements. However, if none suitable exists, a new terminological ontology must be built reusing, if possible, existent knowledge resources.

- Management and access to terminological ontologies: An information retrieval system must rely on an efficient and robust ontology management service to filter and select the most appropriate ontology for each specific context. It must consider many different types of terminologies for discovery, visualization, and access; each one with their own specific characteristics. In this context, a unified management system is required to simplify the access and control of the terminologies used along the infrastructure.

- Applicability of terminological ontologies to information retrieval systems: Last, this book has addressed the integration of terminological models in information retrieval components related to search and presentation of information (catalog services, user applications, structure of content repositories and data/service catalogs) with the objective of simplifying classification of resources and improving information retrieval. Three main areas where the terminological ontologies have applicability have been reviewed: classification, discovery, and browsing of resources.

Following this division of main issues in four categories, the rest of the chapter points out the concluding ideas and areas for future work that have been identified.

A representation framework for terminological ontologies

In order to provide a simple and harmonized integration of terminological models in an information retrieval system, a common representation framework has been proposed. The identification of the most suitable representation model and interchange format required the study of different existent ontology models described in the literature, analyzing their characteristics and structure to find the common elements that the different models share. The need to establish the context in which the terminological models fit created the need to review all the main types of ontologies and not only the terminological ones. It has been found that although each otology type has usually associated a set of representation formats used to store and interchange the models, it is also very usual to have many different ad-hoc formats created for organizations to represent their models. As result of the analysis, the SKOS format [141] has been identified as the most suitable format for the representation of terminological models. SKOS has a broad coverage and it is simple to define extensions to adapt it to specific user requirements. In addition, as it is shown by Lacasta et al. [117], the SKOS format is very suitable for their integration in the discovery components of an information infrastructure, and it starting to be used for organizations and companies that publish relevant terminological models.

Additionally, the proposed representation framework also provides support for representing mappings between terminological ontologies. Nowadays, there is a need to relate the ontology models of the information infrastructures to improve their functionality. It has been required to integrate different terminological models.

The objective is to facilitate a bridge between the terminology used in one system and the terminology used in other systems. Additionally, it may also help to perform transformations between data models using different terminologies, a scenario that has been found to be quite common. The use of many different vocabularies to classify information by different content creators has created the need of relating them to provide a single access point to different data collections, which use not only ontologies with different degree of formalism but also different versions of the same ontology. The representation for mappings proposed in the framework has the following characteristics:

- It is based on the thesauri model, the mapping nomenclature and definitions described in the BS-8723 [27] standard. The structure of relations allows defining *exact*, *partial* and *inexact* equivalences. With respect to composite relationships the *intersection*, *union*, and *difference* have been the selected. Additionally, the model is open to facilitate the addition of new relationships if required.
- The representation format is RDF based in the same way as SKOS mapping one, but the structure of mappings relations is adapted to the nomenclature of concepts and relationships used in the BS-8723 standard, and the number of tags required to define the relationships is reduced.

Ontology learning for terminological ontologies

The integration of many terminological models in one system has required the use of the selected representation formats (SKOS) for all of them. This has simplified the management and it has made the input of the processes working with the ontologies homogeneous. However, because of the heterogeneity of models and sources, it has been shown that this is not a straightforward process. In this context, different ontology learning alternatives are proposed to generate terminological models from sources such as data corpora, dictionaries, schemata, or other knowledge models.

In particular, two use cases have been studied: one describing a process to being able to adapt existent models to the desired use; and another one focusing in the creation of a new model through the merging of pre-existent thesauri.

In the first case of study, we faced the problem of adapting existing terminological ontologies available with different electronic formats. It is common to find that although terminological ontologies are available for a specific project or study, the format of transfer files does not conform to a recognized standard and must be converted into a SKOS-compliant version.

With respect to the transformation of terminological models to SKOS, given that information translation processes are usually ad-hoc processes, a translation generation process has been defined to simplify the creation of a new translation software for each scenario. The process includes the steps to follow and a series of general techniques to apply. The purpose behind the definition of this process is to reuse as much as possible the pieces of software that must be applied for each transformation. Additionally, since the destination format is always SKOS, an architectural pattern providing the common elements in all the translation processes has been created to facilitate the construction of new translation tools. Some conclusions have been extracted from this process:

- Transformation approaches described in the literature lack an homogeneous description of the source, destination models and formalism in the specification of the definition of relationships between the two models. This issue has been solved by defining a representation model to store the structure of the models and the relations between them.
- Part of the software created for previous translation processes can be reused. In this context, following the defined architectural pattern, to create the software for a new translation it is only needed to define a new reader for the source format and a set of translation functions to perform the transformation between the models.
- Errors in source formats are common and have to be properly managed. Therefore, it is needed a validation step to verify that the generated model is correct according to the structure that is supposed to follow.
- The generated process is reusable and applicable to a very different set of terminological models. Around 70 different terminological models have been translated to SKOS using it. Most of them have been simple controlled vocabularies used for classification purposes such as the international codes for languages defined in ISO-639 [82] or the controlled lists contained in ISO-19115 [84], but the process has been also applied to some more complex models such as AGROVOC, EUROVOC, GEMET, and UNESCO thesauri or the Spanish and French Administrative Units Model.

In cases where the required terminological model does not exist and has to be created, a method to build a new ontology has been proposed. It uses as input the knowledge found in other ontologies partially focused on the required theme. The generated model cannot be directly used, but it provides a knowledge core that can be refined to obtain the desired model.

The process is based on the merging of concepts from different thesauri. It uses a glossary of concepts desired in the target model as core and it prunes those concepts from the selected thesauri that are not related to them. The domain ontology obtained has several advantages in comparison with the thesauri used as source and the thesaurus used for filtering in the following areas:

- Consensus and focus: The concepts of the output network have been selected by consensus thanks to the mappings among the different sources, removing those concepts that are neither common nor focused on the desired thematic.
- Relations: With respect to the relation structure, the total number of available relations is bigger than the existent ones in each of the original sources. Besides, each relation has a weight that indicates its relevance.
- Multilingual support: Thanks to the combination of different sources of knowledge with multilingual support, the output network is enriched with alternative terminology in different languages.

Partial versions of this approach have been applied for the generation of thesauri in the urban domain [121], the hydrology domain [124] (as part of an information retrieval system), and some initial experiments in the formalization of terminological ontologies [152, chap. 11].

As future work, the merging methodology could be improved with the aim of obtaining better results. A possible research line could be the use of *grandparent* and *grandchildren* relations between the concepts in the input thesauri in order to define the relations between concept clusters (the generated output concepts) with a higher precision.

Formalization of terminological ontologies

In the same way as terminological ontologies can be created using other ones, this book has analyzed the feasibility of using terminological models to construct formal ones. The proposed method focuses on deriving *is-a* relationships from the *broader/narrower* relationships of thesauri. The objective is to find how much the original model structure directly fit into a formal model.

This prototype has been tested with a set of thematic thesauri (see section 1.3.4), and other thesauri generated in the previous merging. The results obtained have shown that the complexity of the formalization depends greatly on the structure of each processed model. For instance, it is much easier to formalize the EUROVOC thesaurus than the UNESCO thesaurus because it has a much higher percentage of *is-a* relations. With respect to the formalization of thesauri obtained as a result of the merging method, the results show clearly that the most common relations (those that are contained in a higher number of source models) have a much higher chance to be an *is-a* relationship. Additionally, the obtained results can be used as a measure of the structural quality of each thesaurus. They can be used as an additional factor in the decision of the thesaurus to select for each purpose.

Finally, it must be noted that the identification of semantics behind underspecified *broader/narrower* and *related* relations is still an open research line. A possible to way for improving the refinement of their semantics would lie in exploiting the text found in the definitions, examples, and naming patterns of the properties in the original concepts. The analysis of this text would help, for example, to identify whether *broader* relations can be refined as *part of*, *instance of* or *generalization* relations.

Access to terminological ontologies

The uniform use of terminological models has required the definition of a suitable management system for these models where their status and the relations with other models can be managed.

In order to facilitate the access to terminological models to other information components, the architecture of a ontology web service has been provided. The description of the ontologies using metadata facilitates their thematic location and access through search services. This architecture acts as an ground layer to construct on top of it the required management components:

- So as to fill the repository and have control of the life cycle of the stored terminological ontologies, a tool called *ThManager* has been designed. *ThManager* provides the functionality to create, describe, update, and delete terminological ontologies stored in a repository and it is distributed as open source software. Partial versions of the design of *ThManager* have been published in [151] and [117].
- In order to provide access to the ontologies contained in the repository, to the components requiring, it a centralized web service called *Web Ontology Service* (WOS) has been created. It has been designed as a centralized service where to facilitate access two different interfaces are provided: one for general access and the other one compliant with the OGC Web Services Architecture specification. The final version of the WOS is based on the work developed in different previous research works [116, 115].

Additionally, from the analysis and development of the described management components the following results have been obtained:

- The performance of the management system is suitable for the required purpose. This performance has been proved through a series of experiments on the management of a selected set of thesauri. The efficiency of the proposed storage model has been compared with respect to other models that load the terminological ontologies directly from a RDF file. In particular, the time spent for the graphical loading decreases, easing the browsing of the contents, as well as other typical operations like sorting or change of visualization language.
- The layered architecture of all the defined elements simplifies the integration of the developed components in other applications that need to use thesauri or other types of controlled vocabularies. For example, some *ThManager* components have been integrated within the Open Source *CatMDEdit* tool [210], a metadata editor tool for the annotation of resources, with special focus on the description of geographic information resources.

A future extension of these management and access components should be the support for formal ontologies. As it has been already explained, formal ontologies have an important number of possible applications in information infrastructures such as the definition of data models or metadata schemas. To integrate them, it is needed to expand the proposed framework to take into account the use and management of formal models, analyzing where their use can provide a significant improvement of functionality. For example, SKOS could continue being the format used for terminological models, but for formal models OWL could be selected. This would not imply a complete redesign of the components architecture because SKOS is already based on both RDF and OWL.

Applicability of terminological ontologies to information retrieval

All the previous described elements were developed with the final objective of simplifying the integration of terminological models for information discovery and access. Three areas have been analyzed: annotation, search, and browsing.

Within the annotation area, the integration of *ThManager* and the *Web Ontology Service* technology into a metadata editor called *CatMDEdit* has been studied. The integration of *ThManager* management technology for terminological ontologies provides the metadata creator with the terminological models he needs to complete those elements in the metadata records whose values belong to controlled vocabularies. Additionally, it makes possible to validate already created metadata and suggest alternative terms contained in the stored terminological ontologies.

With respect to the classical information retrieval context, an information retrieval model is proposed to integrate the management of terminological model through the WOS. The WOS is used to provide the terminological ontologies used for term selection and the query construction interface. It has been used to provide terminological ontologies of catalog search systems guided by controlled vocabularies such as the search interfaces of IDEE (Spanish spatial data infrastructure), SDIGER [116], and IDE-Ebro (spatial data infrastructure of the Ebro river basin district). Additionally, the terminological ontologies are used to expand queries by adding terms equivalent in meaning to those originally used in the query. The WOS provides the required terminology and relations between models required for the defined expansion processes. The expansion is based on the use of alternative concepts and translation to different languages and it has been extended to match the query terms with respect to different terminological ontologies (functionality provided by the WOS) to obtain additional elements to expand the query.

The last use of terminological ontologies is related to browsing information. It is described how to extract a topic map from a collection of geographic metadata records. The method proposed assumes that the terms used in the keywords section have been selected from a well established thesaurus, and the aim of the method is to extract a hierarchical topic map that reduces significantly the size of the original thesaurus. Additionally, the method proposed also suggests a formula to obtain an even more reduced set of representative nodes (a 1-dimensional cluster), which summarizes the main themes of the collection at a first glance. A preliminary version of these processes has been published in [119].

Following the line of obtaining a reduced set of representative categories for a collection, some techniques to automatically generate a classification of a collection of metadata records using the elements of their keywords section have been proposed. Lacasta et al. [118] shows a summary of the process described here. These techniques have been based on hard (*K-means*) and fuzzy (*C-means*) clustering and have into account the hierarchical structure of the concepts contained in the terminological ontologies used to select these keywords. A first approach has encoded each thesaurus concepts as a numerical value that maintains the inner structure of the thesaurus. Then, this encoding has been used as the property for the definition of the thematic clusters. This approach has shown as deficiencies the limitation of the concepts to be into a single terminological model and the impossibility to process keywords not contained in this model. In order to solve this issues, a second approach that considers the keywords in the metadata collection as free text has been proposed. This approach uses the hierarchical *broader/narrower* relationships of the thesauri used for classification to add the terms in the hierarchy of ancestors to the set of keywords.

The generated topic map has proven to be applicable to facilitate the selection of the terms in a query system because it provides a synthesized and accurate summary of the contents of the metadata collection. With respect to the classifications obtained, they can be used to create metadata identifying the collection content, or as part of a general browsing interface that show the collection content according to its main topics.

References

[1] Agirre, E. and Rigau, G. (1996). Word Sense Disambiguation using Conceptual Density. In *Proceedings of the 16th International Conference on Computational Linguistics (Coling'96)*, pages 16–22, Copenhagen, Denmark.

[2] Ahmed, K. (2000). Topic maps for repositories. In *XML Europe*, Paris, France.

[3] Alani, H., Jones, C., and Tudhope, D. (2000). Associative and Spatial Relationships in Thesaurus-based Retrieval. *Lecture Notes in Computer Science. Research and Advanced Technology for Digital Libraries: 4th European Conference, ECDL.*, 1923/2000:45–55.

[4] Albertoni, R., Bertone, A., Demšar, U., Martino, M. D., and Hauska, H. (2003). Knowledge Extraction by Visual Data Mining of Metadata in Site Planning. In *Proceedings of the 9th Scandinavian Research Conference on Geographic Information Science, ScanGIS2003*, pages 119–130, Espoo, Finland.

[5] Aleksovski, Z., Klein, M., ten Kate1, W., and van Harmelen, F. (2006). Matching unstructured vocabularies using a background ontology. *Lecture Notes in Computer Science*, 4248:182–197.

[6] Alfons, J. (2005). Reconeixement de Formes. Technical report, Universidad Politecnica de Valencia.

[7] Amann, B., Fundulaki, I., and Scholl, M. (2000). Integrating ontologies and thesauri for RDF schema creation and metadata querying. *International Journal on Digital Libraries*, 3(3):221–236.

[8] ANSI/NISO (2003). Information Retrieval: Application Service Definition and Protocol Specification. Final draft for review Z39.50, Z39.50 Maintenance Agency. American National Standards Institute (ANSI). http://lcweb.loc.gov/z3950/agency/profiles/collections.html.

[9] ANSI/NISO (2005). Guidelines for the Construction, Format, and Management of Monolingual Thesauri. ANSI/NISO Z39.19-2005, American National Standards Institute (ANSI). Revision of Z39.19-1983.

[10] Antoniou, G. and van Harmelen, F. (2004). *A Semantic Web Primer*, chapter Ontology engineering, pages 205–222. Massachusetts Institute of Technology.

[11] Astrova, I. (2004). Reverse engineering of relational databases to ontologies. In *Proceedings of the 1st European Semantic Web Symposium (ESWS)*,, volume 3053 of *LNCS*, page 327341.

[12] Astrova, I. and Stantic, B. (2005). An html-form-driven approach to reverse engineering of relational databases to ontologies. In *Databases and Applications*, pages 246–251.

[13] Baeza-Yates, R. and Ribeiro-Neto, B. (1999). *Modern Information Retrieval*. New York. ACM Press, Addison Wesley.

[14] Ball, G. and Hall, D. (1965). ISODATA, A novel method of data analysis and pattern classification. NTIS AD699616, Standford Research Institute, Standford, California.

[15] Batschi, W.-D., Felluga, B., Legat, R., Plini, P., Stallbaumer, H., and Zirm, K. L. (2002). SuperThes: A New Software for Construction, Maintenance and Visualisation of Multilingual Thesauri. In *Proceedings of the Environmental Communication in the Information Society*, Vienna.

[16] Bechhofer, S., van Harmelen, F., Hendler, J., Horrocks, I., McGuinness, D. L., Patel-Schneider, P. F., and Stein, L. A. (2004).   *OWL Web Ontology Language Reference*.   W3C, W3C Recommendation 10 February 2004. http://www.w3.org/TR/2004/REC-owl-ref-20040210/.

[17] Bermudez, L. and Piasecki, M. (2006). Metadata Community Profiles for the Semantic Web. *Geoinformatica*, 10:159–176.

[18] Berry, M., Drmac, Z., and Jessup, E. (1999). Matrices, Vector Spaces, and Information Retrieval. *SIAM Review*, 41:335362.

[19] Binding, C. and Tudhope, D. (2004). KOS at your Service: Programmatic Access to Knowledge Organisation Systems. *Journal of Digital Information*, 4 Issue 4. 26 pages.

[20] Borgida, A., Brachman, R. J., McGuinness, D. L., and Resnick, L. A. (1989). CLASSIC: A Structural Data Model for Objects. In *Proceeedings of the 1989 ACM SIGMOD International Conference on Management of Data*, pages 59–67.

[21] Borgo, S. (2007). *Ontologies for Urban Development*, volume 61 of *Studies in Computational Intelligence*, chapter How Formal Ontology can help Civil Engineers, pages 37–45. Springer Berlin / Heidelberg.

[22] Boulos, M. N. K., Roudsari, A. V., and Carson, E. R. (2001). Towards a Semantic Medical Web: HealthCyberMaps Dublin Core Ontology in Protégé-2000. In *Fifth International Protégé Workshop*, SCHIN, Newcastle, UK.

[23] Bouquet, P., Serafini, L., Zanobini, S., and Sceffer, S. (2006). Bootstrapping semantics on the web: meaning elicitation from schemas. In *Proceedings of the 15th international conference on World Wide Web table of contents*, pages 505 – 512, Edinburgh, Scotland.

[24] Brachman, R. J. (1983). What IS-A Is and Isn't: An Analysis of Taxonomic Links in Semantic Networks. *Computer*, 16(10):30 – 36.

[25] British Standards Institute (1985). Guide to establishment and development of multilingual thesauri. BS 6723, British Standards Institute (BSI).

[26] British Standards Institute (1987). Guide to establishment and development of monolingual thesauri. BS 5723, British Standards Institute (BSI).

[27] British Standards Institute (2007). Structured vocabularies for information retrieval. Guide. BS 8723, British Standards Institute (BSI).

[28] Calvanese, D., Giacomo, G. D., and Lenzerini, M. (2001). A framework for ontology integration. In *Proceedings of the 1st Internationally Semantic Web Working Symposium (SWWS)*, Stanford, CA, USA.

[29] Chaudhri, V. K., Farquhar, A., Fikes, R., Karp, P. D., and Rice, J. P. (1998). Open Knowledge Base Connectivity 2.0. Technical Report KSL-98-06, Knowledge Systems Laboratory, Stanford, CA.

[30] Cimiano, P. (2006). *Ontology Learning and Population from Text. Algorithms, Evaluation and Applications*. Springer Science+Business Media, LLC, New York.

[31] Clark, P., Thompson, J., Holmback, H., and Duncan, L. (2000). Exploiting a thesaurus-based semantic net for knowledge-based search. In *Proc 12th Conf on Innovative Application of AI (AAAI/IAAI'00)*, pages 988–995.

[32] Cohen, W. W., Ravikumar, P., and Fienberg, S. E. (2003). A comparison of string metrics for matching names and records. In *Proceedings of the KKD Workshop on Data cleaning and Object Consolidation*, pages 73 – 78, Washington (DC US).

[33] Compatangelo, E. and Meisel, H. (2002). Intelligent support to knowledge sharing through the articulation of class schemas. In *Proceedings of the 6th International Conference on Knowledge-Based Intelligent Information & Engineering Systems*, Crema, Italy.

[34] Cross, P., Brickley, D., and Koch, T. (2001). RDF Thesaurus Specification. Technical Report 1011, Intitute for Learning and Research Technology.

[35] Cutting, D. R., Karger, D. R., Pedersen, J. O., and W.Tukey, J. (1992). Scatter/Gather: A Cluster-based Approach to Browsing Large Document Collections. In *Proceedings of the 15th annual international ACM SIGIR conference on Research and development in information retrieval*, pages 318–329, Copenhagen, Denmark.

[36] d'Aquin, M., Baldassarre, C., Gridinoc, L., Sabou, M., Angeletou, S., and Motta, E. (2007). Watson: Supporting next generation semantic web applications. In *Proceedings of the WWW/Internet conference*, Vila real, Spain.

[37] Davis, R., Shrobe, H., and Szolovits, P. (1993). What is a knowledge representation? *AI Magazine*, Spring:17 33.

[38] Demšar, U. (2004). A visualization of a Hierarchical Structure in Geographical metadata. In *Proceedings of the 7th AGILE Conference on Geographic Information Science*, pages 213–221. Heraklion, Greece.

[39] Denny, M. (2002). Ontology building: a Survey of Editing tools. *XML.com*, November:1–4. http://xml.com/pub/a/2002/11/06/ontologies.html.

[40] Dewey, M. (1876). *A Classification and Subject Index for Cataloguing and Arranging the Books and Pamphlets of a Library (Dewey Decimal Classification)*. Project Gutenberg Literary Archive Foundation.

[41] Ding, L., Finin, T., Joshi, A., Peng, Y., Cost, R. S., Sachs, J., Pan, R., Reddivari, P., and Doshi, V. (2004). Swoogle: A semantic web search and metadata

engine. In *Proceedings of the Thirteenth ACM Conference on Information and Knowledge Management*.

[42] Doan, A., Madhavan, J., Domingos, P., and Halevy, A. (2002). Learning to Map between Ontologies on the Semantic Web. In *The Eleventh International WWW Conference*, Hawaii, US.

[43] Doerr, M. (2001). Semantic Problems of Thesaurus Mapping. *Journal of Digital Information*, 1, Issue 8(52):1–25.

[44] Dubes, R. C. and Jain, A. K. (1988). *Algorithms for Clustering Data*. Prentice Hall.

[45] Ehrig, M. (2007). *Ontology Aligment: Bridging the Semantic Gap*. Semantic Web and Beyond: Computing for Human Experience. Springer, 1 edition.

[46] European Union Commission (1994). Report on Europe and the Global Information Society: Recommendations of the High-level Group on the Information Society to the Corfu European Council. EU Commission - COM Document Supplement No. 2/94, European Union Commission. Bangemann Report.

[47] Euzenat, J., Bach, T. L., Barrasa, J., Bouquet, P., Bo, J. D., Dieng, R., Ehrig, M., Hauswirth, M., Jarrar, M., Lara, R., Maynard, D., Napoli, A., Stamou, G., Stuckenschmidt, H., Shvaiko, P., Tessaris, S., Acker, S. V., and Zaihrayeu, I. (2004). State of the art on ontology alignment. Technical Report D2.2.3, Knowledge Web.

[48] Euzenat, J. and Shvaiko, P. (2007). *Ontology Matching*. Springer Berlin Heidelberg New York.

[49] Faro, S., Francesconi, E., and Sandrucci, V. (2007). Thesauri kos analysis and selected thesaurus mapping methodology on the project case-study. TENDER N 10118 - EUROVOC Studies LOT2 1.5, ITTIG-CNR Institute of Legal Information Theory and Techniques.

[50] Farquhar, A., Fikes, R., and Rice, J. (1996). The Ontolingua Server: A Tool for Collaborative Ontology Construction. Technical Report KSL 96-26, Stanford University, Knowledge Systems Laboratory.

[51] Federal Geographic Data Committee (FGDC) (1998). Content Standard for Digital Geospatial Metadata, version 2.0. Document FGDC-STD-001-1998, Metadata Ad Hoc Working Group.

[52] Fellbaum, C., editor (1998). *WordNet. An Electronic Lexical Database*. MIT Press.

[53] Fernández-Breis, J. T. and Martínez-Béjar, R. (2002). A cooperative framework for integrating ontologies. *International Journal of Human-Computer Studies*, 56(6):665–720.

[54] Fikes, R. and Kehler, T. (1985). The role of frame based representation in reasoning. *Communications of ACM*, 28(9):904–920.

[55] Fisher, D. H. (1987). Knowledge Acquisition Via Incremental Conceptual Clustering. *Machine Learning*, 2:139–172.

[56] Fisher, D. H. (1998). *Structures and relations in knowledge organization: proc. 5th Int. ISKO Conference*, chapter From thesauri towards ontologies?, pages 18–30. Number 18-30. Würzburg: Ergon, Lille (France).

[57] Foskett, D. J. (1997). *Readings in Information Retrieval*, chapter Thesaurus, pages 111–134. Morgan Kaufmann.

[58] Friedman-Hill, E. (2003). *Jess in Action: Rule-Based Systems in Java*. Manning Publication Co.

[59] Garshol, L. M. (2004). Metadata? Thesauri? Taxonomies? Topic Maps!. Making sense of it all. Technical report, Ontopia.

[60] Geller, J., Chun, S. A., and Jung, Y. (2008). Toward the Semantic Deep Web. *Computer*, 41(9):95–97.

[61] Genesereth, M. R. and Fikes, R. E. (1992). Knowledge Interchange Format, Version 3.0 Reference Manual. Technical Report Logic-92-1, Computer Science Department, Stanford University.

[62] Giarratano, J. and Riley, G. (1998). *Expert Systems: Principles and Programming*. PWS-Kent, Boston, MA., 3rd edition.

[63] Gil-García, R. J., Badía-Contelles, J. M., and Pons-Porrata, A. (2003). *Progress in Pattern Recognition, Speech and Image Analysis*, volume 2905 of *Lecture Notes in Computer Science*, chapter Extended Star Clustering Algorithm, pages 480–487. Springer.

[64] Giunchiglia, F. and Shvaiko, P. (2003). Semantic matching. *The Knowledge Engineering Review*, 18(3):265–280.

[65] Gómez-Pérez, A., Fernández-López, M., and Corcho, O. (2003). *Ontological Engineering*, chapter Methodologies and Methods for Building Ontologies. Springer-Verlag, London (United Kingdom).

[66] Gómez-Pérez, A. and Manzano-Macho, D. (2003). A survey of ontology learning methods and techniques. Deliberable 1.5, OntoWeb Consortium.

[67] Golbeck, J., Fragoso, G., Hartel, F., Hendler, J., Parsia, B., and Oberthaler, J. (2003). The national cancer institute's thesaurus and ontology. *Journal of Web Semantics*, 1(1):1–5.

[68] Gonzalo, J., Verdejo, F., Peters, C., and Calzolari, N. (1998). Applying EuroWordNet to Cross-Language Text Retrieval. *Computers and the Humanities*, Special Issue on EuroWord-Net(2-3):185 207.

[69] Gruber, T. (1993). A translation approach to portable ontology specifications. *ACM Knowledge Acquisition, Special issue: Current issues in knowledge modeling*, 5, Issue 2(KSL 92-71):199–220.

[70] Gruber, T. R. (1992). Ontolingua: A mechanism to support portable ontologies. Technical Report KSL-91-66, Stanford University, Knowledge Systems Laboratory,. Revision.

[71] Guarino, N. (1998). Formal Ontologies and Information Systems. In Amsterdam, I. P., editor, *Proceedings of FOIS'98*, pages 3–15, Trento, Italy.

[72] Guarino, N. and Boldrin, L. (1993). Ontological requirements for knowledge sharing. In *Paper presented at the IJCAI workshop for knowledge sharing and information interchange*, Chambery, France.

[73] Guarino, N., Masolo, C., and Vetere, G. (1999). OntoSeek: Content-Based Access to the Web. *IEEE Intelligent Systems*, 14(3):70–80.

[74] Heath, B., McArthur, D., and Vetter, R. (2005). Metadata lessons from the iLumina digital library. *Communications of the ACM*, 48(7):68–74.

[75] Heery, R., Johnston, P., Beckett, D., and Rogers, N. (2005). JISC metadata schema registry. In *5th ACM/IEEE-CS joint conference on Digital libraries*, page 381.

[76] Hepp, M. and de Bruijn, J. (2007). Gentax: A generic methodology for deriving owl and rdf-s ontologies from hierarchical classifications, thesauri, and inconsistent taxonomies. In *LNCS, Proceedings of the 4th European Semantic Web Conference (ESWC 2007)*, volume 4519, pages 129–144, Innsbruck, Austria. Springer.

[77] Hodge, G. (2000). *Systems of Knowledge Organization for Digital Libraries: Beyond Traditional Authority Files*. The Digital Library Federation, Washington DC.

[78] Horrocks, I. and Patel-Schneider, P. (2003). Foundations of the semantic web: Three theses of representation in the semantic web. *Proceedings of the Twelfth International World Wide Web Conference*, 1:39 – 47.

[79] International Council on Archives (2004). International Standard Archival Authority Record for Corporate Bodies, Persons and Families. Technical Report ISAAR (CPF), International Council on Archives (ICA).

[80] International Organization for Standardization (1985). Guidelines for the establishment and development of multilingual thesauri. ISO 5964, International Organization for Standardization (ISO).

[81] International Organization for Standardization (1986). Guidelines for the establishment and development of monolingual thesauri. ISO 2788, International Organization for Standardization (ISO).

[82] International Organization for Standardization (2002). Codes for the representation of names of languages. ISO 639, International Organization for Standardization (ISO). ISO/TC 37/SC 2.

[83] International Organization for Standardization (2003a). Computer applications in terminology - terminological markup framework. ISO/DIS 16642, International Organization for Standardization (ISO).

[84] International Organization for Standardization (2003b). Geographic information - Metadata. ISO 19115:2003, International Organization for Standardization (ISO).

[85] International Organization for Standardization (2003c). Information and documentation - The Dublin Core metadata element set. ISO 15836:2003, International Organization for Standardization (ISO).

[86] International Organization for Standardization (2003d). Information technology – SGML applications – Topic Maps. ISO/IEC 13250, International Organization for Standardization (ISO).

[87] International Organization for Standardization (2005). Geographic information - Services. ISO/DIS 19119, International Organization for Standardization (ISO), ISO/TC 211.

[88] International Organization for Standardization (2007a). Geographic information – Metadata – XML schema implementation. ISO/WD 19139, International Organization for Standardization (ISO), ISO/TC 211.

[89] International Organization for Standardization (2007b). Information technology – Common Logic (CL): a framework for a family of logic-based languages. Technical report, International Organization for Standardization (ISO).

[90] International Organization for Standardization (2008a). Language resource management lexical markup framework (lmf). ISO FDIS 24613, International Organization for Standardization (ISO).

[91] International Organization for Standardization (2008b). Terminology and other language and content resources computer applications in terminology termbase exchange format specification (tbx). ISO/DIS 30042.2, International Organization for Standardization (ISO).

[92] International Organization for Standardization (2010). Thesauri and Interoperability with other Vocabularies. Technical report, International Organization for Standardization (ISO).

[93] International Terminology Working Group (1996). Guidelines for Forming Language Equivalents: A Model Based on the Art&Architecture Thesaurus. Technical report, Getty Information Institute.

[94] Isaac, A. and Summers, E., editors (2009). *SKOS Simple Knowledge Organization System Primer.* W3C Candidate Recommendation. W3C. http://www.w3.org/TR/skos-primer/.

[95] Jain, A. K. and Dubes, R. C. (1988). *Algorithms for Clustering Data.* Prentice Hall.

[96] Janée, G. and Frew, J. (2002). The ADEPT digital library architecture. In *Proceedings of the second ACM/IEEE-CS joint conference on Digital libraries*, pages 342 – 350, Portland, Oregon, USA.

[97] Janée, G., Ikeda, S., and Hill, L. L. (2003). The ADL Thesaurus Protocol. Technical report, Alexandria Digital Library Project.

[98] Jannink, J. (1999). Thesaurus entry extraction from an on-line dictionary. In *Proceedings of Fusion '99*.

[99] Johannesson, P. (1994). A Method for Transforming Relational Schemas into Conceptual Schemas. In Rusinkiewicz, M., editor, *10th International Conference on Data Engineering*, pages 115 – 122, Houston. IEEE Press.

[100] Jones, C. B., Alani, H., and Tudhope, D. (2001). Geographical Information Retrieval with Ontologies of Place. *Lecture Notes in Computer Science*, 2205:322–335.

[101] Kalfoglou, Y. and Hu, B. (2005). CROSI Mapping System (CMS) Results of the 2005 Ontology Alignment Contest. In *Integrating Ontologies workshop at the 3rd International Conference on Knowledge Capture*, Banff, Canada.

[102] Kalfoglou, Y. and Schorlemmer, M. (2002). Information Flow based Ontology Mapping. In *1st International Conference on Ontologies, Databases and Application of Semantics (ODBASE'02)*, Irvine, CA, USA.

[103] Kalfoglou, Y. and Schorlemmer, M. (2003a). If-map: an ontology mapping method based on information flow theory. *Journal on Data Semantics*, 1:98127.

[104] Kalfoglou, Y. and Schorlemmer, M. (2003b). Ontology Mapping: The state of the art. *The Knowledge Engineering Review*, 18(1):1–31.

[105] Kalyanpur, A., Parsia, B., Sirin, E., Cuenca-Grau, B., and Hendler, J. (2005). Swoop: A 'Web' Ontology Editing Browser. *Web Semantics: Science, Services and Agents on the World Wide Web*, 4(2):144–153.

[106] Kang, S.-S. (2003). Keyword-based document clustering. In *Proceedings of the Sixth International Workshop on Information Retrieval with Asian Languages*, pages 132–137.

[107] Kashyap, V. (1999). Design and creation of ontologies for environmental information retrieval. In *12th Workshop on Knowledge Acquisition Modeling and Management (KAW'99)*, Banff, Canada.

[108] Kaufman, L. and Rousseeuw, P. J. (1990). *Finding Groups in Data: an Introduction to Cluster Analysis*. John Wiley & Sons.

[109] Kawtrakul, A., Imsombut, A., Thunkijjanukit, A., Soergel, D., Liang, A., Sini, M., Johannsen, G., and Keizer, J. (2005). Automatic Term Relationship Cleaning and Refinement for AGROVOC. In *Workshop on The Sixth Agricultural Ontology Service*, Vila Real, Portugal.

[110] Kietz, J. U., Maedche, A., and Volz, R. (2000). A method for semi-automatic ontology acquisition from a corporate intranet. In *Proceedings of Workshop Ontologies and Text, EKAW'2000*.

[111] Klein, M. and Fensel, D. (2001). Ontology versioning for the Semantic Web. In *International Semantic Web Working Symposium (SWWS)*.

[112] Koch, T., Neuroth, H., and Day, M. (2001). *Subject Retrieval in a Networked Environment: Papers Presented at an IFLA Satellite Meeting*, chapter Renardus: cross-browsing european subject gateways via a common classification system (DDC), pages 1–8. IFLA Section on Classification and Indexing & IFLA Section on Information Technology.

[113] Kotis, K. and Vouros, G. (2004). The HCONE Approach to Ontology Merging. *Lecture Notes in Computer Science*, 3053:137–151.

[114] Krowne, A. and Halbert, M. (2004). An Evaluation of Clustering and Automatic Classification For Digital Library Browse Ontologies. Metacombine project report, htttp://metacombine.org.

[115] Lacasta, J., Muro-Medrano, P. R., Nogueras-Iso, J., and Zarazaga-Soria, F. J. (2005). Web ontology service, a key component of a spatial data infrastructure. In *Proceedings of the 11th EC GI & GIS Workshop, ESDI Setting the Framework*. 10 Pages.

[116] Lacasta, J., Nogueras-Iso, J., Béjar, R., Muro-Medrano, P. R., and Zarazaga-Soria, F. J. (2007a). A Web Ontology Service to facilitate interoperability within a Spatial Data Infrastructure: applicability to discovery. *Data & Knowledge Engineering*, 63(3):947–971.

[117] Lacasta, J., Nogueras-Iso, J., López-Pellicer, F. J., Muro-Medrano, P. R., and Zarazaga-Soria, F. J. J. (2007b). ThManager: An Open Source Tool for creating and visualizing SKOS. *Information Technology and Libraries (ITAL)*, 26(3):39–51.

[118] Lacasta, J., Nogueras-Iso, J., Muro-Medrano, P. R., and Zarazaga-Soria, F. J. (2007c). Thematic clustering of geographic resource metadata collections. *Lec-*

ture Notes in Computer Science (LNCS), 7th International Symposium on Web and Wireless GIS (W2GIS 2007), 4857:30–43.

[119] Lacasta, J., Nogueras-Iso, J., Tolosana-Calasanz, R., López-Pellicer, F. J., and Zarazaga-Soria, F. J. (2006). Automating the Thematic Characterization of Geographic Resource Collections by Means of Topic Maps. In *Proceedings of the 9th AGILE International Conference on Geographic Information Science*, pages 81–89. Visegrád, Hungary.

[120] Lacasta, J., Nogueras-Iso, J., Torres, M. P., and Zarazaga-Soria, F. J. (2003). Towards the geographic metadata standard interoperability. In *Proceedings of AGILE 2003: 6th AGILE Conference on Geographic Information Science*, pages 555–565.

[121] Lacasta, J., Nogueras-Iso, J., Zarazaga-Soria, F. J., and Muro-Medrano, P. R. (2008). *Conceptual Models for Urban Practitioners.*, chapter Generating an urban domain ontology through the merging of cross-domain lexical ontologies, pages 69–84. Società Editrice Esculapio, Bologna.

[122] Lacher, M. S. and Groh, G. (2001). Facilitating the exchange of explicit knowledge through ontology mappings. In *Proceedings of the 14th International FLAIRS Conference*, Key West FL, USA.

[123] Lassila, O. and MacGuinness, D. (2001). The Role of Frame-Based Representations on the Semantic Web. Technical Report KSL-01-02, Knowledge Systems Laboratory, Standford University, Standford, California.

[124] Latre, M. A., Lacasta, J., Mojica, E., Nogueras-Iso, J., and Zarazaga-Soria, F. J. (2009). An approach to facilitate the integration of hydrological data by means of ontologies and multilingual thesauri. In Sester, M., Bernard, L., and Paelke, V., editors, *Advances in GIScience. Lecture Notes in Geoinformation and Cartography (LNGC)*, pages 155–171.

[125] Latre, M. A., Zarazaga-Soria, F. J., Nogueras-Iso, J., Béjar, R., and Muro-Medrano, P. R. (2005). SDIGER: A cross-border inter-administration SDI to support WFD information access for Adour-Garonne and Ebro River Basins. In *Proceedings of the 11th EC GI & GIS Workshop, ESDI Setting the Framework*, Alguero, Italy.

[126] Lauser, B., Sini, M., Salokhe, G., Keizer, J., and Katz, S. (2006). Agrovoc Web Services: Improved, real-time access to an agricultural thesaurus. *Quarterly Bulletin of the International Association of Agricultural Information Specialists (IAALD)*, 1019-9926(2):79–81.

[127] Lenat, D. B. (1995). CYC: A large-scale investment in knowledge infrastructure. *Communications of the ACM*, 38(11):33–38.

[128] Lenat, D. B. and Guha, R. V. (1991). The evolution of CycL, the Cyc representation language. *ACM SIGART Bulletin, Special issue on implemented knowledge representation and reasoning systems*, 2(3):84 – 87.

[129] Lesk, M. (1997). *Practical Digital Libraries*. Morgan Kaufmann, San Francisco.

[130] Lieberman, J., editor (2003). *OpenGIS Web Services Architecture, v0.3*. Number 0.3 in OGC. Open Geospatial Consortium.

[131] Lim, E.-P., Srivastava, J., Prabhakar, S., and Richardson, J. (1993). Entity identification in database integration. In *Procceedings of the 9th International Conference on DAta Engineering (ICDE)*.

[132] Lindberg, D., Humphreys, B., and McCray, A. (1998). The unified medical language system. *Journal of the American Medical Informatics Association*, 32(4):281 291.

[133] Maedche, A. and Staab, S. (2002). Measuring similarity between ontologies. *Lecture Notes In Computer Science*, 2473:251 – 263.

[134] Masolo, C., Borgo, S., Gangemi, A., Guarino, N., Oltramari, A., and Schneider, L. (2003). Wonderweb deliverable d17: The wonderweb library of foundational ontologies. Technical report, ISTC-CNR.

[135] Matthews, B. M., Wilson, M. D., Miller, K., and Ryssevik, J. (2001). Internationalising data access through LIMBER. In *Third international workshop on internationalisation of products and systems*.

[136] McGuinness, D. L., Fikes, R., Rice, J., and Wilder, S. (2000). An environment for merging and testing large ontologies. In *Proceedings of the Seventh International Conference on Principles of Knowledge Representation and Reasoning (KR2000)*, pages 12 – 15, Breckenridge, Colorado.

[137] McIlwaine, I. C. (1998). The Universal Decimal Classification: Some factors concerning its origins, development, and influence. *Journal of the American Society for Information Science*, 48(4):331 – 339.

[138] McIlwaine, I. C. (2000). *The Universal Decimal Classification: A guide to its use*. Number P035 in UDC Publication. UDC Publication, 3rd edition.

[139] Miles, A. and Bechhofer, S., editors (2009). *SKOS Simple Knowledge Organization System Reference*. W3C Candidate Recommendation. W3C. http://www.w3.org/TR/skos-reference/.

[140] Miles, A. and Brickley, D., editors (2004). *SKOS Mapping Vocabulary Specification*. W3C. http://www.w3.org/2004/02/skos/mapping/spec/2004-11-11.html.

[141] Miles, A., Matthews, B., and Wilson, M. (2005). SKOS Core: Simple Knowledge organization for the WEB. In *Proceedings of the International Conference on Dublin Core and Metadata Applications*, pages 5–13, Madrid, Spain.

[142] Miles, A., Rogers, N., and Beckett, D. (2004). Migrating thesauri to the semantic web - guidelines and case studies for generating rdf encodings of existing thesauri. Technical Report Deliverable 8.8, SWAD-Europe.

[143] Minsky, M. (1981). *Mind design. Philosophy, Psychology, and Artificial Intelligence*, chapter A framework for representing knowledge, pages 95–128. MIT Press, Cambridge MA.

[144] Missikoff, M., Velardi, P., and Fabriani, P. (2003). Text mining techniques to automatically enrich a domain ontology. *Applied Intelligence*, 18:323.340.

[145] Mizoguchi, R., Vanwelkenhuysen, J., and Ikeda, M. (1995). *Towards Very Large Knowledge Bases: Knowledge Building & Knowledge Sharing*, chapter Task Ontology for Reuse of Problem Solving Knowledge, pages 46–59. IOS Press.

[146] Navigli, R., Velardi, P., and Gangemi, A. (2003). Ontology learning and its application to automated terminology translation. *IEEE Intelligent Systems*, 18(1).

[147] Nebert, D., editor (2004). *Developing Spatial Data Infrastructures: The SDI Cookbook v.2.0*. Global Spatial Data Infrastructure (GSDI), http://www.gsdi.org.

[148] Network development and Marc Standard Office (2006a). Marc 21 Concise format for Authority Data. MARC 21, Library of Congress.

[149] Network development and Marc Standard Office (2006b). Marc 21 Concise format for Bibliographic Data. MARC 21, Library of Congress.

[150] Niles, I. and Pease, A. (2001). Towards a standard upper ontology. In *Proceedings of the international conference on Formal Ontology in Information Systems*, pages 2 – 9, Ogunquit, Maine, USA.

[151] Nogueras-Iso, J., Bañares, J. A., Lacasta, J., and Zarazaga-Soria, F. J. (2003). A software tool for thesauri management, browsing and supporting advanced searches. In *Geodaten- und Geodienste-Infrastrukturen - von der Forschung zur praktischen Anwendung. Beiträge zu den Münsteraner GI-Tagen 26./27. Juni 2003*, volume 18, pages 105–118, Münster, Germany. IFGIprints.

[152] Nogueras-Iso, J., Lacasta, J., Teller, J., Falquet, G., and Guyot, J. (2010). *Ontology Theory, Management and Design: Advanced Tools and Models*, chapter Ontology learning from thesauri: an experience in the urban domain (chap. 11). IGI Global Publisher. ISBN 978-1615208593.

[153] Nogueras-Iso, J., López-Pellicer, F. J., Lacasta, J., Zarazaga-Soria, F. J., and Muro-Medrano, P. R. (2007). *Ontologies for Urban Development: Interfacing Urban Information Systems*, volume 61 of *Studies in Computational Intelligence*, chapter Building an Address Gazetteer on top of an Urban Network Ontology, pages 157–167. Springer.

[154] Nogueras-Iso, J., Zarazaga-Soria, F. J., Lacasta, J., Béjar, R., and Muro-Medrano, P. R. (2004a). Metadata Standard Interoperability: Application in the Geographic Information Domain. *Computers, Environment and Urban Systems*, 28(6):611–634.

[155] Nogueras-Iso, J., Zarazaga-Soria, F. J., Lacasta, J., Tolosana-Calasanz, R., and Muro-Medrano, P. R. (2004b). Improving multilingual catalog search services by means of multilingual thesaurus disambiguation. In *Proceedings of the 10th European Commission GI&GIS Workshop, ESDI: The State of the Art*, Warsaw, Poland. 14 pages.

[156] Nogueras-Iso, J., Zarazaga-Soria, F. J., and Muro-Medrano, P. R. (2005). *Geographic Information Metadata for Spatial Data Infrastructures - Resources, Interoperability and Information Retrieval*. Springer Verlag.

[157] Noy, N., editor (2005). *Representing Classes As Property Values on the Semantic Web*. W3C.

[158] Noy, N. F., Fergerson, R. W., and Musen, M. A. (2000). *Proceedings of the 12th European Workshop on Knowledge Acquisition, Modeling and Management*, volume 1937 of *Lecture Notes In Computer Science*, chapter The knowledge model of Protégé-2000: Combining interoperability and flexibility, pages 17–32. Springer-Verlag, Juan-les-Pins, France.

[159] Noy, N. F. and Musen, M. A. (1999). SMART: Automated Support for Ontology Merging and Alignment. In *Twelth Workshop on Knowledge Acquisition, Modeling, and Management*, Banff, Canada.

[160] Noy, N. F. and Musen, M. A. (2000). PROMPT: Algorithm and tool for automated ontology merging and alignment. In *Proceedings of the 17th NAtional Conference on Artificial Inteligence*, pages 450–455.

[161] Online Computer Library Center (2003). *Dewey Decimal Classification System, 22nd edition*. Online Computer Library Center (OCLC).

[162] Palma, R., Haase, P., and In, A. G.-P. . . (2006). Oyster: sharing and re-using ontologies in a peer-to-peer community. In ACM Press, New York, N., editor, *Proceedings of the 15th International Conference on World Wide Web*, pages 1009–1010, Edinburgh, Scotland.

[163] Pepper, S., Moore, G. (eds.) (2001). XML Topic Maps (XTM) 1.0. Technical report, http://www.topicmaps.org.

[164] Podolak, I. and Demšar, U. (2004). Discovering structure in geographical metadata. In *Proceedings of the 12th conference in Geoinformatics*, pages 1–7, Galve, Sweden.

[165] Prasad, S., Peng, Y., and Finin, T. (2002). Using explicit information to map between two ontologies. In *Proceedings of the AAMAS Workshop on Ontologies in Agent Systems*, Bologne, Italy.

[166] Rahm, E. and Bernstein, P. A. (2001). A survey of approaches to automatic schema matching. *The VLDB Journal The International Journal on Very Large Data Bases archive*, 10(4):334 – 350.

[167] Rahm, E., Do, H.-H., and Maßmann, S. (2004). Matching large xml schemas. *ACM SIGMOD Record archive*, 33(4):26 – 31.

[168] Ranganathan, S. R. (1962). *Elements of library classification*. Asia Publishing House, Bombay.

[169] Resnik, P. (1995). Disambiguating noun groupings with respect to WordNet senses. In *Proc. of the 3rd Workshop on Very Large Corpora*. MIT.

[170] Rigau, G., Rodríguez, H., and Agirre, E. (1998). Building accurate semantic taxonomies from monolingual mrds. In *Proc. 17th International Conference on Computational Linguistics and 36th Annual Meeting of the Association for Computational Linguistics COLING-ACL'98*, Montreal, Canada.

[171] Roussey, C. (2005). Guidelines to build ontologies : A bibliographic study. Technical report nr. 1, COST Action C21. http://www.towntology.net/Documents/guidelines.pdf.

[172] Schaerf, A. (1994). *Query answering in Concept-Based Knowledge Representation Systems: Algorithms, Complexity and Semantic Issues*. PhD thesis, Dipartimento di Informatica e Sistemistica. Università di Roma 'La Sapienza'.

[173] Schlieder, C. and Vögele, T. (2002). Indexing and Browsing Digital Maps with Intelligent Thumbnails. In *Spatial Data Handling 2002 (SDH'02)*, Ottawa, Canada. 12 pages.

[174] Schlieder, C., Vögele, T., and Visser, U. (2001). Qualitative Spatial Representation for Information Retrieval by Gazetteers. In *Proceedings of Conference*

of Spatial Information Theory COSIT, volume 2205, pages 336–351, Morrow Bay, CA.

[175] Sigel, A. (2006). From traditional Knowledge Organization Systems (authority files, classifications, thesauri) towards ontologies on the web. In *Workshop Introducing Terminology-based Ontologies at the 9th International Conference of the International Society for Knowledge Organization (ISKO)*, pages 3–53, Vienna, Austria. Published electronically on E-LIS (E-prints in Library and Information Science, http://eprints.rclis.org), 2006-07-14.

[176] Soergel, D., Lauser, B., Liang, A., Fisseha, F., Keizer, J., and Katz, S. (2004). Reengineering Thesauri for New Applications: the AGROVOC Example. *Journal of Digital Information*, 4(4):1–19.

[177] Soualmia, L., Goldbreich, C., and Darmoni, S. (2004). Representing the mesh in owl: Towards a semi-automatic migration. In *Proceedings of the 1st Intl Workshop on Formal Biomedical Knowledge Representation (KR-MED 2004)*, page 8187, Whistler, Canada.

[178] Sowa, J. F. (1996). Ontologies for Knowledge Sharing. In *Manuscript of the invited talk at Terminology and Knowledge Engineering Congress (TKE '96)*, Vienna.

[179] Steinbach, M., Karypis, G., and Kumar, V. (2000). A comparison of document clustering techniques. In *Proceedings of the KDD Workshop on Text Mining*, pages 1–20, Boston, USA.

[180] Stock, K., editor (2009). *OGC Catalogue Services OWL Application Profile of CSW. Version 0.3.0*. Open Geospatial Consortium (OGC).

[181] Stojanovic, L., Stojanovic, N., and Volz, R. (2002). Migrating data-intensive web sites into the semantic web. In *Proceedings of the ACM Symposium on Applied Computing SAC-02*, Madrid.

[182] Stumme, G. and Maedche, A. (2001). Ontology Merging for Federated Ontologies on the Semantic Web. In *Proceedings of the International Workshop for Foundations of Models for Information Integration (FMII-2001)*, Viterbo, Italy.

[183] Sure, Y., Angele, J., and Staab, S. (2002). *On the Move to Meaningful Internet Systems 2002: CoopIS, DOA, and ODBASE*, volume 2519/2002 of *Lecture Notes in Computer Science*, chapter OntoEdit: Guiding Ontology Development by Methodology and Inferencing, pages 1205–1222. Springer Berlin / Heidelberg.

[184] Sussna, M. (1993). Word sense disambiguation for free-text indexing using a massive semantic network. In *Proc. of the Second International Conference on Information and Knowledge Management (CIKM-93)*, Arlington, Virginia.

[185] Tennis, J. T. (2005). SKOS and the Ontogenesis of Vocabularies. In *Dublin Core Conferece: Vocabularies in Practice*.

[186] Tolosana-Calasanz, R., Alvarez-Robles, J. A., Lacasta, J., Nogueras-Iso, J., Muro-Medrano, P. R., and Zarazaga-Soria, F. J. (2006a). On the problem of identifying the quality of geographic metadata. *Lecture Notes in Computer Science (LNCS), Research and Advanced Technology for Digital Libraries, ECDL 2006*, 4172:232–243.

[187] Tolosana-Calasanz, R., Nogueras-Iso, J., Béjar, R., Muro-Medrano, P. R., and Zarazaga-Soria, F. J. (2006b). Semantic interoperability based on Dublin Core hierarchical one-to-one mappings. *International Journal of Metadata, Semantics and Ontologies*, 1(3):183–188.

[188] Tolosana-Calasanz, R., Portolés-Rodríguez, D., Nogueras-Iso, J., Muro-Medrano, P. R., and Zarazaga-Soria, F. J. (2005). CatServer: A Server of GATOS. In *Proceedings of AGILE 2005: 8th Conference on Geographic Information Science*, pages 359–366.

[189] Torra, V., Miyamoto, S., and Lanau, S. (2005). Exploration of textual document archives using a fuzzy hierarchical clustering algorithm in the GAMBAL system. *Information Processing and Management*, 41:587–598.

[190] Tudhope, D., Alani, H., , and Jones, C. (2001). Augmenting Thesaurus Relationships: Possibilities for Retrieval. *Journal of Digital Information*, 1, Issue 8(41, 2001-02-05). 22 pages.

[191] Tudhope, D. and Binding, C. (2005). Towards Terminology Services: experiences with a pilot web service thesaurus browser. In *Proceedings of the International Conference on Dublin Core and Metadata Aplications*.

[192] Tudhope, D., Binding, C., Blocks, D., and Cunliffe, D. (2006a). Query expansion via conceptual distance in thesaurus indexed collections. *Journal of Documentation*, 62(4):509–533.

[193] Tudhope, D., Koch, T., and Heery, R. (2006b). Terminology services and technology. jisc state of the art review. Technical report, UKOLN.

[194] United Nations Educational, Scientific and Cultural Organization (UNESCO) (1995). *UNESCO Thesaurus: A Structured List of Descriptors for Indexing and Retrieving Literature in the Fields of Education, Science, Social and Human Science, Culture, Communication and Information.* UNESCO Publishing, Paris. http://www.ulcc.ac.uk/unesco/.

[195] U.S. Congress (1991). *High Performance Computing and Communications Act of 1991.* Superintendent of Documents, Congressional Sales Office, U.S. Government Printing Office, Washington, DC 20402.

[196] Usländer, T. (2005). Trends of environmental information systems in the context of the European Water Framework directive. *Environmental Modelling & Software*, 20(12):1532–1542.

[197] van Assem, M., Malaisé, V., Miles, A., and Schreiber, G. (2006). A Method to Convert Thesauri to SKOS. In *Proceedings of the 3rd European Semantic Web Conference (ESWC-06)*, pages 95–109, Budva, Montenegro.

[198] van Assem, M., Menken, M. R., Schreiber, G., Wielemaker, J., and Wielinga, B. (2004). A method for converting thesauri to RDF/OWL. In McIlraith, S. A., Plexousakis, D., and van Harmelen, F., editors, *Proceedings of the Third International Semantic Web Conference (ISWC 2004)*, Hiroshima, Japan. Springer.

[199] van Heijst, G., Schreiber, A. T., and Wielinga, B. J. (1997). Using explicit ontologies in KBS development. *International Journal of Human-Computer Studies*, 46(2-3):183 – 292.

[200] van Heist, G., Schreiber, A. T., and Wielinga, B. J. (1997). Using explicit ontologies in kbs development. *Int J Hum Comput Stud*, 46(2/3):183292.

[201] Velardi, P., Fabriani, P., and Missikoff, M. (2001). Using text processing techniques to automatically enrich a domain ontology. In *Proceedings of the international conference on Formal Ontology in Information Systems, FOIS 2001*, pages 270–284.

[202] Volz, R., Oberle, D., Motik, B., and Staab, S. (2003). KAON SERVER - A Semantic Web Management System. In *12th World Wide Web, Alternate Tracks - Practice and Experience*, Hungary, Budapest.

[203] Vossen, P. (1998). Introduction to EuroWordNet. *Computers and the Humanities (Special Issue on EuroWordNet)*, 32(2-3):73–89.

[204] Vretanos(Eds), P. (2005). Filter Encoding Implementation Specification, Version 1.1. OpenGIS project document OGC 04-095, OpenGIS Consortium Inc.

[205] Whiteside, A., editor (2007). *OGC Web Services Common Specification. Version 1.1.0.* Open Geospatial Consortium (OGC).

[206] Wielemaker, J., Schreiber, G., and Wielinga1, B. (2005). Using Triples for Implementation: The Triple20 Ontology-Manipulation Tool. *Lecture Notes in Computer Science (LNCS)*, 3729:773–785.

[207] Wielinga, B. J., Schreiber, A. T., Wielemaker, J., and Sandberg, J. A. C. (2001). From Thesaurus to Ontology. In *Proceedings of the 1st international conference on Knowledge capture*, pages 194 – 201, Victoria, British Columbia, Canada.

[208] Zarazaga-Soria, F., Nogueras-Iso, J., Latre, M., Rodríguez, A., López, E., Vivas, P., and Muro-Medrano, P. (2007). *Research and Theory in Advancing Spatial Data Infrastructure Concepts*, chapter Providing SDI Services in a Cross-Border Scenario: the SDIGER Project Use Case, pages 107–119. ESRI Press.

[209] Zarazaga-Soria, F., Torres, M., Nogueras-Iso, J., Lacasta, J., and Cantán, O. (2003a). Integrating geographic and non-geographic data search services using metadata crosswalks. In *Proceedings of the 9th EC-GI&GIS Workshop: ESDI: Serving the User.* 12 pages.

[210] Zarazaga-Soria, F. J., Lacasta, J., Nogueras-Iso, J., Torres, M. P., and Muro-Medrano, P. R. (2003b). A Java Tool for Creating ISO/FGDC Geographic Metadata. In *Geodaten - und Geodienste-Infrastrukturen - von der Forschung zur praktischen Anwendung (Beiträge zu den Münsteraner GI-Tagen)*, volume 18 of *IFGIprints*, pages 17–30, Münster, Germany.

[211] Zeng, M. and Chan, L. (2004). Trends and issues in establishing interoperability among knowledge organization systems. *Journal of American Society for Information Science and Technology*, 55(5):377 395.

Index